PENGUIN BOOKS

WOODY AND NORD

'A refreshing slice of biographic[...]
The Times

'Engrossing . . . An excellent re[...]

'A critique of the modern game that will become required reading for England squad members . . . astute, forthright, moving' *Daily Telegraph*

'Every now and again a football biography comes along that sidesteps the usual garbage with a neat shimmy. Gareth Southgate and Andy Woodman have pulled it off . . . wonderfully refreshing' *Four Four Two*

'A football memoir with a sensitive side . . . the Third Division versus Premiership lifestyles is the real eye-opener . . . worth reading' *Daily Mirror*

'Exceptional' *Daily Telegraph* (Sport)

'A searingly honest and amusing behind-the-scenes portrait of footballing life' *Birmingham Evening Post*

'A heartwarming story that will restore your faith in the game . . . A powerful human insight into a unique and lasting friendship' *Oxford Mail*

'Both men write with great humour, honesty and candour . . . a resounding triumph' *Caterham Advisor*

'Provocative, forthright and hard-hitting' *Teesside Evening Gazette*

Woody and Nord

A Football Friendship

GARETH SOUTHGATE AND
ANDY WOODMAN WITH
DAVID WALSH

PENGUIN BOOKS

PENGUIN BOOKS

Published by the Penguin Group
Penguin Books Ltd, 80 Strand, London WC2R ORL, England
Penguin Group (USA), Inc., 375 Hudson Street, New York, New York 10014, USA
Penguin Books Australia Ltd, 250 Camberwell Road, Camberwell, Victoria 3124, Australia
Penguin Books Canada Ltd, 10 Alcorn Avenue, Toronto, Ontario, Canada M4V 3B2
Penguin Books India (P) Ltd, 11 Community Centre, Panchsheel Park, New Delhi – 110 017, India
Penguin Group (NZ), cnr Airborne and Rosedale Roads, Albany, Auckland 1310, New Zealand
Penguin Books (South Africa) (Pty) Ltd, 24 Sturdee Avenue, Rosebank 2196, South Africa

Penguin Books Ltd, Registered Offices: 80 Strand, London WC2R ORL, England

www.penguin.com

Published by Michael Joseph 2003
Published in Penguin Books 2004
1

Copyright © Gareth Southgate and Andy Woodman, 2003
All rights reserved

The moral right of the authors has been asserted

Typeset by Rowland Phototypesetting Ltd, Bury St Edmunds, Suffolk
Printed in England by Clays Ltd, St Ives plc

To my late mum, Gail Penelope Woodman, who I know would have been proud of me no matter what I did. God bless, Mum. I love you.

And to my two beautiful children, Freddie and Isobelle, who have given me so much joy. I hope that one day you will read this book and be proud of me. I love you, guys.   Dad

To Mia and Flynn

I would like to thank many people, but words will never be enough to repay the faith, commitment and loyalty they have all shown me. I hope they have enjoyed the triumphs and not been too down with the disappointments that I have had. My wife, Anna, has been there first-hand to witness all of these and never once left my side, for which I am eternally grateful. My dad Colin has been with me every step of the way, driving too many miles to mention. I will never be able to thank you enough and just hope I can be as supportive to my children as you have been to me. My big brother Peter spent his first week's wages to buy me some top goalie gloves and has never once been envious of me but always proud. I feel it would be unjust not to mention my in-laws, Beryl and John, for their support on and off the field.

I must also take this opportunity to thank David Walsh for the excellent job he has done in bringing this dream together; Ashley Woolfe for working on our behalf; Rowland White at Penguin Books for believing in the book from day one and also bringing it together.

Lastly, I must thank Nord, for he has reached the dizzy heights that we aspired to, but not once has he forgotten where we both started. A true friend in every respect of the word.

Andy

I hope I have acknowledged the help of the many who have helped me within this book. I wanted to make particular mention of certain people, though.

In many respects our lives are dictated by fate from the outset; we have no choice as to the situation we are born into. I am incredibly fortunate to have been born into the family that I was. For all of us our parents have a huge influence on our character and personality, and I will always be grateful to my mum and dad for giving me such a stable and supportive upbringing – I hope the thousands of miles of travelling have been worth it!

I have learnt from all the teachers, coaches and managers who I've worked with, and I hope they have all taken pleasure in following my career. In particular, though, Alan Smith has shown belief in me from the outset. The dictionary definition of 'mentor' is 'an experienced and trusted adviser'. Alan, you've been that and much more. Also, Steve Harrison, who has coached me at all three of my clubs and spent more hours than anyone improving my game. The coaching has been excellent and the entertainment has made my career all the more enjoyable – Killawayadoodoo!

The idea for this book was sketchy; my thanks to Ashley Woolfe for pursuing that idea and to Rowland White at Penguin for giving us the platform to tell the tale as we wanted. Ashley must also take great credit for introducing David Walsh to us. The highlight of this project has been working alongside and forming a friendship with such an outstanding and perceptive sports writer. The thoroughness of your work has been incredible. I look forward to many a rematch in Portugal!

Which just leaves the woman behind the man. The highs and lows of life are pretty futile unless you have someone special to share them with. My wife, Alison, has lived with a professional sportsman for eight years – understood the sacrifices; put up with the moods that come with injury, bad performances and defeat; tolerated me being habitually late for her; and been forced to move further and further from home! I look forward to the years ahead that we will enjoy with our wonderful children.

Gareth

Gareth Southgate

Name: Gareth Southgate

Age: 33

Club: Middlesbrough

Married to: Alison

Children: Mia and Flynn

Do you love the game?
Love, yes; like, no

Football hate:
Players who don't make
the most of their talent

Best football moment:
First England cap

Best coach / manager:
Terry Venables

Favourite film:
One Flew Over the
Cuckoo's Nest, an every-
day tale of football folk

Favourite book: Still Me –
Christopher Reeve.

Best friend: A. J. Woodman,
Esq.

Andy Woodman

Name: Andy John Woodman

Age: 32

Club: Oxford United

Married to: Anna

Children: Freddie and Isobelle

Do you love the game?
100 per cent

Football hate:
Depressed Premiership
players

Best football moment:
Penalty save at Wembley

Best coach/manager:
Jack Pearce, Bognor Regis

Favourite film:
Goodfellas

Favourite book:
Muhammad Ali: His Life and
Times – Thomas Hauser
and Muhammad Ali

Best friend: Gareth Southgate

Introduction

Get not your friends by bare compliments, but by giving them sensible tokens of your love.
    Socrates

Gareth

Mitcham train station in south London was a desolate waste-land on the line between West Croydon and Wimbledon. The trains left West Croydon every half-hour and often we got to the station twenty seconds late. A game of pool that had gone on a minute too long meant a twenty-nine-minute wait. There was just one platform and we slumped on to the benches, with barely enough energy to talk about that morning's training or Saturday's match or why the manager made us do so much running. Track-suited young appren-tices, we were, on a collision course with the realities of professional football.

Years before, you were a kid in the back garden placing shots into the roof of an unguarded net. It had seemed so simple then. Manchester United and England, they were the future. Bryan Robson, Captain Marvel. Then you arrived at a professional football club and your cosy expectations were shattered. You never knew how hard it was going to be. Deep-lying insecurities came to the surface and you worried:

'Do you think the manager likes me?'

'Yeah, he does. It's me he doesn't fancy.'

'I'm just hoping to stay in the youth team.'

The first team at Crystal Palace was like a beacon shining in the distance; the more you looked at it, the further away it seemed. You kept going because of stubbornness and the dream was still a dream, even when it seemed impossible. Some days I got to Three Bridges station, near my home in Crawley, found Dad's car and, too exhausted to walk the last mile and a half, waited for him to finish work and give me a lift home.

John Budden and Barry Ellis were my companions at Mitcham station in those early months. Good lads who gave it a shot but for whom it didn't work out. John, I think, is teaching in Kent now; Barry is a fireman – both in professions more honourable than mine. Andy Woodman turned up a little later. Woody, we called him. Of all of us, he made the worst start to his apprenticeship. The goals flew past him, sometimes three or four, another day six and finally, seven. He was a thin, spindly goalkeeper, a year younger than the rest of us and physically weak. That difference of a year meant everything but none of us would admit that. It was easier to let Woody shoulder all the blame.

He often ate an orange at Mitcham station, and as we talked he would toss the peel on to the tracks. He asked if I thought he would make it. 'You'll be okay, mate. You're still young enough for the youth team next year.' You always encouraged because you too needed reassurance. To get it, you had to give it. It was Woody's sense of humour and spirit that brought us together. No matter how often he was knocked down, he got back up and there was nothing that he couldn't laugh at. He had the knack of making me laugh. In his company, I could even be half-funny. In time I would get beyond the laughs and find the deeper Woody. Not a lot of people know that guy.

We would sit on the platform and try to see into the future. Would we make the Palace first team? 'You definitely will, not sure about me.' Would we drive the flash cars, play for England and appear on *A Question of Sport*? We didn't talk about the possibility of one of us making it and the other being let go. Too close to the bone and anyway, it was something over which we had no control. Once it developed, our friendship was in our own hands. Something the game could not destroy.

Why did it survive to become such an important part of our lives? What is it that makes two people close? Trust, loyalty, shared experiences? I don't know. Why did that tall, lanky teenager who tossed his orange peel on to the tracks become my best friend?

Ask me anything about football and I've got an answer. But the question about Woody and I, that's harder. We met at a time when we were young, vulnerable and single. We had nothing but we had it all; £27.50 a week and your only worry was not getting in the side for the weekend's game. Saturday afternoon on the football pitch, Saturday evening in the nightclub: it was an intense and brilliant time in our lives and we shared it. The legacy was a bond that has proved unbreakable.

Andy

I was back at Mitcham station not so long ago. Nothing has changed; still the same single platform, the same bench we once sat on. Except the orange peel has gone. All those years ago, there was a dream that I dared not tell the lads about. I kid you not, this was a recurring dream for me. In it, I was the star of an edition of *This Is Your Life*, my old team-mates appeared from behind the curtain and my mum was there in the front row, as proud as Punch. During the dark days of my first two years at Palace, I clung to that dream. That was the night-time dream. By day I dreamed of playing for Palace's first team, being involved in big matches at packed grounds, being part of something successful. Things turned out differently, but not badly.

It was Wally Downes who first called Gareth 'Nord'. Wally was on the coaching staff at Crystal Palace and he came up with 'Nord' because Gareth's deliberate way of speaking reminded Wally of Denis Norden, presenter of *It'll Be Alright on the Night*. Soon you will find out what Wally called me. It wasn't funny. Not even remotely funny.

Sitting on that bench at Mitcham station, I once asked Nord where we would be ten years on. Would we still be friends? Married? Kids? Ten years on we were married, Nord had played in the European Championship for England and I had my own moment of glory with Northampton Town at Wembley. Back then it was so innocent, it never dawned on me that football was such a dog-eat-dog business, a game in which loyalty didn't pay and honesty was a rarity.

We would talk of the good things that would come if things went well. The car, the house, being set up for life. To me, the car didn't actually matter that much, the house wouldn't have to be special, but an expensive watch, that's what I wanted. Ian Wright and Tony Finnegan were senior lads at Palace and they had agreed that if one of them got a decent contract, he would buy the other a nice watch. True to their pact, when Tony signed for Blackburn he sent Ian a watch. Nord and I struck the same deal.

My career didn't pan out as I hoped it would. Though I spent seven years at Palace, I never played in the first team in a competitive match. Since making a bitter exit from the club, my career has been in the backwaters of the Nationwide League: divisions two and three. It's been a great life and it's still going. As I write this, Oxford United have just missed getting into the promotion play-offs, a goal four minutes from time by Lincoln in their match with Torquay did for us. To make it even more heartbreaking, Torquay missed a penalty.

Ah well, the rewards for me these days tend to be spiritual rather than material. I drive to training in a Ford Ka and share the driving and the petrol expenses with my team-mate Andy Scott. We should do better, but though I still care, I am more philosophical about our results now. I ain't a kid any more.

Two years ago I celebrated my thirtieth birthday. Anna, my wife, had a marquee erected in our garden and invited all our friends. Gareth couldn't make it because Middlesbrough had a game that afternoon. Alison, his wife, came down and as we spoke in the kitchen beforehand she gave me a present from Nord. It was a very classy mobile phone, top-drawer job. I was thrilled.

'Woody, there's something else in there,' Ali said.

'No, Ali, the bag's empty.'

'Look again.'

There was a card and inside it a cheque for £6,000. 'Fuck me, what the fuck is this?'

All the card said was, 'Get yourself that watch. Gareth.'

It took me a while to find the right Rolex but it's on my wrist now, a reminder of what football has given me. I am not talking medals or caps or money; it gave me precious little of those. This game we play, it knocks you down more than lifts you up. It has taken more from me than it has ever given to me. I owe it just one debt and that is my friendship with Nord.

The bird a nest, the spider a web, man friendship.
  William Blake

Gareth

The possibility of writing a book had always been in the
background and for many years that's where it stayed. It
didn't appeal to me. What story could I tell that would keep
people interested for 200 pages?

'Nice guy, that Southgate. Bit boring, though.'

Apart from being the man who missed the penalty at the
European Championship of 1996, what was there? More
than fifty caps for England so, yeah, there could be a few
chapters on my international career. I was, after all, drafted
into the middle of the defence on that famous evening
in St Etienne when we had our penalty shoot-out against
Argentina and there, too, when Sven-Goran Eriksson led us
off to the Far East. Something could be written about the
early years at Crystal Palace and Alan Smith, a one-time
Palace manager, who once looked into my seventeen-year-
old eyes and said, 'Son, no fucking chance.' Alan was one of
the good guys.

That age of innocence could be resurrected and we could
exhume the not-so-innocent years at Aston Villa. The seasons
there began well, promised much but delivered little. Little,
that was the name of my first manager at Villa Park. When

Brian departed, we weren't sure whether it had been a voluntary exit or whether Villa's eternal chairman, 'Deadly' Doug Ellis, showed him the way out. We suspected Doug. My own feeling is that Brian Little was a good man brought down by expensive signings that failed. If there is a managerial graveyard, you'll find the headstone commemorating Brian was erected by Stan Collymore and Sasa Curcic.

After Brian Little came John Gregory. Ah, John Gregory, remember him? Touted once as a future England manager, John rose without trace and has had a similar fall. They say if you don't have something good to say about someone, better to say nothing. Ideally, I should stop now. But four years is a long time in a football career and they were two years too many for John and I. At first you support the manager, then you lose respect for him and, finally, you end up disliking him. It is a cycle not uncommon in the world of football.

When all of the bits of my career are added together, they don't amount to that much. Ask me to list my achievements and I will ask you if you've got five seconds to spare. A Division One title from 1994, a League Cup winners' medal from 1996 and that's pretty much it. Neither is there much by way of controversy: one sending-off in twelve seasons and a supporting actor's role in the drama of Roy Keane's sending-off in the 1995 FA Cup semi-final at Villa Park. Roy stamped on me, got a red card and I got a nomination for best supporting actor.

If I avoided red on the pitch, I stayed clear of all colour off it. I have never been good at gambling/drinking/fighting/tantrums/celebrity. Too much like Clive, my dad. And the small scars you see on my body, they're not from football, but from book publishers touching me with 40-foot barge poles.

Then one thought struck me as worthwhile. Woody.

Why not with Woody? Andy Woodman, known to me and countless others as Woody, has been my best friend since our apprentice days at Crystal Palace. We grew up together in football, shared our dreams and our disappointments. He got us into scrapes, I got us out of them; I fell down, he lifted me. We hoped our friendship was more than football's norm, that we weren't just ships passing in the night. My career went in one direction, Woody's went in another, but we never lost touch. He's played at places we never dreamed of: Exeter City and Bognor Regis, Brentford and Northampton, Southend and Peterborough, Colchester and his current club, Oxford United. I went to Villa and Middlesbrough, but geography was only an inconvenience.

Ours is a long story. The starting point was his naturally charismatic personality. How could anybody be so confident and uninhibited? At first it made me a little suspicious, almost resentful, but that soon disappeared. I think it was on a pre-season trip to Italy that we first shared a room and after that, so much else. During our years at Palace, we always paired up. They were unforgettable times.

Wherever our careers took us, our friendship remained intimate. There had been too many good times for it not to. When Woody and his wife, Anna, first started going out together, I was the sidekick that inevitably tagged along. In the end Anna expected me to be there and the three of us spent a lot of time together. When I bought my first flat, it wasn't far from where Woody lived with his dad, Colin. When Colin cooked, I got the call: 'Gareth, I'm cooking dinner. Want to come round? Spaghetti bolognese this evening.' It was always spaghetti bolognese.

I went with Colin to watch Woody play for the Palace reserves and winced when he made a mistake. All the time our relationship developed. Woody was best man when

Alison and I married. I was godfather to their first child, Freddie, and our wives, Alison and Anna, have become very close. As for Woody and I, there's hardly been a day when we haven't spoken on the phone.

And from our friendship came the idea for this book. Convinced a story about Gareth Southgate wasn't really what the reading public wanted, I thought, 'What about a book about our friendship and our contrasting lives in football?' There are two sides to the world of professional football but you wouldn't know it from the way the game is reported in the media. The glamour and wealth of the Premiership bear no resemblance to the reality Woody has faced at Brentford, Northampton, Colchester and other far-flung places. Yet we both earn our living playing the same game.

When we started out, we earned £27.50 a week as apprentices at Crystal Palace. Now I earn almost as much in one week as Woody does in a year. That isn't right, but it is how it is in the entertainment industry. From Woody, I have some understanding of what it is like to have to wash your own kit and travel by bicycle and train to training. Woody could speak for himself and countless other unknown players in the lower reaches of the Nationwide League.

There were other reasons for wanting to share this stage with my mate. Woody is a more colourful character than I am. He has always had the ability to light up a dressing room; to light up any room for that matter. His story would tell as much about the football world as mine would, and coming from Woody, it would sound better.

It was going to be more fun with Woody, but there's no getting round the fact that sharing the stage with him would also earn him some money. What we get is split fifty-fifty and though the amount is not going to make or break me, it will mean something to Woody and Anna and their family.

Yet, it's a funny thing about a book and something I discovered almost the second we committed to doing it: once you start recalling memories and typing them into your laptop, it takes on a life of its own. The money can seem irrelevant. Woody, I know, would have done this book for nothing and, once he was involved, I knew I'd enjoy it.

In the Premiership we do not want for attention, neither can we claim to be undervalued, but in the lower leagues, it is very different. They live their careers in virtual anonymity, yet we were all apprentices once, sharing the same dream. They are forced to accept less, to play their football for six or eight years before five or six thousand people and then move on. Who knows they exist? People can now discover Andy Woodman, a big man of the small leagues. He, too, played at Wembley, and unlike his best mate, he can remember a penalty kick in that stadium with nothing other than joy.

While reading about our friendship and our football lives, I hope people will learn something about the many sides of the professional game.

Andy

We can't all be David Beckhams. But a lot of fellows could be Andy Woodman.

Football has been my life since Crystal Palace signed me as an apprentice sixteen years ago. Fifteen years old then, there were seven of us taken on that summer. Gareth Southgate would go on to play more than fifty times for his country, five didn't make it in professional football and then there was me. I would be telling a lie if I said it's been everything I'd hoped for. I spent five years at Palace but never once played for the first team. That was a big disappointment and it remains a regret. Palace never understood how much I loved their damn club.

Since then it's been an adventure through the heartlands of the Nationwide League. A roller-coaster ride, I call it. I'm thirty-two now, at that point where a footballer begins to see a new contract not as an opportunity but as an act of survival. My last move took me from Colchester United to Oxford United and though it meant dropping from the second to the third division, the two-year deal offered by Oxford persuaded me. It's a guarantee of bread and butter on the table for two years and a licence for me to carry on playing. In our football world there's much to complain about and the smile on my face is often forced, but as long as I am paid, I will play on. When I fell for the game, it was hook, line and sinker. Like me, there are a lot of players who expected something great and settled for less. I ain't complaining. There's plenty to tell about where I've been, what I've seen.

Anna and I have often talked about my life as a footballer. How people think of it as glamorous when the reality is so different. At most clubs I've had to wash my own kit and spend two hours driving to and from training. Four hours commuting each day, £900 a week and all for the glory of the occasional Oxford United chant: 'Woody for England'. I'm a sucker for it and love the game as much today as I did the day I walked into Crystal Palace as a starry-eyed apprentice.

Anna constantly reminds me of the reality and some time ago she suggested writing a book to let people know just how ordinary our lives are. It was, though, more a pipe dream than a serious ambition: who had heard of me, who would want my story? The idea died. It came back to life a year or so later.

It was early one morning in our kitchen. Gareth and Alison had stayed over, we'd been out the night before and the men were nursing slight hangovers. We spoke about my almost forgotten dream of writing a book and it may have been one of the girls who talked about doing something together. We joked about a title for the book but it was a bit of fun, not a plan.

Typical Gareth, he said little at the time, and I thought no more about it. A few months later we met and went for a coffee in Croydon. He wanted to know if I was still interested in the idea of doing a book together. That afternoon we talked about it as newlyweds might discuss the prospect of their first kid. What we wanted was a book that would honestly reflect our lives, both in football and beyond. So I've got to say here and now, the money is important to me. My current salary from football is £40,000 a year, but if you take from that the cost of driving from south London to Oxford five or six times a week, the money isn't as good as it sounds. Anna works three days a week for the Home Office and without her salary, I don't know how we'd make ends meet. The money from this book is extra and I want to use it to help when football is finished with me and I've got to move on. The money will also be welcomed by Paul Joyce, the manager at my local bank. He's been good to me. When the book became a reality, I thought, 'Paul's gonna like this.'

But money has never been a driving force in my life. I would have done the book for nothing other than the satisfaction of having something that proved I played the game for a living. When our two children, Freddie and Isobelle, grow up, I want them to be able to show their children the book and say, 'Before Granddad got really old and grumpy, he used to be a footballer and this is a book about his life and his friendship with a man called Gareth Southgate.'

That's the future. More immediately, there's my nan, Daphne. From the moment I told her Gareth and I were doing a book, she asked if she could have the first copy signed by the two of us. Daphne is my mum's Mum and she and my granddad, Thomas, lived in a prefabricated house in West Norwood that for years and years was the heart of our family. When Anna and I first started going out, we couldn't meet on Sunday afternoon because that was the day I went to my nan's. Anna complained until one Sunday she came with me. Then, after one afternoon in my nan's house, she never complained again.

Thomas died last year but my nan is still with us, thank God. Every time I see her now she wants to know if the book is finished. She talks about Gareth as if he too was her grandson, but then he was a regular in the prefab at West Norwood. Sometimes we would go for breakfast, other times we would turn up at night for toast. Nan was always there and always made us feel special. I also want Colin, my dad, and my brother, Peter, to know more about the football life I have led. Because I've always been a master at showing the sunny side they may not have understood what it was really like. I hope Alan Smith, my former manager at Crystal Palace, reads this book and cringes. I want Al to realize the impact of how he handled my exit from Palace. What people at football clubs sometimes forget is that they are not simply running a team, they are dealing with people's lives.

There are two final wishes, and they relate to Gareth and my mum, Gail. It seems an eternity ago that Gareth and I became friends. He was this well-spoken and highly uncool lad from somewhere out in the sticks. He used words we couldn't understand and wore clothes we wouldn't have been buried in. But there was something about him, something different. I was a streetwise kid from one of London's tougher areas, South Norwood. Loud, cocky and exactly the kind of young lad you would have expected Gareth Southgate to run a mile from.

A pretty odd couple but that didn't stop us; I could make him laugh and, sometimes, he could make me see sense. I've often felt people look at us together and think, 'Ah, he did well to hold on to Southgate's friendship.' Funny, I've never thought of it like that. I knew Gareth when he was on £27.50 a week and his friendship was as important then as it is now. I could fill this book with stories of fellows who were inseparable at football clubs, then one of them got a move and they hardly ever spoke again. 'Ever hear from Richard now?' 'Nah, not since he moved to the Midlands.'

Gareth and I survived that.

Most of all I want to use this book to talk about things that are dear to me. My mum, Gail, died from cancer at the age of forty-four, when I was seventeen. I loved her as much as any son could love a mother and her death destroyed me. Though my dad, my brother and I have always been close, our home was never the same without Mum. Fourteen years have passed since her death and I haven't really got over it. Maybe I am not meant to. But by talking in this book about Mum, I can pay my respects to her memory and let my own family know exactly how I feel.

2

A simple friend thinks the friendship is over when you have an argument. A real friend knows it's not a friendship until after you've had a fight.

Unknown

Andy

They tell me I was born on the eighth floor of King's College Hospital in Brixton, 11 August 1971. Don't recall much about that but I do remember the first-floor flat at Claylands Court in West Norwood. That's where I spent the first six years of my life. It was a nice place to live, right opposite Norwood Park. There were swings and a roundabout and when the ice-cream van came we would all shout up to our mums: 'Mum, Mum, throw us 10p for an ice-cream.' It was okay for me, but the boy whose mum lived at the top, he had to really scream. We all gathered in the car park for the Silver Jubilee celebrations in 1977 and there was a great community spirit about the place. Dad would take my brother Peter and me to Dulwich Park to play football. Dulwich was a nice area, the pitch was always cut and it was free of dogs' muck. Keen as mustard, Dad was.

But our days at Claylands Court ended suddenly and violently. I'm sure it was a Friday night because Friday night was bingo night and Mum and her dad, Thomas, were at bingo in Streatham. Dad was looking after Peter and me. We were sitting together watching television. I was seven, Peter was twelve. Outside we could hear this bloke having a conversation beneath our window. It was a black guy on the street talking to his friend, who was leaning from a window in a house across the road. Dad opened our window and shouted down: 'Excuse me, mate, do us a favour and walk across the road to talk to him – I've got two kids trying to sleep here.' I think the black guy said something like, 'Fuck you, man, come and make me.' That was a red rag to a bull.

'Just wait here, boys, I've got something to sort out,' Dad said.

On his way Dad called to our neighbours, Sheila and Bill Campbell. 'Just keep an eye on the boys for a second,' he said. As Dad walked towards him, the black guy sensed what was going to happen and took off his coat and hat – he was wearing a big trilby. Then someone shouted, 'Col, he's picked up a bottle.' Peter and I were watching from our window as Dad just walked straight up to the man, who tried to hit him with the bottle. Dad ducked and caught the guy with a combination and he went down. Then Dad belted him with punch after punch.

From across the road, the other black man rushed to help his friend and then Dad's mate, Paul Huggett, came out of his house with a golf club in his hand. Loads of people had heard the commotion and were watching from their windows. On the front of our flat, we had thick glass with corrugated wiring through it and as we were watching, Peter somehow put his knee through that.

For a seven-year-old and his twelve-year-old brother, it was terrifying. There was now a group of people on the road; Dad, the guy he had beaten up, his mate from across the street and Paul Huggett. The mate and Paul were grappling over the golf club and Dad had just about finished with the first bloke. 'Right, that's it,' he said, 'you've had enough now, you're gonna fuck off now. I've had enough too.'

The bloke was screaming. Then he became quieter and it seemed like everything was about to die down. But the guy Dad had beaten got up and started shaping up to my dad as if he was Muhammad Ali.

A mistake.

What happened next was terrible. Dad picked up the golf club, which had fallen on to the ground, and smashed it across the guy's head. His face was cut, his cheekbone must have been in bits. The man went down, his mate tried to look after him and Dad turned and walked away, the golf club still in his hand. When he came inside he just said, 'Calm down, it's all sorted now.'

I don't remember if an ambulance came for the man. It was a bad fight and if it happened now, it would be seen as racist. We weren't a racist family and Dad wasn't a racist. He would have reacted the same if a white man had taken him on; his fiery nature didn't differentiate between black and white. About an hour or so later, things seemed to have settled down. The three of us were watching telly again when the first brick came through the window. Then another and another. Dad grabbed Peter and me and took us next door. When the bricks stopped and the fellows who were throwing them dispersed, Dad took us round to our nan's in West Norwood. He decided we would hole out there until things quietened down in Claylands Court. Not long afterwards Dad went back with a mate to see how things were; the flat was all boarded up, though inside everything was as we had left it.

They were spotted as they went in, and within minutes some guys were outside and they hadn't turned up to welcome Dad back. 'I'm going to call the cops, Col,' his mate said. 'We're sitting targets here.'

My dad, being my dad, didn't see it like that. 'Don't worry,' he said. General Custer was prepared for his last stand, ready to fight to the death. As he opened the door two of the guys tried to brick him in the face, so he shut it, then, opened it again quickly and chased his would-be attackers with a screwdriver. They got away and Dad's mate persuaded him to call it quits and get the hell out of there. Dad was still adamant that we would return to Claylands Court but Mum, who was not a violent person at all, said she would never go back. That was it, we never did. Dad bought a house in South Norwood, 3 Lonsdale Road, and it became our home.

I'd be interested to know if that black guy is still around. He can't not remember that night. Even now it almost makes me sick. The episode nearly drove my mum to a nervous breakdown and it wasn't a nice time for our family. To be honest, Dad didn't bat an eyelid. One of those things that had to be sorted; that was him.

Over the years that night was recalled at different family gatherings and Dad would be asked to tell the story again. He would never boast about it, nor would he express much sorrow. Where he came from, there came a point in every argument where your fists did the talking. It was violent but it wasn't guns-and-knives violent and Dad brought us up to look after ourselves. Peter used to have Dad's temper but he's calmed down a lot. I'm not a violent person, but even so, the bit in the Bible about turning the other cheek never made much sense to me.

Dad's own father, Ernie Woodman, was the same. He never backed down. Ernie was a bare-knuckle fighter and sparring partner for Tommy Farr, who was British heavyweight champion in the 1930s and fought Joe Louis for the world title in New York. Dad was supposed to have been sensational in the ring and was meant to go to New York to train out there. But he got a taste for drinking and womanizing at an early age and that spoiled him. In the end his biggest claim to fame was that he was Terry Downes's sparring partner. Downes won the world middleweight title in 1961. Granddad never forgave his son for not making the most of his boxing talent. When Dad was into middle age, Ernie would still introduce him to his friends as 'My son Colin, you know he could've been a fighter.' Always that qualification about what Dad could have been.

Ernie was a well-respected man. He was big into gambling and ran a bookmaking business at a time when betting shops had not yet been legalized. He had a pitch at Hove dog track and at Epsom racetrack. At the dogs, Granddad's friends would slip me a fiver or even a tenner. 'Don't take that, just say "No, thank you,"' Dad would say before Granddad overruled him: 'Let the boy take it.' At the end of the night, no one could tell whether Granddad had won or lost money. The smile was always the same. Back at his house, he would say, 'Count the money, son, what's there?' And if you asked, 'How did you do tonight, Granddad?', he would just say, 'Good, son. Yeah, good.'

He was a very upright man, both in his build and in his mentality. Once, when he was sixty, a punter at the dog track claimed my granddad had diddled him over the odds of a dog. There was one thing you didn't do to Granddad and that was call him a cheat. He got down off his bookmaker's box and, even though the punter was about twenty years younger than him, Granddad knocked him clean out. The police turned up but they knew Ernie and didn't even question him; the punter must have had it coming.

Granddad never lost his love for the fight game and for a long time was chairman of the Sussex Ex-Boxers' Association. He would write the newsletter, arrange the reunions and keep the thing going. We loved visiting him, although there was always one moment of dread. Just before Mum and Dad took us home, Granddad would say, 'Okay boy, let's see you shape up before you go.' So I would put up my fists and get into position.

'No, no, you're a southpaw,' he would say.

We would have a little spar. Not too little. He had these big, shovel-like hands and Mum, bless her, could not bear to see her little diamond getting roughed up. To Granddad, it was the slightest tap, but to me it felt like my brain was rocking inside my head. The tears would well up but I wouldn't cry. You couldn't cry in front of your granddad and your dad.

We saw just as much of my other set of grandparents, Thomas and Daphne. Their prefab house in West Norwood was the place where the family congregated, especially on Sundays. The ladies would go into the kitchen and make sandwiches, the men would sit around the table in the living room and play cards. They played kaluki, which is thirteen-card rummy, three-card brag and a game called nap. My cousin Darren and I would be bankers for our dads, counting their change, stacking it into neat piles and learning to play by watching them. Years later I introduced Gareth to kaluki and we have had many sessions. My nan's home in West Norwood was one of those houses that no member of the family would walk past. She used to leave the back door open.

Now and again I find myself back in West Norwood thinking, 'This isn't a place you'd want to live in.' It's like many of the London suburban areas: crime-ridden, dour, sad really. Then I think, 'Was it that much different when I was growing up?' Cousins from the country used to visit us and although they never said anything, you could tell from their reactions they thought it was rough. But when you're in there, you're familiar with the territory and the tough guys are people you know well. My memories of Claylands Court are happy ones; the same goes for Lonsdale Road.

Ours was a fairly happy home. Mum and Dad had rows, as most couples do, and generally they were about money. Peter and I never went without but money was tight. Mum, though, held things together. She was a very loving person and backed Peter and me no matter what. She loved us, dressed us, cooked for us, cleaned for us and argued for us. If we said white was black, Mum said, 'Well, then it must be.' It wasn't easy for Dad, because he would sometimes reprimand us, only for Mum to take our side. Her personality was the source of the happiness in our home. Mum, you see, was the sort of woman that lit up a room as soon as she walked into it. She was the life and soul of every family gathering and people just took to her. In her company, Dad was always quieter and would naturally slip into the background. As we got older, she moved with the times and encouraged us to discuss everything with her. It wasn't a problem talking to Mum about girlfriends, the problem was finding one good enough to take home. I tried it once. Mum wasn't impressed and I knew there was no point.

When Peter and I started going to dances and nightclubs, Mum would sleep lightly until we got in. She would hear the taxi – it might be two, three or even four in the morning – and still she'd come down to the kitchen: 'I'm sure you wouldn't say no to a cup of tea and some toast.' She knew we had been drinking and reckoned the tea and toast would help offset the effects of the alcohol. During those years there were lots of times when Peter's comings and goings got him into trouble and Dad always seemed to be hard on him.

Although Peter wasn't a bad footballer, he preferred girls and Dad didn't think that was right. Part of the problem was Peter and Dad were so alike – both had quick tempers – but Mum was brilliant at protecting Peter. Because I was more like her and could cheekily talk my way out of situations, Mum didn't have to work as hard for me.

It helped, too, that I was so into football. Dad trained Peter's school team and I was allowed to train with them. My football education continued at St Luke's Primary School in West Norwood, where Mr Cooper was our sports teacher. Apart from the opportunity to play football, school didn't interest me at all. Mum didn't see it as that important either and she didn't push me. If I didn't want to go, I didn't have to: 'Okay, you can stay at home today, son, if you're not keen to go.'

But I was no thicko; I passed an exam to get into a private

school called Trinity. Mum and Dad couldn't afford the fees but under some scholarship scheme or other, all I had to do was pass the entrance exam. I got through it but when we sat down to talk about it at home, all we could see was the fact that this school played rugby and not football. On that basis we turned it down. Even then, football was more important than school and my education would come on the streets rather than in the classroom.

In the middle of my O levels, I went down to Basingstoke, where my cousin was having a stag week. He was twenty-three and I was fifteen and don't ask me how, but I got into a club called Martine's, where I drank eleven or twelve pints of lager. Dad made sure when I was going out with my cousins that there was money in my pocket. For three or four days we were on a bit of a binge. Being in Basingstoke meant missing two exams but that wasn't a big deal. People will be horrified, but that's the way it was back then. There was always the feeling that I would land on my feet. I was the kind of fellow who could turn a bob or two, selling this, selling that, doing odd jobs. Even now, when I try to remember a particular time in my youth, I am likely to wonder, 'Was that the Christmas I was selling the fake perfume?' Probably.

Gareth

Ah, childhood: football, rugby, cross–country running, and then some more football. Everything was fine until our school team lost. Then the journey home on the minibus was a nightmare.

We had a good team at Pound Hill in Crawley and an excellent football teacher in Mr Cripps, Christopher Cripps. I was eleven or twelve at the time and though we were good, we lost a few games. Days I still remember. I would try to get a seat by the window because there the other boys wouldn't notice me so much. Losing upset me, always had me close to tears and sometimes I just couldn't hold them back. Embarrassed and imagining everyone was looking at me, I went for a seat by the window and pretended to look out.

Once my mum joked in front of the other boys, 'If you don't win, you don't get any dinner.' For them, that explained it: 'No wonder he's cryin', he's not going to get any dinner.' I just hated to lose and couldn't deal with it when it happened. It wasn't just at football. At school we had a rounders tournament, boys and girls playing together, and it seemed everyone knew how desperate I was to win. If our class got beaten, they would taunt me because they knew I would bawl. On one particular day I decided, 'I've got to stop myself doing this' and dug my fingernails into the palm of my hand. It didn't work; the disappointment of losing was greater than the pain of fingernails pressed into flesh. So the tears still flowed.

It has never changed. I've always been a terrible loser. Even in a simple game of Scrabble with Woody, I have sat there for hours, desperately coming up with two- and three-letter words that do not exist. Or a game of head-tennis at training; it's got to be won. Professional footballers are competitive and, for most of us, the post-match mood depends upon the result. Defeat wrecks my head. One experience stands above all the others. It was New Year's Eve 1994; Palace had lost 1–0 at home to Blackburn Rovers and I blamed myself for the goal. Playing midfield at the time, I let a runner go and he scored. Not many saw the goal as my fault, but that didn't matter. We lost and it *had* been my fault. At the time I was single, living alone in a flat, and all the boys were going to clubs to ring in the new year. Not me. I sat in, replaying the goal in my head, torturing myself and then reminding myself our next game was just two days away. Pathetic, but that's how I was. Over the years, I have become a little more discreet, but not much different.

You mature and deal better with the game's inevitable disappointments. Getting married and starting a family has helped. On a Saturday evening our children, Mia and Flynn, are not bothered whether their dad's team has won or lost. Neither does Alison fret too much about football and this is how I like it. Regardless of the result, it's up to me to ensure that no one's evening is ruined because of things that happened on a football field. The agonizing waits until Alison and the kids are asleep. Then I lie awake: 'Why didn't you do this, why didn't you do that?'

It isn't easy to explain where the manic will to win comes from. Not from my dad, anyway. Clive Southgate has always been a calm man, almost easygoing. I don't think he's ever lost his temper in my presence and though he was a keen sportsman, he believed in losing with dignity. He did athletics, played football and, later in life, turned out for a junior rugby club in Hertfordshire. Luton Town signed him on schoolboy terms but he didn't consider football a realistic career option. The money wasn't great, there was no security and he believed he would be better off getting a proper job. That meant IBM, where he worked as a facilities manager. Anything that went wrong in the IBM building where he was stationed was his responsibility.

I was born in Watford but we lived there for just three years before Dad was transferred to a branch of IBM in Bolton. Not long afterwards he was moved to Bury. We spent three years up North, but as we left before I started school there is little that I remember. From a very early age, Manchester United were my football team and I'm sure that was the result of living in Lancashire. After Bury, Dad was transferred to Portsmouth and we spent over three years down there. Portsmouth was where I started school but the most vivid memory I have of our time there was of the day we left. The primary school I attended was due to have its first football match on that very day, but because we were moving, I couldn't play. To me it was a terrible injustice and I held it against my mum. After Portsmouth, Dad was transferred to IBM at Croydon in south London and we moved to the new town of Crawley. At last we had a permanent home.

Mum and Dad met when both were representing Hertfordshire at an English Schools' athletics meeting. Barbara, my mum, was a hurdler, Dad was a javelin thrower. When I began to play football, they would come to watch and when my sister, Michelle, arrived, she too was dragged along to the games. Dad was very supportive but always in an understated way. He watched quietly, didn't get overexcited and though he offered constant encouragement, he never interfered from the sideline. When another parent came and said how well I had played, you could sense Dad's embarrassment and he always tried to find something positive to say about the son of the person who had approached him.

Occasionally in matches, I might get injured and have to be treated off the pitch. Other parents would come over to see how I was, but though his concern was obvious, Dad never made a fuss. 'Are you okay?' he would ask quietly. At home he was boss and if Mum wanted to win an argument with me, she only had to say, 'Wait till your father comes home.' It wasn't in my nature to push things and as there was just my sister Michelle and I, Dad didn't have to be much of a disciplinarian.

In his quiet way, Dad has had an enormous effect on my life. He and my granddad, my mum's dad, Arthur Toll, were the two men that I wanted to be like. Dad lost his mum when he was an infant and his dad never came back from the Second World War; it was presumed he had been killed. Dad was raised by an aunt and his nan. Decades later he discovered his father had not been killed but had met another woman and emigrated to Canada. He died eight years ago. It wasn't something Dad ever spoke about and my feeling was he didn't want to burden us with it. Instead he put everything into his own family. We always came first. There have been times in my career when I've put football before family and a voice in my head has whispered, 'Dad wouldn't have done that.' Without ever asking to be, he has been my guiding light.

Mum and he were alike in that way. Expressions of emotion were not their style, but they had a way of making me feel loved. Mum and I have always got on well and she still speaks of me as if I'm her little boy. During the fall-out after the penalty miss at Euro 96, her naivety in the face of the media interest caused her a lot of hurt. As a kid I used to practise penalties in the back garden, endlessly driving the ball into an empty goal and I used to tell Mum that if ever I had to take an important penalty, I would blast it. So when we spoke on the night of the missed penalty, she ruefully lamented that I hadn't honoured my boyhood promise. 'I thought you said you would belt it.'

'Yeah, but not really, Mum.'

Then, the following day, journalists doorstepped her, following her to the school where she worked and asking if she wouldn't mind posing for a photograph. They wondered if she had spoken to me. What had been said? Mum had never spoken to a reporter in her life and she innocently said, 'I asked him why he didn't belt it like he said he would.' For the newspapers, that was perfect. In the following day's *Daily*

Telegraph, Mum was pictured on the front page with the headline 'Why didn't you just belt it, son?' A few days later there was a cartoon of me practising in the garden, 100 balls in the net, Mum standing at the back door and me saying to her: 'I've been belting them all night, Mum, can I come in now?'

It seems funny now but at the time it deeply upset Mum. She felt she had betrayed me when I was feeling low and had added to my problems. Knowing the way these things work, it didn't bother me in the slightest, but Mum was down about it for days afterwards. From that day, she has never spoken to another journalist.

Arthur Toll, my granddad, lived in Watford. His grand-children all called him 'Grumpy' which was the oddest thing because he was anything but. When I was young we would spend Christmas with Granddad and my nan. The first game of football I ever saw was Watford on Boxing Day. One of Granddad's friends was a devout Watford fan who saved the match programmes until I arrived each Christmas. I studied those programmes for hours on end. Granddad and Dad were the men to first kick a ball with me and yet that's not what I most recall about them. Before everything else, they placed good manners and respect for others. In their world, you didn't know how to behave if you didn't stand when a lady entered the room. Any kind of bad language was unheard of and everything had to be done properly. Their attitude had an enormous impact on me.

Granddad, especially, was a real old-style English gentle-man. He had been in the Royal Marines and it was natural for him to get up at 5.30 or six in the morning. Hearing him, I would go down to the kitchen and watch as he put shaving foam on his face or maybe polished his shoes. How he shined those shoes! Though he used a walking stick, he was a strong walker and would go into the centre of Watford each morning, a three- or four-mile journey. He dressed immaculately: shirt, tie, waistcoat, overcoat and hat. For an occasion of any sort, he wore a suit. Had to be a suit. His hair, of course, was always Brylcreemed back. I wanted to live up to his standards, and when I first started to use public transport, it was a shock to find men who sat and read their papers while ladies stood.

One of the only rows I've had with Woody was over him wearing a cap in a restaurant. We were in the south of Spain on holiday with Woody's dad, Colin, and a few of Colin's friends. Sitting round a table, waiting to order, I said to Woody: 'Would you take off your hat?'

'No, no, no. *He's* my father, not you,' he said pointing to Colin.

'You're showing no respect for other people,' I said.

'Look, mate, don't tell me what to do.'

'I'm only saying what's right.'

'You're not my effing father.'

It was a hell of a row. The rest of the lads were aghast, because they had never seen Woody and me argue. Understandably, he resented me telling him how to behave, but it was a big thing in my eyes. We've talked about it afterwards, argued some more, but I notice he's changed his view and ticks off the young lads at his club when they wear caps in the canteen. 'Take your cap off, it's not right when you're eating.'

The goalkeeper turned gamekeeper.

3

When you're looking for a friend don't look for perfection, just look for friendship.
    Unknown

Gareth

Ian Botham once said he always knew he would be a cricketer and go on to play for England. It was similar for me; not that I was convinced about playing for England, but in my mind I never was going to be anything other than a footballer. My results at school were good enough to take me as far as I wished to go in education but the thought of going to university never entered my head. Football was going to be my life. How did I know? I just did.

Maybe it was in the way I could influence the game when playing with my schoolmates. It is natural for kids to play selfishly, to beat as many players as they can and then score themselves. I would beat as many as I could but then lay on a pass for someone else to score. I didn't need or even want the limelight. You looked around and not many of the other boys could resist that.

Along the way there were other signs. At the age of nine, I played for our local Sunday under-12 team, Crawley Traders, even though you were supposed to be ten before you played at that level. During my second year at Poundhill, I would regularly go to watch the school team. It was for third- and fourth-year students but when the older boys saw me at the matches, they would say, 'Oh, sir, he should be playing.' Mr Cripps, the football teacher, wouldn't have it, though. Chris Cripps was a very good coach and though I played centre midfield, he said, 'You'll end up as a centre-back.' 'No chance,' I said. Bryan Robson was my hero and the kind of player I wanted to be.

When it comes to football, kids are not stupid. Among their peers, they know who can play and what it means to be selected for the district team. All the time they compare themselves to the other boys; how did I do against him, was I better? Every moment of the match is relived. When I played a game for the school, one that Dad couldn't attend because he was working, I replayed every move that evening for him and though he was often tired, he always listened.

At comprehensive school it was harder to make the team and when the teacher made me captain, that was a sign that I could play. I also made the county side and felt comfortable at that level. All of this encouraged me to believe in myself and made me more determined to be a footballer. It was a dreamy sort of ambition because I knew nothing of the realities of life as a professional footballer. Because Dad had a realistic attitude regarding my ability, he would never offer false hope. I might praise a certain player from an opposing team and Dad would say, 'You're as good as he is, son.' Or, talking about another player, he would say, 'He's stronger in the air than you are.' Though he never overpraised me, neither did he discourage me.

From twelve to sixteen, the quality of my life was measured by what happened on the football field. One year Dad paid for me to go on a summer course run by Bobby Nash, who played for a local side in Crawley but also worked for Southampton. Towards the end of the week another coach came up from Southampton and he and Bobby picked out three of us and asked if we would like to train with them at a centre Southampton had at East Grinstead. Around this time, the Southampton youth set-up was magnificent. As well as the East Grinstead centre, they had another one in Newcastle and, of course, the main one was at the club itself in Southampton. We trained at East Grinstead on Friday evenings and occasionally we would travel to Southampton and play against the centre there. Lads came from the Newcastle centre as well and I'm sure I played against Alan Shearer in one of those games.

Southampton's interest in me was shortlived. Convinced I would not be big enough to cope with the rigours of professional football, they released me. The news came in a letter and it shattered me. 'Dear Gareth Southgate,' it began, 'we will not be offering your son a place at the Slough/East Grinstead/Newcastle/Southampton centre of excellence . . .' It was the standard. 'Dear Gareth Southgate' was handwritten and while I understand that clubs have to send out hundreds of these letters, the kid who is rejected receives only one. It bothered me too that they confused my first name with Dad's.

Playing with Southampton had set me apart from my friends, some of whom were training with Crystal Palace. After the letter, I lost my status. I became the boy 'let go by Southampton'. That difference was everything. I kept the letter and still have it. A reminder to me that people did not believe I was good enough and it was up to me to prove them wrong. Invariably, I have responded well to being put down or criticized.

The Arsenal scout Fred Ricketts watched me play for a Crawley district team. He spoke with my dad afterwards and suggested I needed to play in a stronger league. Fred gave Dad his card – it had the Gunners' logo on it – and Dad passed it on to me. Countless times I gazed at that card and wondered. Fred's advice sent Dad and me in search of a more competitive league. We ended up going with Selsdon Juniors in the Shirley and District League at Croydon. Derek Millen ran the team and was also a scout for Palace. Derek knew a good player when he saw one and was able to persuade the best to join Selsdon. Our team at Selsdon was close to invincible and we played in a league where it was customary to have scouts watching the games.

John Whitfield was one of those scouts and he watched most of Selsdon's matches. John was friendly with Alan Smith, who ran the youth team at Palace, and many Selsdon players had the option of training with Palace. At fifteen, I trained there on Thursday evenings. It became a routine: train from Crawley to Croydon, link up with Dad at IBM and then drive to Palace's training ground at Mitcham. Not long after I started, the youth development officer, Peter Prentice, approached me and said. 'Look, we want you to travel with the third team on Saturday, they're playing at Oxford.' Without knowing what team he was talking about, I agreed. That evening I went home and looked up a programme to see if Palace had three youth sides. They hadn't. There was the first team, the reserves and their South East Counties side, effectively their third eleven. It was an adult team and, at the age of fifteen, I was involved.

That first experience was just a ten-minute role as substitute and though I did well enough, it was an eye-opener. This was the professional game: faster, more intense, more physical, more brutal than anything I'd seen. At half-time the players got shouted at and bollocked in a way that I could hardly believe. At that moment I got an inkling of the reality of being a professional footballer. In this world you would be questioned like never before, you questioned yourself and the insecurities that followed stayed with you for the rest of your career.

Gone for ever was the easy confidence of the kid in the Sunday league team and the certainty that, come hell or high water, you could perform at that level. Even from that first taste of the professional game, there was the message that good preparation is the key to everything. If you were unprepared for what you had to face, there would be a price to pay.

You'd think that with time and experience this would stop being a problem. Not true. The 2001–02 season, my first with Middlesbrough, was one of the best of my career. Lucky to have avoided any injury, I played consistently well. One exception was the match against Newcastle at St James' Park on Boxing Day. As a team our preparation was wrong. Bad weather meant much of the training was indoors and when we met on Christmas Day, we allowed the festive season to affect our focus. From my own point of view, we had moved into our new house in Yorkshire a week before and I felt bad leaving Alison and Mia on Christmas Day. Had there been family staying with us, it wouldn't have been a problem but that Christmas Day I felt lousy leaving the house. For probably the only time in my career, family came before football and, not properly tuned in to the match, I played badly. Physically fit and mentally sharp, I know I will play well and it is my responsibility to make sure that when I get on that pitch, I am ready.

Even though it was a huge leap for a fifteen-year-old, playing for the South East Counties team helped me enormously. John Salako, Chris Powell and Richard Shaw were in the side and in that first season I played twelve or thirteen times and came on as a sub in a lot more. Being part of that team brought a little reality to my dream and it ensured that the people at Palace saw me play far more than other fifteen-year-olds. At school it was O-level year and my parents, especially Mum, wanted me to stay on to do A levels. That wasn't going to happen. In early spring, the people at Palace spoke to me: 'We'd like to take you on as a full-time apprentice next year.' They told me to go away and think about it. My mind was made up, but not my parents'.

At school I competed for all the teams: football, rugby, basketball, cricket and cross-country. Homework was fitted into the gaps between matches and training; often it had to be left until the fifteen minutes before the first lesson the next morning. But I kept up and my eight O levels weren't bad; two As, four Bs and two Cs. Certainly good enough to encourage Mum to press the case for staying on at school, but even though I was just sixteen, my parents were prepared to leave the decision to me. Dad was cautious but inclined towards the football route. 'You might not get the chance again,' he said. Mum leaned towards further education. I was the person with the most definite view: it had to be football. My O-level results were okay but in terms of my future, I knew they were irrelevant.

It quickly became clear that it had been the right decision. Two of the other boys offered places by Palace opted to stay in school and train at Palace for a couple of days each week. Alan Smith encouraged them and said how important it was that they kept up their education, but with the best will in the world, the two student-footballers weren't treated the same as the rest of us at the football club. Because they didn't have to do the boot-cleaning, floor-cleaning and toilet-cleaning, they weren't treated as equals by the other lads. If someone had to be left out of the team, it would be one of the lads still going to school. After all, they had something to fall back on. It gave the coaches an out and it even gave the boys themselves one too. If you give people an out in life, they will take it.

The summer before the start of my apprenticeship at Palace, I played for their under-16 side. Our first game was at Wimbledon's training ground and the occasion has stayed in my mind because our goalkeeper was Andy Woodman. We had seen each other before; he played for Selsdon Juniors at the time but as he was an age-group down, we didn't get to know each other. It was the same at Palace, although my dad had met and talked with his dad. And then on this Saturday afternoon, we were together for the first time on the same side. We were dressed in our Palace blazers, tie and grey flannels and as we waited for the minibus to take us to the game, you might have expected a certain awkwardness as young lads got to know each other.

Woody wasn't like that. Full of chirpiness, he made jokes and gave the impression he had seen it all before. 'Who is this guy?' I thought. 'How can he be so cocky?' For over a year, that's how I saw him. Confident, even too confident, and with too much to say. 'Not my cup of tea,' I thought.

Andy

The day I signed for Crystal Palace was as good as it gets. It wasn't just I who signed, but my whole family. South Norwood was a stone's throw from Selhurst Park. Palace was in our blood: we loved the club. At the age of ten, I won a goalkeeping competition and the prize was a week's training with Paul Barron, Palace's keeper at the time. Alan Mullery was the manager and I spent a week at the club's training ground in Mitcham. It was a fantastic experience for a kid, standing in goal and trying my best as the first team fired in shots. Billy Gilbert was a hero of mine and I was diving this way and that, trying to keep his shots out. There is a photograph of me and Paul Barron from that week and it still has pride of place in Dad's house.

Dad supported Palace with a passion. When we lived in the flat at Claylands Court, he and a group of mates who were also avid Palace fans would travel all over the country following the team. Every week they would bet on the first goalscorer. Their number dwindled as fellows got married and had families. Dad still went and when I was growing up, there was never any question about the club I would support. I was on the terraces at Selhurst Park on the day the team beat Burnley to earn promotion to the First Division. Fifty-two thousand people attended that game and I can easily remember Dave Swindlehurst scoring the winner. My mum worked in the Palace lottery office and during school holidays, I would tag along when she went to the club. While she was working, I went to the café up the road, Bertos, and I would hang around until the players turned up for breakfast. Vince Hilaire, Kenny Sansom and Billy Gilbert were the three I remember most.

At the age of thirteen and fourteen, I was getting a good reputation as a young goalkeeper and was offered a trial for Arsenal's under-15 side. As I had signed schoolboy forms with Palace, this wasn't proper but I told a few white lies and played with the Arsenal lads. It was a great experience and I loved it. They were impressed with me, asked me to come back and said they were interested in signing me. But when it came down to it, Palace was my club and I was committed to them. There was no way I could have gone home and told my family that I was switching to Arsenal. It would have led to murder.

Whatever I was as a goalkeeper was down to Dad. He was the driving force and without him, it wouldn't have happened. At the beginning I was an outfield player but switched to goalkeeper during a school game when our keeper got injured. From that one experience in goal, I was recommended for trials for South

London. For thirteen weeks, the trials went on; each week some of the fellows were discarded and the numbers were gradually whittled down. At the time I was ten, maybe eleven, and couldn't see the point of so many trials. 'I'm not getting anywhere, I don't want to go no more,' I said to my dad. He said if I stuck at it, he'd buy me a video recorder. 'Jesus Christ,' I thought, 'a video recorder, a bloody video recorder.'

I made the South London team and then went on to play for London.

After our move to South Norwood, I went to Ingram High School and, outside the London catchment area, I now had to play for Croydon Schools and then Surrey. Mr Jones, a teacher at Ashburton High School, was manager of the Croydon and Surrey teams and there was a goalkeeper from his school that he preferred to me. Kevin Keel was the lad's name and I was understudy to him for a couple of years. Eventually, he just gave up and my turn came. Getting into that side seemed such a breakthrough at the time. I loved playing, loved the banter and the fun of being in a team. And Dad wanted it almost more than I did.

Was he making sure I didn't waste my natural talent for football, as his dad used to say he had done with boxing? From the moment I began playing until I got married and moved away from London, Dad didn't miss a match. Every school game, every district game, every county game, every youth-team game and every reserve-team game: he was always there.

People ask who was the greatest influence on my career; Mum was important, my brother, Peter, too, but no one was greater than Dad. After a bad game, I felt I had let him down and would be more disappointed for him than for myself. We would argue on the way home from matches: 'You should have come for that cross, you should have held that shot, you should have done this, should have done that.'

After we became friends, Gareth copped how I glanced over

at my dad after making a mistake in a game. Dad desperately wanted me to do well and I could read his disappointment from a mile off; the way he would shake his head or just look at me. When things went well, he wasn't the kind who would get hold of you, give you a hug and say, 'You was out of this world today, son.' No, he would just say, 'You did all right, son, but you kicked one ball badly.' People thought he was hard on me, but I didn't. Dad was just Dad and thank God. For the last sixteen years, I've been lucky to earn a living from the game. Without his encouragement and pushing, I wouldn't have made it. He believed in me.

At the age of eleven, I joined Selsdon Juniors, who were the top club in the Shirley and District League in Croydon. Selsdon always had players who were being watched and courted by the professional clubs. Charlie Hartfield, who joined Arsenal, played on our side at Selsdon, as did Lee Sauthion, who was taken on by Palace. I was fourteen when Palace signed me as a schoolboy and I always believed that when the time came, they would take me on as an apprentice. As it turned out, I got that place but it was close.

Carl Ramsey was the other goalkeeper and we were both at Palace and played in under-16 games. Every Monday and Thursday we trained, so the youth team coach, Alan Smith, had plenty of opportunity to assess us. Carl wasn't a bad goalkeeper and he was a really nice guy. He had big curly hair and we used to call him Joey Boswell after the character from the television series *Bread*. But playing for Palace was my destiny and I believed I would be the chosen one.

Alan Smith called both of us into his office at the same time. He looked at us and paused. It struck me that this was no sure thing and suddenly the pause seemed like an eternity. 'Between you two,' he said, 'there's nothing. *Nothing*. But I'm going to let you go, Carl. We'll have you on a non-contract basis where you can still come in and train.' He then looked at me. 'I'm going to take you, Woody, as an apprentice.'

It was the happiest day of my life. There was no reason for me to have been as confident as I was. Alan Smith was right; there was nothing between Carl and I, but I was the chosen one and, at that moment, that was all that mattered.

4

Do not protect yourself by a fence, but rather by your friends.
   Czech proverb

Gareth

Do I remember the first summons to the manager's office? Actually, I do. It came about two months into my apprenticeship at Crystal Palace; at a time when the contrast between dream and reality was at its most striking.

The call came on a Friday afternoon, the caller was our youth-team manager, Alan Smith. I imagined he was going to ask about my injury. Alan had been telling us we were physically weak and not aggressive enough. We needed to put our foot in. Results were horrendous. Alan was entitled to say whatever he wished. Woody was letting in hatfuls of goals but it wasn't down to him. The whole team was playing poorly. Everyone felt under pressure, lads were afraid in training and the atmosphere was terrible. As for enjoyment, it didn't come into it.

That Friday morning I tried to put Alan's advice into practice and went into a fierce tackle and though I came out with the ball, there was a deep gash on my shin. Alan had little sympathy and told me to go and get it seen to. At the hospital I had six stitches, and after I returned to the training ground at Mitcham, Gary O'Reilly, the former Tottenham player who was at Palace, offered me a lift home. He lived in Crawley and it wasn't that much out of his way. As we were leaving the training ground Alan said he wanted to see me. 'How is it?' he asked.

'Fine,' I said. 'I got six stitches in it.'

His mood changed. This was a little speech he had been preparing and, in hindsight, he may even have found it hard. That didn't stop him. 'Sit down,' he said, 'let me tell you how I think you're doing.'

'Okay.'

'You've been crap, absolute crap. Since you've come here you've done nothing, given us no indication that we were right to take you on.'

He could see my devastation. 'You're sitting there, feeling sorry for yourself, thinking you're going to miss tomorrow's game. I'm telling you now, son, you wouldn't have been playing anyway.'

Never in my life had I been dropped from a team. It just didn't happen to me.

Alan saw the tears welling up in my eyes. 'You have to fucking toughen up, mentally and physically; otherwise you're no good to this football club, no good to yourself, no good to anyone. When you came here, I had high hopes for you. I admit if you were my son, I'd be proud of you. As a travel agent or an estate agent, you'd be perfect. As a footballer, no fucking chance.'

All I could do was keep back the tears. Knowing Alan liked me just made it harder. I didn't want to hear what he was saying, yet I knew it was the truth. By the time I got to Gary's car I was in tears. He was brilliant. After Alan, I needed someone's sympathy. Gary listened patiently as I recounted the biggest bollocking I'd ever got. He told me how hard it had been for him coming through at Tottenham and gave me a lot of encouragement. Some of the senior pros at Palace were dismissive of him because of his injuries, but he couldn't have been nicer to me. It wasn't just that day. He continued to be friendly and helpful to me until he moved on three seasons later.

The mauling from Alan was a turning point though. Physically I was soft and had to toughen up. Mentally I was developing but I wasn't hard enough. Alan's brutal assessment left me with a choice: go under or push on. It was no contest. From that day, I was going to show people how much I wanted to be a professional footballer. You see, I was the lad who had gone to school and had a string of good O levels – something to fall back on – and that was how I was playing. If this didn't work, I could get a proper job. Stuff the exam results, stuff the five years' schoolwork, stuff the proper job: they were crutches that held me back. What did it matter that you had good school results if Chris Powell lapped you on a circuit of the training ground at Mitcham? The guys who made it were hard and single-minded. There were plenty of tough lads in our dressing room and they were going to find I wasn't soft.

Next day I went to Mitcham for our game against Oxford. Injured or dropped or, in my case, injured and dropped, you were expected to be there in your Palace blazer, grey flannel pants and club tie. We were hammered 6–2. As I had to fetch the half-time and full-time teas, I couldn't follow the match that closely but it wasn't difficult to get the drift. Oxford destroyed us. At the end of the game our youth development officer, Peter Prentice, told me the Oxford lad who scored five was only over on trial from Ireland. And then there was Joey Beauchamp. Every Palace boy who played in that game remembers him; he ripped us apart and his crosses must have led to four or five of the Oxford goals.

The lads filtered into the dressing room, I was there helping with the teas. Players who miss a bad defeat will often turn up in the dressing room just to hear the bollocking: 'You can't blame me, I wasn't playing.' But I felt none of that. Alan had told me what he thought of my football the day before. Now he was about to tell the lads what he thought of them. He was calm at first, pointing out things that were wrong and speaking in a general way about the poor performances. We weren't hard enough; we thought we were better than we were. Then he snapped and started on individuals, dissecting each one and finding nothing that was any good. When a manager loses it, players sometimes feel as inclined to laugh as cry, but during this performance we all knew it would have been suicidal to laugh.

At first some of the lads tried to say there were logical reasons why the team wasn't producing but that just fuelled Alan's anger. After a while, there was no point and you leaned close to the wall and hoped he didn't notice you.

Alan slaughtered everyone who had played. Though I didn't feel comfortable, I thought that the previous day's bollocking and the fact that I hadn't played might save me. Fat chance. 'You're sitting there,' he said, 'and you haven't even played. Well don't be sitting there looking smug in your blazer and trousers. You've done nothing at this club.' He then repeated what he had said to me in his office. I was a smashing kid. But a footballer? 'No fucking chance.'

Alan's tirade lasted nearly two hours. Once he got into his stride, there was no stopping him. Every player was getting it. And we all knew where it would end up. Woody was going to be a big target. He had let in twenty-one goals in six games, he was a year younger than most of us and it was obvious that he wasn't physically strong enough. One of the second-years said it was hard if you were always conceding soft goals and that was the cue into Andy.

Andy

One goal from that infamous 6–2 hammering by Oxford has stuck with me all these years. It can't have been one of the early ones because it was the kind of goal that comes when your confidence is shot to pieces. The cross came over, no more than four or five yards from goal. As it arrived Chris Powell shouted, 'Woody, come!' I wasn't sure. Then it was too late. At the last second, Powelly realized I wasn't coming and lunged to hook the ball away. Instead he just turned it past me. I can still see it; Powelly's look, the stare, the utter disbelief, turning away, shaking his head: 'For fuck's sake, Woody.'

When the game ended, we had a 200-yard walk to the dressing room. We were in the one used by the pros when they trained at Mitcham. I would have preferred a 20-mile walk, anything to put off what was coming. I was dreading it. Alan Smith wasn't going to let this go and everyone knew that if you conceded six goals, the goalkeeper must have been crap. To be fair, I was crap.

At sixteen, you don't know a lot. I thought it best to accept responsibility for the goals that went past me. I'd put my hand up: 'Should have done better on that one.' The thing about accepting blame is that once you go down that road, there's no stopping. Everything becomes your fault – 'Yeah, that was my fault too' – and you talk yourself into being a really bad goalkeeper. The more I accepted responsibility, the more I lost confidence. Of course, the rest of the lads liked it when I owned up. How can you defend properly with a crap goalkeeper? Outfield players never accept blame for a goal unless it is totally obvious. Come on, it's the goalkeeper. Always the goalkeeper.

Inside the dressing room, I sat behind the door, to the left as you came in. We sat down, everyone looking glum but not daring to look up. The inevitable was coming. The first act in the drama was the sound of the door slamming. We didn't have to look up to know Alan was there. I didn't dare lift my eyes and I doubt if anyone did. You didn't want to remind him of your presence. At first he spoke of just how bad we were as a team. 'Fuck my granny' was one of his favourite expressions, but it wasn't meant as a joke and no one smiled. As Alan spoke there wasn't a sound from the players, no one with the balls to say, 'Just hold on, gaffer.'

Everyone was cut to pieces. The rest of the boys thought it was wrong they were getting the blame because they felt it was all my fault. But Alan kept going, one player after another and not a mention of me. Might I be getting away with this? Someone said something about conceding a lot of goals, but Alan didn't pick up on that. Maybe, just maybe, he wasn't going to turn on me. Then he looked in my direction. His voice grew softer, almost sympathetic, 'You all blame Woody, that's too easy. It's a cop-out.'

For a fraction of a millisecond, I thought, 'Yes – it's not going to be me.' Then his voice grew louder. I sensed something coming.

'Yeah, Woody. You all want to blame Woody. He's let in the goals. It's too easy. Too fucking easy. Soft fucking target. You can't blame Woody, because Woody's . . . just a cunt.'

He said a few more things, but they went clean over my head. I was shell-shocked, the most miserable I'd ever felt in my life. What am I doing in this game? What made me think I could be a footballer?

By the time I came round, Alan was back shredding players that had already been cut to pieces. He slaughtered them, slaughtered us all. I don't know how the other lads felt but it knocked me for six. No one stirred. All you had to do was reach down to undo a bootlace and you would have qualified as the bravest man to ever play for Palace's youth team. I don't remember how long it went on for, but it was a good two hours. It felt like three.

By the time Alan arrived back to where I was sitting he could have said what he liked. What did I care any more?

'Fuck my granny. What am I going to do with you, Woody? Tell you what, son, go out and pick up your P45 because you're never going to make it as a goalkeeper.'

When I got to the car park, Colin was waiting. He knew well why we were late. My dad wasn't one for shying away from the truth. On the way home he conducted his own inquest. He went through every one of their six goals with a fine-tooth comb, what I had done and what I should have done. I always knew he wanted the best for me, but I could have done without the second post-mortem. Hugs weren't our thing but, that afternoon, I wouldn't have said no.

Gareth

There was no immediate improvement in our fortunes. Stuart Scott, Alan's assistant, took the youth team to North-ampton for the following week's match. We were hammered 7–0. That was the last youth game Woody played that season.

Those defeats and Alan's brutal assessment of my worth completely changed my outlook. As an apprentice, I'd had no idea what was involved. A good runner at school, I presumed the physical training would be okay. No one would out-run me, and after a year in the youth and reserve teams, it would be the first team. When we went down to Devon for a first pre-season tour, we were out on the pitch before our game against Ottery St Mary signing autographs. The kids were looking for Palace's big-name players, Ian

Wright and Mark Bright, not realizing we were the youth team and a pretty bad youth team at that. But we strutted around as if we were the bee's knees.

When Alan told me on the day before the Oxford game that he wasn't going to play me, it was an unbelievable shock. He was very hard and he could be cruel but everything he said made sense to me. I hated those early weeks at Palace. The training was killing me and stronger players were just pushing me aside in games. 'Two years playing like this and you'll be out in the real world looking for a job,' I kept telling myself.

Though I was still living at home, it wasn't as if Dad could sort out the situation. It was something I had to do on my own. At the time we were doing a lot of stamina work; plenty of cross-country runs, a set of eight 400m runs, eight 200s. I realized I was going to have to win every cross-country race and every 400m and 200m repetition.

The lads looked at me a little differently. I spoke like a middle-class kid and had come from a comfortable background. Too soft, they thought. How could I have the hunger of a lad who came from a tough working-class background? It played on my mind. Maybe more than it should.

During pre-season training, I overheard Steve Coppell talking to Mark Bright and Ian Wright. 'Gareth's got eight O levels,' said Steve.

'Don't know if I want them to know that,' I thought . . .

Brighty just said to Steve: 'Yeah, but can he fucking play?'

It would be an issue all through my career as the O levels would often be mentioned in newspaper articles. I don't consider they're significant. It's not like I did A levels and then got a university degree. There are plenty of footballers with qualifications. Lots of players are bright, even if they haven't had much formal schooling. Anyway, when you're seventeen and trying to prove that you have what it takes to be a footballer, your eight O levels are no advantage whatsoever.

I tried to take in what Alan Smith said because he was the boss and he seemed to know the game. 'The fellow on the production line says, "Can you pass me that hammer?" You lot are fucking mutes.' Alan wanted us to see football as work and never to lose sight of the realities.

In the second half of my first apprentice year, I started to play for the reserves. Saturday morning with the youths, Saturday afternoon with the reserves, it was a tremendous experience. Because of a shortage in personnel, we would occasionally drag in non-league players from Carshalton and Sutton United to fill out our reserves team. Bobby Armitt from Carshalton was a regular; he would later become the kit man at Arsenal.

In the mornings Bobby worked at a flower stall or on one of the fruit and vegetable stalls at Covent Garden and he would come and play for us in the afternoon. We were the full-timers, the kids with futures in the game, whereas Bobby's life was early mornings on the stall and a little football in the afternoon. 'I have to get Bobby Armitt in,' Alan would say. 'He's been up since six o'clock this morning, he's had a day's work done before he gets here and he's our best fucking player.' It just emphasized how far I had to go.

Andy

If you had gone round the Palace dressing room that Saturday afternoon and asked every member of the youth squad whether young Andy Woodman should have picked up his P45, quite a few would have said yes. They didn't think I could do it. At different times over the following sixteen years, similar doubts would be expressed. Don't know why, but I always felt it would work out. 'Don't worry,' I have said to Anna many times, 'this is going to work out better than you expect. Something will turn up.' I am proud of having survived sixteen years in the game. In 2002–03, my sixteenth season, Oxford played an FA Cup tie against Arsenal at Highbury and though we got done 2–0, I made a couple of good saves from Dennis Bergkamp and Sylvain Wiltord.

Between loans and transfers, I have played at eight different clubs. The last move was from Colchester United to Oxford. Who should I see when I walked into the Oxford dressing room? Joey Beauchamp. The same Joey who had bamboozled us at Mitcham all those years ago. Flying down the left wing and me not knowing whether or not to come for his crosses. Generally I got caught somewhere in between. If you'd asked me that evening who was going to make it: Southgate or Beauchamp, it wouldn't have been Gareth. Don't get me wrong, Gareth was promising but Joey Beauchamp was class.

My first thought on entering the Oxford dressing room was, 'Christ, Joey, what are you doing here?' He had gone to West Ham for £1m but didn't like the pressure and the expectations at a big club. Just wasn't his cup of tea. He was ridiculed for publicly admitting that. Before returning to Oxford, he spent some time at Swindon but that didn't work out either. He was a favourite at the old Manor Ground and was welcomed back with open arms. When I told Gareth that Joey was a team-mate, he wanted to know what he was like. Was he the top man?

Nah, he wasn't. Extremely quiet, he seemed likeable enough but was struggling with injury when I arrived. Some of the lads weren't sure how badly he wanted to be fit. Though he had all the talent in the world, it seemed to some that Joey didn't have the heart and the head for it. A few months into my time at

Oxford, he was moved on. Someone said he had joined a non-league team. We never saw him again.

I never did tell Joey Beauchamp I was goalkeeper the day he waltzed through the Palace youth team at Mitcham. To admit that would have been to confess to my part in the humiliation. I wasn't prepared to give him the satisfaction.

5

Andy

It was close to seven o'clock on a Sunday morning in November 1988. Dad walked into the bedroom, and woke me but before he could say anything, I spoke. 'Mum's died, hasn't she?'

'Yeah, son,' he said.

Mum was forty-four, I was seventeen and to this day I swear she came into my dreams that night and said, 'I'm going now, son, you be strong. I love you.' She had come to say goodbye. Later that day we went to the hospice. Mum had become abnormally thin because of her cancer and I didn't want to see her. Bill Kemp, a family friend, pulled me to one side and said I should. The Kemps and the Woodmans go back a long way: Bill worked as caretaker at the South London college where my mum worked. For many years our two families went on holidays together to the south of France; long drives, hot days, radiator overheating, no one able to speak French – the usual fun. Bill is a born-again Christian and on our holidays we needed someone like him.

'You should see your mum,' he said. I couldn't say no. I went and kissed my mum goodbye. She was stone cold. But there was no pain on her face and that was lovely. Bill was so right.

God, it was a hard time. Everyone was amazed at how well I

coped. At the funeral, I didn't cry. My brother, Peter, says that I didn't grieve for Mum and therefore have never got over her death. Maybe. But I did cry a lot in my room, especially at night when I was in bed. It was a massive loss, something I felt I could deal with but was never going to get over. Mum was always my idol. My earliest memories are of her kisses and hugs and of always being under her wing.

She was so proud of her boys. She would come to most of my games and, if she didn't, there would be a good reason. Mum brought the flask of tea and the oranges and never hid her belief in me. When she got sick, I convinced myself it was something she would recover from. Dad tried not to let her illness affect Peter and me. We thought everything would be fine, just a matter of time. People of her age didn't die. Ron Noades, the chairman at Crystal Palace, once arranged for her to come to an FA Youth Cup game at Selhurst Park. It was against Charlton Athletic, a big game for us. Ron arranged for a corporate box to be opened and he laid on nice food for Mum, Dad, my nan and a couple of aunties. Mum couldn't eat but she beamed with pride. From the pitch, I could look up and see this one, lone, lighted box. It was the last time Mum saw me play. I had one of the best games of my life.

Soon afterwards, Mum was moved to the hospice. I thought a hospice was a place where people convalesced, a kind of resting place before they got back into the swing of things. They would build her up and she'd be on her way home. One night at the hospice, Mum asked Peter and me to draw the curtain round the bed and sit close to her. 'I am going to die, boys,' she said, 'and you must be strong.' We told her she was wrong. 'Mum, you're not going to die, you can fight this.' We were heartbroken and cried our eyes out as we spoke to her. Outside in the car park, I tried to take it all in but just couldn't. My mum wasn't going to die. Okay, she had cancer, but it was cervical cancer and didn't people recover from that? I couldn't accept she was going to die but the cancer spread and she deteriorated fast.

Alan Smith cancelled youth-team training on the morning of Mum's funeral and got some of the lads to attend, wearing their Palace blazers. It was a nice thing to do. Afterwards, family and friends went back to the house while the boys had to go in for afternoon training – there was a big FA Youth Cup game against Southampton a couple of days later. At the house people were drinking, eating sandwiches and laughing. I couldn't get my head around that. My mum had just died. Not able to stay there, I packed my bag and went training. The first-team lads saw me coming through the corridor. 'You all right, kid? You doin' okay?' All trying to say the right thing but not knowing what that was.

There were lots of people around. It's a blur to me now, but I could sense everyone wondering why I'd come in. The only person I can remember is Gareth. He was washing a pair of boots in the cold sink at the back of the changing room. We were just getting to know each other at the time. He looked at me in amazement. Can't remember what he said, but I remember the way he looked at me. There was concern on his face. Somehow or other I knew from how he reacted towards me that we would get to know each other better.

Gareth

Though Woody and I began as apprentices together in July 1987, we hardly got to know each other through the first year. He used to travel to training with one of the lads from South Norwood and would wave at us as we headed for the train station while he was chauffeured home. He probably felt I was a bit of a goody-two-shoes, as I was one of the few who got on well with Alan Smith. They would joke as if I was Alan's son: 'Would you mind asking your father what time we're to be here for tomorrow's game?' Actually, I've got that at every club I've played. Alan used to bring a couple of us to his house, which was called the Wend, to chop trees and do other bits and pieces around his garden. As we were doing nothing most afternoons, the extra £10 came in handy. Of course, it was the two guys who had broken through to the reserves, myself and Dave Stephens, who were invited.

Woody would ask, 'Where are you off to this afternoon – the Wand, I suppose?'

'It's not the Wand, Woody. It's the Wend.'

So there was that hint of friction between us, at first, though it was nothing serious. I became more aware of Woody at the time of his mum's illness. She was coming to the games and we knew she was unwell. When she died, I didn't feel close enough to Woody to go to the funeral. He came in for training that afternoon. I saw him and told him, 'I'm really sorry.' 'What was I going to do?' he said. 'Sit around all day?'

I was envious of how comfortable Woody was in the dressing room. He knew how to be one of the boys, what to say, how to dress. Me? I was a total disaster. Crawley, where I came from, was a new town and my upbringing had been very sheltered. Football was my life, girls hadn't entered into it and before going to Palace, I'd never played with a black player and all the lads seemed more streetwise than me. First day I turned up in my old school trousers and shirt, the tie in my trousers pocket because I didn't know if you had to wear a tie every day. My shoes were grey Hush Puppies, very unfashionable. The lads looked at me as if I was from another planet, some kid from the sticks who hadn't a clue.

Fashion had never even crossed my mind. Mum picked out my clothes from catalogues or bought them at Marks and

Spencer. They seemed fine to me. Slazenger jumpers were a favourite, like the ones Ronnie Corbett used to wear. All the guys at Palace had their Adidas tracksuits and their Lacoste jumpers. This was a big deal; they were cool south Londoners, I was a bumpkin from the country. To the lads, I looked like I'd fallen off the set of *A Question of Sport*, wearing David Coleman's hand-me-downs.

One day I walked into the apprentices' dressing room and Chris Powell was dancing across the floor *à la* Fred Astaire. Everyone was keeled over laughing and then I twigged why. Chris was wearing my grey Hush Puppies. The lads saw me and were embarrassed. Not half as much as I was. 'This is what they do when I'm not around,' I thought. It was excruciating.

Larking about once with Dave Stephens I said something half-smart to him. 'Hark at Leo Gemelli!' he said, referring to the brand name of the jumper I was wearing. It was one of Mum's specials, bought with the best intentions in the world but, sadly for me, another naff brand. 'Hark at Leo Gemelli' was all Dave had to say and the boys were falling about laughing and banging the floor. I just wanted the ground to open up and swallow me. Normally Woody would have been in the middle, laughing with the others. But this time, he didn't see it as funny. Instead he came over and tried to reassure me. 'Look mate, don't let it get to you.'

Barry Ellis, a 6ft 4in beanpole who played centre-half, took pity on me. We had played together at Selsdon and were friendly. 'Come on,' he said, 'we'll go and get you sorted.' We started with the basics. We had to wear grey trousers with proper shoes and also the club blazer and tie. Barry suggested I get trousers with turn-ups and a pair of Ravel shoes to replace the Hush Puppies. I remember arriving for the next match and all the boys going 'Whooh!' But it wasn't until I had the money to buy the right gear that I could walk into the dressing room and not be noticed, which was what it was all about.

Andy

The lads used to give Gareth a bit of stick, not that he didn't attract it. His clothes were horrendous. I can still see that Leo Gemelli jumper. It was white and green and red. Where I came from, a jumper like that got you into serious trouble. But it wasn't just his gear. His hair had this peculiar bit at the front and in other ways he was different from the rest of us. He was educated and could murder any one of us with a long word none of us had ever heard before – let alone understood.

But I thought nothing of the slagging Gareth was getting, just saw it as a bit of banter that wasn't malicious. It's how it is in a dressing room. What really struck me was the way he used to clean the floors; he went into the corners and made sure every inch was spotless. Everyone else just wanted it done as quickly as possible. After sweeping the leaves and cutting the bushes in Alan Smith's garden, he was invited back to do other jobs and would stay over at Alan's house. Alan was involved in different things and he once asked Gareth to measure a piece of land for him. The tape measure wasn't nearly long enough for the field but still he carried on regardless, measuring it meticulously and taking for ever. That was Gareth, he wouldn't cut corners. Alan really took to him.

Gareth

Steve Coppell was in charge of our first training session at Palace. Seven of us made up the new batch of apprentices and we didn't have a clue what to expect. One of the first things Steve asked us to do was a twelve-minute run round the 400m track, something that should have been okay for me. I was always naturally fit and had done cross-country at school. Chris Powell, who was then a second-year, took off so fast I wondered if he realized it was twelve minutes. 'Extra running for anyone who gets lapped,' shouted Steve Coppell. Close to the end, Chris lapped me. It was such an eye-opening experience; how could anyone be so fit? It was the result of training full-time the previous season and the work Chris had done during the summer break. 'I'm never going to be able to survive this,' I thought, but Woody had been lapped twice by Chris. He was only fifteen at the time, younger than the rest of us and physically very weak.

But Alan saw something in me. I wasn't tough enough and my sheltered upbringing compounded this. Inside the Palace dressing room, I was the guy who had come from the comfortable and secure background: my dad had a good job, my mum was a teacher. Being doubted by the other lads or being hammered by Alan Smith only made me more determined though.

Two or three months after that disastrous start, 6–2 at Oxford, 7–0 the week after, things improved. They moved me to right-back and started picking me for the reserves as well as the youth side. If you were in both teams, it wasn't unusual to play for the youths on Saturday morning and the reserves in the afternoon. You would be taken off with ten minutes left in the youths game, quick shower and change, jump into the back of Alan's Jaguar and off through the London traffic for a match at White Hart Lane or the Valley or wherever. The Jag was designed for two people. You squeezed into the back at an awkward angle that made for an unbelievably uncomfortable ride, but no one dared complain. For one particular game at Spurs, Palace started with nine men and didn't have a full eleven until we arrived in the Jag, ten minutes into the action. You got changed fast, ran straight on and got stuck in. Warm-up? You didn't even think about it. John Chiedozie and Johnny Metgod played for Spurs that day. I can still remember the way they looked at us as we ran on ten minutes late.

Nowadays, young lads in an academy are restricted to around twenty-five games each season. The authorities would look back and say what we did was a shocking way to nurture young players. I wouldn't change a thing. It toughened me up.

Andy

It went badly for me from that first game down in Devon. Ottery St Mary were an adult team and I was challenging for crosses against them. They were men and I was a boy. I'm not being funny but it was the worst thing in the world for me. My dream of becoming a top goalkeeper and getting into the Palace first team began to seem stupid. As the goals flew in and Alan Smith made his feelings known, life changed. Football wasn't fun any more. I loved being at Palace, loved the banter in the dressing room and the whole idea of being a professional footballer. It was the matches that were the problem. Getting dropped after the 7–0 hammering at Northampton was a big moment. 'I'm gonna be out of this in no time,' I thought. George Wood was

Palace's only fit goalkeeper at the time and I was often dragged into the first-team training. It was a nightmare. The first-team guys blamed me for losing the five-a-sides and told me I was useless.

Alan Smith was a fiery, passionate man. He knocked the stuffing right out of me. We had gone from being stars on our Sunday league teams to getting slaughtered. When you're a kid, it's personal: 'This bloke is always picking on me. He just doesn't like me.' It wasn't that Alan didn't like you, he didn't like the way you played. When he told me to go and collect my P45, I thought to myself, 'Jesus Christ, he really means it.' Then on the Monday after the slaughtering on Saturday, Alan was still pissed off with you. He was like that, Alan. He said a lot of things to kids that if I ever became a manager, I would never say. He had his good points; he took us on tours and showed us the good side of the football life. I just didn't like the way he spoke to some of us.

Sixteen years later I'm still playing professional football, so I must have something. There were other lads who couldn't take it. One couldn't cope with it and just quit. You can say it's the survival of the fittest; the football world sorts out those who can make it from those who can't. Don't know if that's right. Stan Collymore joined us and he was one of those players who couldn't deal with someone having a go at him after a match. 'It's wrong,' he would say, 'to speak to people like that is wrong.' I always felt Stan had a point.

Gareth

Alan used to say to us, 'You are the plankton at the bottom of the ocean and everybody is out to eat you up.' Every time he said it, I thought, 'Yeah, dead right.'

6

A friend is someone with whom I may be sincere. Before him, I may think aloud.

Ralph Waldo Emerson

Gareth

We were very different characters, Woody and I.

He would hustle more in an afternoon playing snooker than we earned in a week as apprentices. I didn't even know where the snooker hall was. As I walked to Mitcham station with Barry Ellis and John Budden, two lads with whom I had played at Selsdon Juniors, Woody would shout at us from a passing car, 'Whooay, enjoy your train journey home!' He used to travel with Paul Raines, our centre-forward, who was a bit of a nutcase. He was a hard player and not exactly a soft touch off the pitch either. 'Woody,' I thought, 'must really know his way round to be a pal of Paul Raines.'

Andy

Without Paul Raines, I would have been buried in that first year. I was left out of the youth team and blamed for the bad start, and people were seeing me as a joke. Except that I was friends with Rainesy and no one treated Rainesy's friend as a joke. With Paul, the fear factor was high. No one dared take a liberty, not with Rainesy, not with his mate. Mention the name and the response was always the same: 'Ah yeah, Rainesy, how is he? Send him my best.' He came from South Norwood. Our family knew his family, his older brother and my older brother were good friends and I'm sure Pete asked Rainesy to keep an eye out for me.

Paul drove a Mark One Escort, a car his grandfather had passed down to his brother, who handed it on to him. The yellow submarine, we called it. Behind the wheel, Paul was a lunatic. Once, on the way to training, we came to an intersection and he said, 'Let's keep going.' I thought it was a joke and he would stop at the last second. Rainesy's idea of a joke was to keep going, straight through the red light. It was one of the scariest moments of my life. Even had I known what he was going to do, I wouldn't have opened my mouth. You didn't tell Rainesy what to do. His attitude was: if we die, we die; if we don't, we'll be in time for training. Russian roulette, that was Rainesy's game.

On our pre-season tour to Devon that first year, a second-year lad, Dave Stephens, played a prank on Rainesy that went too far. So that night Dave was looking for a safe room in the dormitory of the college where we stayed. 'Can't stay in my room, Dave, he's my mate.' It seemed to die down and there was no set-to that night. Next morning we were sitting in the hall, waiting to go training and out of the blue Rainesy went for him. No talk, no warning, no hint of what was about to happen. Just bang, bang, bang and, of course, all the banging came from Rainesy. By the time we had pulled him away, the damage had been done. No one played any more pranks on Rainesy.

He had a little brother who didn't have a football so Rainesy borrowed one after training. It was a proper £40-ball. Next morning Alan Smith said one ball hadn't come back; it must have been lost in the bushes and we weren't to return until we found it. Everyone knew the ball was in South Norwood with Rainesy's kid brother but we silently spent three and a half hours searching the bushes. Not one person, until now, has ever said a word about that ball. Who else could have had twenty-five footballers looking for a ball they knew was elsewhere? That was the respect Paul Raines commanded.

Bad knees destroyed his career. He now works for Otis Lifts but I will always remember how he looked after me during those early months. We came from similar backgrounds and had learned to survive on the same streets. It was Nord who came from another planet.

Gareth

On the day of his mum's funeral, when he amazed us all by coming in for training, I saw a different Woody. A more mellow Woody but a guy who was mentally strong. He dealt with his mum's death unbelievably well. You knew it was killing him but he wouldn't let it show. Around the same time, he took my side when Dave Stephens cracked his Leo Gemelli joke and had everyone rolling around laughing. We were becoming friends.

The Easter after Woody's mum died, Alan Smith organized a trip for the youth team to a prestigious tournament in Italy. Teams came from all over and it was typical of Alan to take us there. Woody would joke that the reason we had so many overseas trips was because Alan liked his suntan. I wouldn't discount that theory entirely! But Alan wanted us to experience foreign countries and to see the rewards that would come through hard work. He also wanted the players to get to know each other better and to develop as people. We would play in the tournament, have a drink on specified nights and as there would be a carnival taking place in the town, it would be a great experience. For Woody and me, it was the beginning of our friendship.

Andy

The town was Viareggio in Tuscany and the hotel was in the centre of the town. Everyone was standing around the reception area, and guys were pairing up and heading off to their rooms. No one wanted to room with me because I was a bit loud and brash. As people disappeared, Gareth was still there; he and I like the last turkeys on the shelf late on Christmas Eve. He was probably a bit too quiet for the other lads. 'Hey, we can share,' I said. 'Great,' he said, and that was the start.

Gareth

I didn't see myself as being in Woody's league. His dad worked on the fruit and veg at Covent Garden and his people seemed so clued-in, far removed from where I came from. Then we were thrown together in that Italian hotel and we hit it off famously. Share a room with a man and you get to know him. We would lie on our beds and talk football; who would get a contract and who wouldn't. 'What do you think of so-and-so?' 'He's a bit too sure of himself, isn't he?' 'Yeah, I think he is.' So our friendship was forged. We were mates.

As the nights passed Woody talked about his mum and what she meant to him. This was the side of him the lads never saw. But it was as much a part of him as the more outgoing and streetwise Woody. He could see the first seventeen years of my life had been sheltered and that when it came to clothes, girls and alcohol, I was a beginner. Even though he was a year younger, in some ways he was taking me under his wing rather than the other way round. With my Adidas tracksuits and Lacoste jumpers, I was now presentable. Woody was prepared to introduce me to girls and alcohol.

Andy

It was a bloody good tournament. Lots of quality teams but it's not the football I recall but the nights on the town. On our first evening off, there was a disco in a nearby town. We needed a lift and this lady said, 'I'll drive you boys up there.' We had only met her about ten minutes earlier; she was an older lady, late thirties. About eight of us went. As the night wore on, lads were slipping off in different directions. Eventually there was just me, Gareth and Chrissy Powell. The Italian women didn't interest us. Or was it the other way round? By now, we were past the curfew and struggling to get back. These guys in a van offered to take us but to my south London eyes, they looked gay. Thanks, lads, but no thanks.

We looked the other way and saw a car pull up at the traffic lights. It was playing my mum's favourite song, Whitney Houston's 'I Want to Dance with Somebody'. 'We'll be okay, that's me mum's favourite song,' I said to Gareth. Soon afterwards another lady offered us a lift.

It was well after midnight when we got back to the hotel. Every door was locked. No way could we ring the bell, so Chrissy scaled a wall, got on to a flat roof and into the room of two of the other lads. We'd got away with it.

Gareth

Taking a drink and socializing were all a bit new to me and one night I drank a bit too much. We were at some get-together and Ron Noades, our chairman, was there. I remember Ron being there because I have been reminded countless times by Woody. He loves telling the story. Normally, my memory is very good but the next morning there was just a vague recollection of what had happened. Woody, of course, remembered every last detail.

Andy

Gareth has always been hazy about the details of our Tequila Slammer evening.

We spent so much time together in Viareggio. It was a new experience for me to be knocking around with someone who was so well-behaved and more of a thinker than I. With me, everything was spontaneous: 'Come on mate, let's do it.' On this particular day we had done well in our game and it was carnival night in Viareggio. We could look out from the balcony in our room and see the procession pass beneath our window. It was a beautiful Italian evening and in our minds, it didn't come much better than this. The evening's victory had taken us to the next stage of the tournament and here we had a night off. Across the road from the hotel, there was a bar we had been to a few times. We would have a cappuccino and carry on as if we were regulars. '*Ciao!*'

When we got to the bar that evening, Ron Noades and his wife, Novello, were already there. They are two of my favourite people, Ron and Novello. People misunderstand Ron. I think he is a terrific man. Some of the old Palace lads will read this and think,

'How can Woody say that?', remembering the wage increase Ron wouldn't agree to or the way he suddenly decided not to spend any more money on the team. Ron has always been fair with me and I got on great with Novello.

Alan Smith was also in the bar, buying a drink for the lads. We'd got a good result, we were in a nice town and everyone was in good spirits. It was our first time out drinking as a team. Novello, though, was the heart and soul of the party. A terrific lady, she could do this trick with a sachet of sugar. She would place it on her eye and then manoeuvre it down into her mouth. Ridiculous, but we couldn't do it and we were all having a fantastic laugh. Novello then decided we should try a Tequila Slammer. Part of our education.

Two Slammers are enough for anyone; we had four, maybe five. This was after a few beers and a game that had left us dehydrated. As bad as I was, Gareth was completely gone. It was the only time in my life I have seen him like that. The walk back to the hotel was the blind leading the blind drunk but I got him there. In the hotel lobby, Ron and Alan were waiting for the lift. I did the talking, hoping they wouldn't notice Gareth. How could they have missed him? I concentrated on pressing the right button inside the lift. With the four of us, there wasn't much room. Then the lift jerked upwards and Gareth just spewed up all over Ron. Jacket, shirt, tie, trousers, shoes, the lot. The smell was terrible and though I'd had a lot to drink, I froze and sobered up pretty quick. Usually I can come up with a joke, but even I could see this wasn't funny.

What could Ron say? Alan was just relieved to have escaped and Gareth was too far gone to be held responsible. A minute later he was lying on his bed, still paralytic. Alan came to the room to make sure everything was okay and then to wind up Gareth. 'What d'you reckon about that John Pemberton?' he asked Gareth about the player keeping him out of the first team.

'Pembo's rubbish, just rubbish, shouldn't be in the team. *I* should be in the team.'

Pembo might have been a bit full of himself, but he wasn't bad. Alan was delighted, though. Gareth wouldn't often say what he really thought about a rival but with a few Tequila Slammers inside him, he was a different man.

As for Ron, his messed-up clothes were outside our door the following morning. They had to be dry-cleaned and we had to organize it. We found a place in the middle of the town and while we waited we sat in a little café drinking cappuccinos. Gareth has never touched a Tequila Slammer since. Scarred him for life, they did. Ron was good about it, and after the clothes were returned there was never another word. Well, that isn't true. The story filtered back to the Palace first team and the boys were thrilled: the choirboy had puked all over the chairman. What could be funnier? And, of course, many of them had their grievances with Ron. To misquote Kevin Keegan, 'I would just love it if I threw up all over the chairman, just love it.'

I've never considered myself a big drinker, or even much of a drinker at all. Gareth will sometimes have a bitter but he's not a drinker either. But that night was special. Gareth had to learn about the evils of Tequila Slammers and learn about them he did. He owes Novello for that lesson. The only thing I don't recall is whether we had to clean Ron's shoes as well as his jacket, trousers, shirt and tie.

Gareth

From then on, we roomed together.

Things just came out. 'Do you think I'm a better player than Pembo?' I would ask.

'Course you are.'

'Arrogant lad, isn't he?'

'Yeah, bit full of himself.' Then Woody would ask, 'Do you think I'm better than Perry [Suckling, first-team goal-keeper]?'

'You are, but you need first-team experience. You have to play in pressure matches.'

'Gareth, will they give me another contract?'

'You'll be all right, Woody. Steve [Coppell] likes having you around. He wouldn't let you go.'

'Hope not. Been thinking about me mum the last few days.'

'Yeah?'

'Me dad does a great job but it's not the same without her.'

'Suppose not.'

'You didn't know me mum, a terrific lady.'

'I remember her coming to the Youth Cup games when she was ill. The light on in the corporate box. You played well that night.'

'Yeah, not bad. Whatever Pete and I did was always right in Mum's eyes. She would wait up for us when we were out. You could tell her nearly everything.'

In the February of my second apprentice year, Palace offered me a professional contract. Two of the seven who had started in our group had already dropped out and that left Woody waiting with three others, uncertain about their futures.

Andy

Steve Coppell pulled me into his office. 'How do you think you've done?'

'I think I've had a brilliant season. Don't think you could have asked any more of me.' I wasn't going to play myself down. As a goalkeeper, you learn that only the mugs take the blame for everything. I went into that meeting thinking, 'Fifteen grand signing-on fee, £400 a week'. If there was any doubt in Steve's mind, I wasn't going to add to it. 'First year was average but I couldn't have done better in my second season.'

'I think you've just scraped it,' he said. 'Skin of your teeth. I'll give you £110 a week for one year. Take it or leave it.'

Afraid he would change his mind, I signed straightaway.

'Next season,' he said, 'come back fitter and stronger, be at the front of the running. I'm not sure you're going to make it. Prove me wrong.'

After me, the other three lads came out. Gutted and crying. 'Jesus Christ,' I thought, 'I've been lucky here.' I sensed the club showed me sympathy because of what happened. 'The kid lost his mum six months ago. If we do this to him now, it could ruin him for ever.' I didn't worry about why they gave me the contract, I was just glad they did.

Gareth

None of us expected Woody to get a contract. He'd had a terrible first year, done better in the second, but we didn't think he'd done enough. Yet of the four who went in, he was the only one who got a contract and this caused a little bit of resentment. A couple of the lads felt that the club took pity on him because of his mum dying. I thought it was because Steve Coppell and Alan Smith liked Woody as a character – he was good to have around. And the fact that he was still young enough to play for the youth team the following season.

It was the same ritual acted out time and again. We would be in our hotel, the night before a game. Woody lying on his bed, thinking about the next day's game and suddenly he's John Motson. 'That's got to be a penalty and Nigel Martyn's in trouble here. It was a clear trip. Yes, the referee is taking out the red card. The keeper is off. What a moment for Andy Woodman to make his debut for Crystal Palace! This is his chance. Woodman rubs his hands together as Shearer places the ball.'

Woody is now standing on the bed, fired up. Shearer hits the penalty, he throws himself full-length, arms outstretched, pushing the ball away, falling on to the bed and all the time, the commentary. 'He's turned it round the post! What a save! No wonder the Palace players are rushing to congratulate the goalkeeper.'

No matter how many times he did it, it was brilliant. And no matter how many times he wished it, it never actually happened. Nigel Martyn didn't get sent off, he never got injured and never got sick: Nigel, the model of consistency; Woody, the eternal substitute. Palace had made Nigel the first £1m goalkeeper when they bought him from Bristol Rovers and he was a tremendous goalkeeper for us. Though I could never have mentioned it to Woody, his bedroom scene created a dilemma for me. It would have been great for him to get his opportunity but if Nigel got a suspension, it was going to cost us. Left to me, I would have given Woody his chance to make that save, on condition that Nigel was back for our next game. Woody spent seven years at

Palace without making one league or cup appearance. He was desperately unlucky because he was on the bench so often you would have thought he had to get a game.

At the beginning of the 1991–92 campaign, we went on a pre-season tour to Sweden, Greece and Spain. Nigel was recovering from a hernia operation and unavailable. The goalkeeping position was between Perry Suckling and Woody. On that tour, Woody played the best I have seen him play at any time in his career. Especially in the game against AEK in Athens. There were 30,000 there and the atmosphere was so hostile, it felt like a normal European cup tie. Both of us did well and as I had only played one league game for the first team at that point, the stakes were high for me too.

Andy

Perry Suckling wanted to move on and Steve Coppell was getting more interested in me. With Nigel injured for the beginning of the 1991–92 season, it went well for me in Sweden and then we had a game against AEK Athens. I remember the gaffer saying to me, 'Woody, you're starting tonight. Perry, you're second half.' As he gave me the shirt, he said: 'Possession, Woody, is nine-tenths of the law.' The shirt was mine to keep. I played really well. Next game, I started again and Perry played second half.

When we came home, the season was about to kick off and Nigel was still unfit. Our first game was against Leeds and it seemed I might play but the match was postponed because redevelopment work at Selhurst Park had caused a problem with the sewerage. 'Shit,' I thought, 'just my luck.'

Our second game was away to Manchester City. This was it. My debut. Dad thought so too, even Gareth believed it was going to happen. Dad flew to Manchester for the match. In the dressing room the team was read out: 'Martyn, Humphrey, Bodin . . .' I was gutted. Perry came in for Nigel in September and having conceded seven goals in two matches I thought Coppell would play me against Oldham. But, no. Perry didn't play well there either and I thought, 'He's *got* to play me in the next.' But Nigel came back and that was it. My chance had gone.

Gareth

I was convinced they would play Woody and me in the scheduled opening game that season, at home to Leeds. Nigel and the centre-half Eric Young were unfit and in my eyes we were the understudies. But the match had to be postponed and you could see Palace weren't too upset. Without Nigel and Eric, the postponement was a result for them. It was always going to be hard for Woody because, at the time, Nigel was the highest rated keeper in the League.

Six weeks later the rearranged Leeds game took place and it was my first home game for Palace. I went on to play thirty league matches by the end of the season.

Andy

Gareth didn't fit into the spivvy football world. Strange thing was though, everyone liked him. Genuine, honest and a grafter: a 100 per cent grafter. He wanted to learn his trade, to be out there training, and he could play. Ultimately it doesn't matter what you do off the field, what you say or don't say in the dressing room; it's out on the pitch you get respect.

One evening at a reserves match Gareth clashed heads with a guy called Gary Strodder. It was one of the worst cuts you've ever seen. The gash went from the middle of his head to his hairline. There was blood everywhere. But no way would he come off. They bandaged his head but the blood seeped through, bright red at first, then darker and darker as the cut continued to bleed. Eventually his head began to spin and he had to go off. Just because he was well brought up didn't mean he was soft. Gareth was never, ever, soft.

Once he was picked for the first team, we all knew he would stay there.

Gareth

For four seasons I played in the Palace reserves. One hundred and twenty games, it's probably a record. It was not one I wanted and it just went on far too long. We played our home matches at Tooting and Mitcham FC, with its one-bar heater in the changing room. Only place in London that could freeze you in early May. For the two years before Steve Coppell put me in the first team, I thought I was good enough. It was frustrating. The club refused to allow me out on loan because there was always some reason why they needed me as back-up; a relegation battle, a promotion push – if it wasn't one, it was the other. They knew that if I got the taste of first-team football, it would be impossible to keep me happy in their reserves. So every time I asked to go on loan, they said no.

The club had ways of keeping us happy. During the run to the 1990 FA Cup final, the first team went off to Tenerife before every round and Woody and I were invited on a few of those trips. We would carry the kit and help the boys get back to the hotel before curfew. When they beat Liverpool 4–3 in the semi-final, Woody travelled and I was taken along to Wembley for the final. It was a thrill for two young guys who were miles away from the team.

A year or so later I made my first team debut at Anfield and marked Ian Rush. Keen to do well, I got too close to him in the first half, he spun the ball round me, turned in a flash and by the time I'd turned, the ball was arrowing into the corner of the net. We lost 3–0 but that goal apart it went okay for me. Alan Smith, who was by then assistant to Steve Coppell, got all of the Liverpool players to sign my match programme.

Once I became established in the Palace side, my football life grew in intensity: the incredible high of promotion from Division One followed by the misery of relegation from the Premiership. Once promoted as Division One champions, twice relegated; that was the story of my four seasons in the first team. The first relegation was bizarre. With three games to go, we were well clear of the third-bottom team, Oldham. In the third-last game, we beat Ipswich at home and put ourselves eight points clear of Oldham, who had three games left. We did a lap of honour at Selhurst Park, mostly because it was our last home game of the season but also because 'eight points clear, no way can they catch us'.

The next afternoon Oldham played at Aston Villa, who were going for the title. I went to the cricket at Arundel. It was Shane Warne's first tour for the Aussies and I was feeling pretty relaxed. But not at the end of the day. Oldham beat Villa 1–0. Next game we drew 0–0 away to Man City and again we thought that would be good enough. But Oldham beat Liverpool 3–2. Now it was down to the last game; they had to play Southampton, we were away to Arsenal. Earlier in the season we had joked about not wanting to go to Highbury needing anything. We were right about that, Arsenal beat us comfortably. Oldham won against South-ampton and we were relegated on goal difference.

Woody and I hadn't the stomach for the coach journey back from Highbury, instead we asked his dad to wait and we would travel home with him. It was well over an hour after the game, I could still see the litter on the streets around the ground and I don't think I'd ever felt as low. People say relegation is a stigma that stays with you for ever. It is.

Things moved on. Steve Coppell resigned at the end of that season and Alan was appointed manager. My relationship with Steve was never what it should have been. I had grown up supporting Man United and he was one of my heroes. I struggled to get beyond that and was in awe of him. The resentment I felt about not being in the first team earlier was bottled up because it didn't seem right for me to challenge him. His view was that he needed experience in the team and, in a way, he was proved right. The first season I had a settled place in the team, we were relegated. But Steve had a lot of ability as a manager and I've always felt he deserved a chance at one of the bigger clubs. Maybe that will still come.

Three games into the following season Andy Thorn got injured and Alan Smith made me team captain. Eric Young and John Humphrey were senior players, I was not quite twenty-three but Alan was prepared to go with me. What Eric and John thought about this unproven kid being made captain is anyone's guess!

The second relegation, two seasons later, was worse than the first because Alan lost his job over it.

There is a view that footballers play for the fans. Up to a point, it is true. But there are other, even stronger motivations. Having a relationship with the supporters is a good thing and it is natural to want to share the joy of a goal or a victory with them. But players move clubs and develop the same relationship with the next set of fans; it is how the game works. It makes me sick to see players kiss the crest on their shirt after scoring when you know that, ultimately, they don't give a damn about the club. Unless you grow up with a club, it is contrived and shallow.

Where there is a good spirit in the dressing room, players want to do well for their team-mates and the manager. When Palace were relegated at the end of the 1994–95 season, I felt bad for Alan Smith. He believed in me, made me captain of the side and I felt I owed him. Managers carry the can for failure in a way that players rarely do. Alan had come up through the ranks at Palace and when he became manager, it was like he was on trial. That season I played for him and wanted us to stay up primarily to keep him in the job.

But the greatest motivation is that which comes from within. You may want to do well for the fans, your team-mates and the manager but, most of all, you do it for yourself. If I allow my standards to slip it is I who will feel bad about that and it is I who will suffer. There may be ten good reasons why it is difficult to play to your maximum on a certain day but, ultimately, nobody cares about that. It is your responsibility to still go out and do your job. Basically, to perform or perish.

Andy

After Steve Coppell gave me that one-year contract at £110 a week, things did improve. Gareth and I began going to the gym together to do weights, and in my third year the youth team won the South Eastern Counties league, something Gareth in his time had not done. That league title has never been forgotten, at least not by me. Or Gareth! 'Nord, show me your SEC league medal,' and he's never been able to.

My wages rose to £175 a week, then £225, £275 in my sixth season and £350 in my final one. That year I was on the bench all season for the first team and getting the promotion bonuses. Earned a lot of money that year. But it was always a battle for me to justify my place in the first-team squad. Did I really believe I should have been in the Palace first team? Not when Nigel Martyn was there. If Nigel had suffered a broken leg, would Palace have gone with me for the season? I'm not sure. What I did enjoy was being part of the club that I and my family had always supported.

In my fourth season, Palace loaned me to the non-league side Bognor Regis. First game was against Marlow; we were smashed 5–0. A guy beat me with a shot from the halfway line; downwind and down the slope, it flew like a rocket into the roof of the net. Still, how could any keeper be beaten from that distance? I expected to be slaughtered by the Bognor manager. After the game, in walked Jack Pearce. 'That's the way it goes sometimes,' he said, 'let's go to the bar and have a drink.' Jack has been manager of Bognor Regis for twenty-five years and he is about the nicest man I have ever met in football. He came to my wedding, he has been to the christening of my children and we speak regularly on the telephone. What does it tell you about football at the top level when the most decent human being you've met happens to be in non-league?

That season Bognor were relegated and I got the supporters' player of the year award. We did much better in my second season and the £100 a week they gave me to cover expenses was a real bonus. Two or three hundred people used to watch Bognor play at home and I loved it there. You could hear every word that every fan shouted. If you were playing shit, you were playing shit and the bloke behind your goal with the hat and the coat and the glasses, would waste no time in telling you so. I have a dream that at the end of my career I will go back to Bognor and play one last season with Jack: we'll have a drink at the end of a bad day and not fall out over one lousy result. It will probably never happen, but I like to think it will.

Gareth

Our friendship brought me into Woody's world. One day he turned up to training with some Gucci leisure suits for sale. They looked good and with the Gucci label the lads couldn't get enough of them. Woody, of course, made the lads feel he had done them an enormous favour. 'Gucci,' he said, 'top-quality brand.' The lads agreed.

'Hey, Woody, where'd you come across these?'

'Ask no questions, you'll be told no lies.'

'Come on Woody, where?

'Let us say, I have my suppliers.'

A couple of weeks later Woody turned up with the same suits, exactly the same pattern, but this lot had the Reebok logo.

'Ah Woody, for fuck's sake, does this mean the Gucci stuff wasn't proper Gucci?'

'Think positive lads, think positive. This consignment may not be proper Reebok.'

With Woody around, we laughed a lot. He had a flair for business, in the same way that Del Boy Trotter has. I, of course, was born for the part of Rodney.

And so Del Boy, Rodney and another friend, Les Samuel, got together and set up a little enterprise that Woody called SAS: Southgate, Andy, Samuel. 'SAS – Who Dares Wins.' We drove to a warehouse near Farnham in Surrey, bought tracksuits, boots and stuff like that. First time down there, we went for Nike tracksuits, brought them back and had no problem selling them to the lads. We made a nice little profit and the plan was to use this car-boot trade as the forerunner to a proper sportswear business. On our second or third visit to Farnham, we got some more Nike tracksuits and bought some trainers for people who had given us orders but Woody always believed that no matter what we bought, he would sell. 'No problem, I'll take 'em down to Beckenham. Sold.'

The stuff piled up in his dad's house. 'Any chance of you boys shifting some of this gear, getting it out of the house?' Colin would ask. 'Yeah, Dad, it's all ordered,' Woody would lie, without missing a beat.

Del Boy couldn't see us failing. One afternoon at the warehouse, one of the salespeople showed us some Lyle & Scott golf jumpers. These were the multi-coloured, diamond-patterned sweaters even I wouldn't have been seen dead in. Del Boy said they were what golfers love.

'We should try five,' I said.

'Nah,' said Woody. 'Fifty. We'll take fifty.'

We were only earning £100 a week at the time; this was a big investment. 'Don't worry,' Woody said. 'I can sell them down at the golf club, no problem.' We agreed to take thirty and they were desperately hard to shift, even for Del Boy.

'You want a Nike tracksuit? How about a Lyle & Scott jumper to go with it?'

A year later we still had twenty-five. Thirteen years on, we still have twenty-five.

Andy

SAS was born at our training ground in Tooting and Mitcham. The reserves played their home matches there and that was how we got to know Les, a Palace fan who went to most of the reserves' games. He was always on the lookout for an opportunity to make a buck or two. He knew of this warehouse where they were giving away sportswear at ridiculous prices. So Les, Gareth and I drove down to Farnham to check it out. Inside the warehouse, I was like a kid in a chocolate factory. Everything there, I could sell. Les was just as excited but Gareth was his usual careful self. 'Look, boys, we can clean up here,' I said. We stuck everything on Les's credit card, thought up the name of SAS Sportswear and dreamed of the money we were going to make.

For a while we did really well, mostly selling out of the boot of the car. There was a lecturer at Heath Clark College called Jim Earl; his students couldn't get enough of our gear. We sold to Palace players and we would have fortnightly meetings to check on what was sold and what still remained. Gareth was our accountant, doing the books and worrying about unsold stock. He couldn't sell for nuts and his enthusiasm for selling, which was never that high, disappeared completely when he got a new contract and better wages. He blames a batch of Lyle & Scott jumpers for the demise of SAS. I just put it down to bad luck.

They were bright-coloured, with a bold pattern down the front. Exactly the kind of jumpers golfers love. Gareth didn't fancy them. 'I think we should take five,' he said. Typical bloody Nord. Les and I agreed on thirty. Unknown to us, Nick Faldo was about to win the 1990 Open Championship at St Andrews and drive a stake through the heart of SAS. He won wearing a bloody Pringle sweater. So everyone in golf then wanted Pringle. We couldn't give away our Lyle & Scott collection. The lads say I brought SAS to its knees but that's not true. It was Nick Faldo.

7

*You have your views and your feelings and I have mine, and I don't
mind in the least if they don't match.*
  Ruth Sargent

Andy

From the ages of fifteen to twenty-two, I was a professional
footballer with Crystal Palace. Nothing in those seven years stands
out like my last day at the club. It was a Sunday afternoon, the
final game of the 1993–94 season, against Watford. We had
been promoted to the Premiership as champions the previous
week; the Watford game was just a celebration. My best mate
would receive the Division One trophy and as I had been part of
the squad all season, it should have been a good day for me too.
It wasn't. As the players were doing the lap of honour, I walked
down the pitch feeling as wretched as I've ever felt in my life. The
club had supplied us with T-shirts with the word 'Champions'
printed on the front. On the back of mine one of the lads had
used a felt pen to scribble: 'For Sale. One Careful Owner. Offers
Considered'. I've got a photo in a drawer of our bedroom of all
of us with the medals around our necks. They look happy. I look
miserable. They were champions. I was out of work.

As I was going out on the pitch to collect my medal, Alan Smith
said: 'You're going to have to give the medal back, Woody.'

'What?'

'You've got to play twelve games to get a medal.'

'Over my dead body will you get this fucking medal back.'

The boys were celebrating on the pitch when I headed towards the dressing room. I got in the shower as quickly as I could and left before they returned. I went to the bar, found my dad and said, 'Come on, let's get out of here.' I didn't say goodbye to anybody, just made my exit from Crystal Palace with a black bin-liner half full of my bits and pieces. Seven years and for it to end like that. I was devastated. Years later, it still leaves a bitter taste in my mouth.

I had been so naïve. Six weeks before the end of the season Alan told a number of players they were getting a free transfer but as he didn't pull me, I assumed everything was fine. You had to put people on the list well before the end of the season, otherwise they would have little chance of finding a new club. I had been on the bench for most of the season, understudy to Nigel Martyn, nothing wrong with that. The bonuses for being in a winning squad were good and, on the bench, you can't play badly. We got promoted at Middlesbrough, had a good time coming back that night on the train and then went out that night and celebrated. If you had asked me about Alan Smith that evening, I would have said, 'Good guy, he's looked after me very well; not as well as he's looked after Gareth, but then Gareth was his favourite.'

On the Thursday after the Middlesbrough game, three days before the end of the season, Alan called me into his office. 'Sit down, Woody.'

'Yeah, no problem.'

'This is the hardest thing I have ever had to do.'

'Well don't fucking do it then – don't do it!' I knew what he was going to say. He had shat on me and he knew he had shat on me. No wonder he felt bad about it.

'We're going into the Premier League,' he said. 'I need an experienced keeper as back-up to Nigel. I've no doubt you'll be a great keeper in your own right, I've always said that, but you need to play in someone's first team at a lower level. Somewhere to find your own way.'

What Alan said actually made sense. But he should have decided to loan me out to some club while I learned my trade. He wasn't proposing that, he was making me redundant at a time when it was virtually impossible for me to get another club. He was also telling me the dream at Palace was over for me.

'That's bollocks, Al, you've told all the other lads six weeks ago, given them a chance to find a new club. But because you couldn't get any other keeper in to sit on the bench, you've used me in this way.'

'I'll help you get a new club,' he said.

'No, that's crap, Al. You can't help me get a club. The season's finished. Everyone's on the list now for the summer. I am fucked, completely fucked.'

'If you don't want to go on the bench on Sunday, I'll understand.'

'I bet you'd fucking well understand. I've been on the bench all season and now we're getting the trophy I'm sure you don't want me on the bench, do you? It'll be embarrassing for you because the way you've treated me is disgraceful.'

He waffled on but nothing he said made the slightest difference. Determined to get promotion and have cover for Nigel right to the end, he shat on me big-time. He may have simply been doing his job, doing what was best for the club, but it was at my expense. And all I could think was that it was all over for me. I hadn't played a league game for Palace, now I never would and it was too late to be looking for a new club.

We then had training and I could tell from their reactions that the lads already knew. Alan had told Gareth and Gareth asked the boys to go easy on me. Unbelievably angry, I played a blinder in training and Eric Young, the centre-back, who was a cold, blunt bastard but not a bad bloke, said to me: 'Woody, too little too late, son. Too little too late.' As cool and as callous as that. But he was right. The misery was only beginning.

I rang Anna, who was working at a Next store in Croydon. She started crying. We were due to get married the following year. Anna rang her mum; her mum cried. I rang Peter, my brother. He was sick. Then I rang Dad. He would have battered Alan Smith if he could have got hold of him that afternoon. Dad had been a Palace supporter all his life; the same season ticket for God knows how long. He swore he would never go to another Palace game. He went the following Sunday just to see me receive my medal and to this day he has never been back. Once Dad makes a promise, that's it.

That evening I went round to Anna's. My situation couldn't have been more desperate. I rang a guy from the club, Terry Byfield. At the time Terry was an up-and-coming PR man and a really decent bloke. 'Terry, I am fucking up shit-creek without a paddle, mate. I need a huge favour, could you get me the names and addresses of the other ninety-one league clubs in the country?'

Not only did he do that, he printed every name and address on a sticky label. That night Anna's mum did me a CV, I put everything I could think of on it and we got all ninety-one letters done that night. Anna's nan licked the stamps; it was a real team effort. Next morning Anna posted them but spread them over a number of letterboxes in case one of the post-office workers thought it was some kind of stupid advertising promotion and decided not to deliver them. Anna had become paranoid, bless her.

On Saturday, the day before the Watford game, Gareth and I had to present trophies at a local football club. Gareth picked me up, we did our bit for the kids and I just wanted to go for a drink. It was my way of saying to Alan Smith and Palace, 'Fuck you, I've done everything right all season and this is how it turns out. Tonight I'm going to piss it up.' Gareth was the team captain and though the title was already won, there was a game the following day. It would have been unfair of me to ask him to join me. But I asked him anyway.

Gareth

We were driving past the Blue Orchid in Croydon, a night-club where a lot of the boys used to hang out. 'Drop me here,' Woody said. 'I'm going to the club tonight and if you're my mate you'll come with me.' I didn't know what to do. He was very down and could have done with company. We had won the Division One title and the following day's match wouldn't change anything, but I couldn't do it. Being out the night before a game, any game, went against the grain.

'I'm probably going to regret this Woody,' I said, 'but I can't.'

I did regret not staying with him that night. He went in there on his own, something you've got to feel pretty low to do. All the way home that night I was torn. I knew I should have stayed with him.

Andy

It annoys Anna that when I meet someone who's pissed me off, I can be totally civil. Maybe there won't be much smiling but there will never be a scene. Anna is an up-front kind of woman, tells people what she thinks, whether it's complimentary or not. I try to see things from the other person's point of view but sometimes that's hard. I couldn't believe Alan Smith had done what he had; not giving me a proper chance to find another club was unforgivable. Everyone else he was letting go was given enough time. But not me. After seven years, he owed me that.

My falling out with Alan was always going to be difficult for Gareth. Alan's been like a father to him and Gareth appreciates what Alan has done for him. I never expected Gareth to shun Alan on my account and would never have put my mate into a situation where he felt he had to. Because we're both mates of Gareth, Alan and I were bound to meet up again. Later Gareth would get me a ticket for an England game and in the seat alongside would be Alan, who had also got his ticket from Gareth. Maybe Gareth hoped that, sitting together, Alan and I would be able to smooth things over. On those evenings, we would talk away normally. I don't resent Alan, but I've certainly got a different view of him now than I had during my years at Palace. In those days, I had a high opinion of him and thought him an unbelievable guy.

Now I see him differently. He has to have the nice house, the tailor-made suit, the flashy car. Always the suntan and the expensive shoes. When I was younger, I would think to myself, 'Love to have that car and that tan.' Now I don't envy him at all, just find him a little self-centred. When we walk out of a players' bar with Gareth, some kid will come for an autograph and I will take Gareth's bag and try to fade into the background. Alan will stand right by Gareth's shoulder. It's all part of his little trip on the ego merry-go-round. I suppose we all have our faults.

The animosity that existed came to a head at Gareth's wedding. Alan was, of course, going to be there; that didn't bother me in the slightest. We had already met a few times and were able to behave normally. Anna hadn't seen Alan and was still upset about the whole episode. There were other things going on at the time. Anna's brother Iain, to whom she is very close, had just been

1. My dear mum, Gail, as a young lady.

2. Palace Guard under-10s winners! The start of every schoolboy's dream.

3. Round Hill Middle School, Crawley 1982–83. Chris Cripps, my first 'coach/teacher', is the manager. I'm in the centre, front row.

4. First Wembley appearance – as a ballboy at the 1987 FA Trophy final. I'm in the front row, third from the left, overlooked by Woody. We were part of a Surrey representative side.

To "Gareth" All you wish yourself for the future!!
Alan Smith 10/10/89

5. Not only did Alan Smith swing the youth-team a trip to Portugal, he got hold of the club blazers too! Pre-season 1989–90.

6. Opening game of the Viarregio youth tournament *v*. Torino, 1990. I'm in the green with Nord to my immediate left.

7. A Palace under-20s side in the Viarregio tournament *v*. Brescia, 1990. Seven of the side played in the Premiership. Chris Powell joined me in the England squad. A testimony to Palace's youth policy.

8. Me and Nord as coaches at a soccer school for kids.

9. A day's training at Crystal Palace with my hero Paul Barron (now at Middlesbrough with Gareth). This is the Mitcham training ground where I went on to do my apprenticeship.

10. At the end of a day's training at Palace. Goalkeepers across the country will relate to this photo.

11. Larking about together as always, at my dad's fiftieth birthday party

12. Palace *v.* Manchester United, 1991. An up-and-coming youngster destined for great things – and a young Ryan Giggs on the left!

13. Clinching promotion at Ayresome Park in 1994 – I scored the opener, number twelve for the season. *From left to right*: Chris Coleman, me, Simon Rodger, Chris Armstrong, Andy Woodman.

14. Division One champions 1993–94. Woody didn't make the celebrations.

15. Captain of the Division One champions 1993–94.

16. A Palace end-of-season trip to Florida. *From left to right, back row*: Dave West (physio), Richard Shaw, Gareth Southgate, Spike (kitman); *front row*: me, Pluto, Simon Osbourn.

17. First season at Villa, which should have been the springboard for a very good ride.

18 Playing in my favourite kit for Northampton – and looking a little worried.

19. 22 June 1997. It rained all day long, everyone got soaked, and we had a great day!

20. 10 June 1995. Clement and Nord, my closest friends, at my wedding.

21. The proudest day of my footballing career. Northampton 1 Swansea 0, 1996. *From left to right*: Ian Atkins (manager), Ray Warburton, me and Jan Molby (Swansea manager).

22. Heading to Wembley, 1997! Celebrations after winning the play-off semi-final at home to Cardiff.

diagnosed with cancer and the family were all very emotional about that. Iain has made a complete recovery but at the time of Gareth's wedding everyone was worried.

Anna was walking along a corridor, having just come from the ladies, when she met Lin Smith, Alan's wife. Lin is a nice woman and had been very kind to Mum when she was unwell. Alan, too, was very good about my mum and their kindness to her has never been forgotten. But that day the scar caused by the way I was released from Palace was still raw.

'Anna, I'm Alan Smith's wife, Lin.'

'Yeah, I know.'

'Alan really did love Andy, you know. He cried when he let Andy go.'

'He didn't cry as many fucking tears as I cried.' And that was Anna's way: she said what she had to say.

Alan might read my account of how my seven years at Palace ended and think I'm out of order. I'm a little bit older now, a little wiser but no matter what he thinks, he can never get away from the fact that, whatever the reasons, I was shat on from a humungous height.

Gareth

At heart, Alan Smith is a great football man. Business and the City made him wealthy but his love for the game is something he has never been able to walk away from. My first experience of Alan came at the age of thirteen – a trial game at Selhurst Park, most of the kids a year older than me. From the moment he introduced himself, you knew this was a man not to be crossed. It was accepted he had a big say in who did or didn't make it at Crystal Palace. His style on the training ground was uncompromising; those who underperformed were crucified. Sink or swim, deliver or be damned. Even in that trial, he tore strips off several of the older group at half-time.

People react differently to criticism. My feeling was that if you couldn't deal with what Alan said, what hope had you in front of 40,000? There was more to him, too, than the brutal sergeant major. It was he who had the vision to plan ambitious overseas trips for his youth team at Palace and the organizational skill to make them happen. He would persuade the club's vice-presidents to cough up some money and used his business acumen to raise more money through sponsorship. He would then dip into his own pocket to make the trips that bit more pleasant for us. We had to look the part as well and Alan ensured that when representing Palace we were neatly dressed in blazer, shirt and tie. It was his way of saying that if we worked hard, the rewards could be considerable. As well as the foreign trips, Alan took us to nice restaurants, put us up at his house if there was a reserve game we could not get home from and paid a number of us to clear trees and leaves from his garden.

When it came to laying down the law in the dressing room or on the training ground, Alan did not treat me differently from anyone else. Yet it was obvious he saw something in me as a player. Our relationship developed as time passed. What impressed me about him was his interest in me as a person as well as a footballer. He talked to me of the spare time young professional footballers had and how, if it wasn't used properly, it could lead to trouble. He gave me some work with a property company he was involved in and to ensure the lads didn't know about this, I would go to training in a tracksuit and have my trousers, shirt and tie hidden in the boot. On the way to the afternoon job, a quick stop in some quiet car park and the tracksuit was swapped for shirt and tie.

The job was to measure properties or sites in order to assess their commercial potential. It gave me some extra money, brought me into contact with people from outside football and forced me to use my brain for something other than heading the ball. Once Peter Wood, one of Alan's business associates at the time, asked me to measure a field in Banstead. Armed with just a 20m tape and a couple of cricket stumps, I was a bit shocked to find the field was five acres. It was like turning up with a spade to dig a quarry. Stump in, extend the tape, mark the end with second stump, walk back, pick up first stump and pull tape a further 20 metres. Five acres, though, is a lot of field: an hour had passed, then another hour and the light was fading when Alan showed up. Shaking his head in disbelief, he took one end of the tape, I had the other and we just kept walking round until the job was done. Don't know which of us looked more ridiculous in the semi-darkness of that field, me with the cricket stumps or him in his pinstripe suit and £200 loafers.

Alan toughened me as a player and made me aware of the realities off the pitch. My dad was unquestionably the greatest influence on my personality but Alan taught me about a world that neither Dad nor I knew much about. When Crystal Palace agreed to sell me to Aston Villa, he introduced me to his accountant, Bernie Hoffman, and Bernie helped me with the contract. Bernie and I have been together ever since. With so much money in football now, players need good people around them and Bernie's advice has always been first class. Alan despised many of the agents who got their tentacles into young players and didn't provide the right guidance. As I've got older, I've tended to rely more on my own judgement but without their schooling I couldn't have done it. Even now, I still run things past them.

There were times during my eight years at Palace when it

seemed my career had stalled. Steve Coppell preferred John Pemberton at right-back and there was no sign of a break-through for me. During that time Alan's faith in me was important. I would be feeling down in the dumps, but then the London *Evening Standard* would print an interview with Alan where he predicted I would go on to play for England. Anchored in the reserves, you appreciated that kind of belief. Of course, Alan had his critics; anyone who bought his suits from Savile Row, drove top-of-the-range sports cars and generally wasn't ashamed of his success is going to turn some people off. But that wasn't the Alan I knew.

Relegation from the Premiership at the end of the 1994–95 season hit me particularly hard because of the effect on Alan's managerial career. This was someone incredibly close to me leaving Palace because of a failure that was partly my responsibility. Once the team went down, Alan wasn't going to be manager any more; once he'd gone, it wasn't hard for me to leave Palace.

Our friendship has thrived since then. He and his wonder-ful wife, Lin, have been key people in my life; not like Mum and Dad but a close second. I feel fortunate to have encountered Alan on my football journey.

But where does that leave me with Woody? Unbelievably divided. Like most people, I have few close friends yet one of them treated another very badly, putting him in a position from which he might not have been able to save his career. Maybe Woody needed to move from Palace and restart his career elsewhere but Alan went about it in totally the wrong way. I know from Alan and Lin it is one of the biggest regrets in his life. For Woody, though, that counts for little. There is no way to justify Alan's actions to him, no way even for me, his best friend, to explain that it was just unintended thoughtlessness on Alan's part.

Ironically, Alan had looked after Woody fairly well before their terrible falling out and, sadly, it destroyed all that went before. Alan always asks after Woody and I sense he is still embarrassed about what happened. Woody and I don't speak about Alan and I can't help but feel I am letting Alan down by not doing so. But they are both dear to me. It may be awkward but I can't change that. Sometimes the thought strikes me that Woody might feel I am being disloyal to him in remaining so close to Alan. Yet that thought is followed quickly by another: Woody is too big a man to see it like that. Our friendship has always been strong enough to deal with whatever has to be dealt with.

8

A true friend never gets in your way unless you happen to be going down.

Arnold Glasow

Andy

I've always believed when one door closes, another opens. After Palace slammed the door in my face, I waited for the next one to open. There were six replies to my ninety-one letters, all of them saying the same thing: 'We will keep your details on file.' On the following Monday, eight days after I walked out of Selhurst Park, there was a phone call from Terry Cooper, the old England international full-back, who was manager at Exeter City. 'Look,' he said, 'we got your CV. We've two reserve games that were postponed and have to be played within a week. If you come down and do well I'll be offering you a contract.' I asked Gareth if he would train with me for a couple of days, just to keep me sharp. His season was over, the last thing he needed was more training but he didn't hesitate for a second. 'Of course,' he said, 'not a problem.'

Dad drove me down to Exeter. They were playing that song from *Only Fools and Horses* on the radio: 'Everyone's Talking About Us'. Del Boy was heading a long way from home. That evening I played for Exeter's reserves. It was a weak reserve side but it went well for me. 'Come and play the final game, I like what I've seen,' Terry Cooper said afterwards. In between the two games Ian Atkins rang me from Doncaster Rovers. 'Don't sign anything there, I've seen you play for Bognor Regis, I know what you're about and I'm going to drive down to watch you play for Exeter's reserves.'

Something good had come out of my two loan spells at Bognor Regis: that pleased me. Ian said he would take me on a three-month contract but Exeter were talking about a twelve-month deal. From my point of view, the nine-month difference was everything. The second game went just as well as the first, I made a lot of saves and afterwards Terry called me to his office. His assistant manager, Trevor Morgan, was also there. 'We've got a year's contract here,' he said, '£350 a week and £3,500 relocation money. We'd like you to sign.' Liking Exeter didn't enter into it. This was all I had, say no and I was on the scrapheap.

'Where do I put my name?' I asked.

Then Ian called. 'I've signed for them,' I said. 'Good luck,' he said with genuine warmth, 'I hope you get on well down there.' Ian had been at Birmingham City with Terry Cooper and they didn't get on. I know he didn't think it would work out for me, but he didn't want to be discouraging.

Anna came down to Exeter and we tried to find a place for me to stay. There was no point in her giving up her job in London when I was only on a year's contract. We couldn't find anywhere nice though. Besides, I didn't want to live on my own. At first I stayed with family friends in Taunton before moving into digs with Ros, a lovely lady who looked after Exeter City players and worshipped the football club. She has since passed away and even though it wasn't the best digs in the world, she made things as good as they could be. Her lodgers were her boys and she could be fiercely protective of us.

From the beginning, Exeter was a shock that my system wasn't ready for. At Palace our kit would be washed, folded and laid out for us in the dressing room. Here you washed your own kit, cleaned your own boots and didn't complain. Now I'm used to it but back then all I knew was the way things were done at Palace. And on a personal level, I struggled too. The lads saw me as a flash Cockney git and I didn't help my situation by driving a Mercedes and having a mobile phone. It was a second-hand Mercedes but there was no point in trying to explain this to the Exeter lads. After a while I left the car with Anna and took trains to and from Exeter. I didn't need the grief. I remained 'a Cockney git', though. Robbie Turner – they called him the Boro Brick – gave me a particularly hard time. I'd walk into dinner and he would say to Gavin, his mate, 'Hey Gav, look at that Cockney boy', then piss himself laughing.

Robbie spent all of his free time in the weights room and he was big, too big to think about squaring up to. I considered it once or twice as it was the only way of saving face. If I took a battering, so be it. Then one weekend I was back in London and I bumped into the Palace player Andy Thorn. 'How's Owen?' he asked.

'We got no one at our place called Owen,' I said.

'Yeah, you have – Robbie Turner. He was at Wimbledon and we called him ''Owing'' because he owed the lads for saving him from getting killed by Fash [John Fashanu].'

'You what?'

'Yeah, he tried to play the big guy. So Fash said, ''Okay, me and you in the dressing room after.'' The lads shut the door and they had a proper set-to. Fash beat the daylights out of him and we had to rush in and pull him off him. So we called him Owing – because he owed us for the rest of his life.'

Not long afterwards Robbie scored a goal in training. 'Good goal, Owing,' I congratulated him. A smile played across his face.

Afterwards in the weights room, he said: 'Who've you been speaking to?'

'Apparently you had a bit of trouble at Wimbledon,' I said.

To his credit, Robbie was open about it. 'I took the biggest pasting of my life from Fash,' he said. He went on to tell me the whole story and from that moment, we got on fine. Never gave me any stick after that. He remained one of the hardest and meanest guys I played with. Gave no quarter on the pitch and a terrific bloke.

I'd have saved myself a lot of trouble if I'd played well at Exeter because that's the only way of getting the dressing room behind you. But we went to Swansea early in the season and I twisted my ankle during the pre-match warm-up. Out for four weeks. As soon as the ankle came right, Terry Cooper had me back in the team because he was determined I would be his number one goalkeeper. A few weeks later we were playing Scarborough and this young guy elbowed me in the face off the ball. I am Colin Woodman's son, so there were no questions. I just smacked him and the two of us were sent off. With my temper still raging and my brain in neutral, I smacked the guy again going down the tunnel. Before this the Exeter fans hadn't liked me; I was a Londoner and hadn't been much good. After the punch-up though, I was a hero.

A week later Exeter had a second-round FA Cup game against Colchester United. The club was short of money, and here was a chance to get a Cup run going. 'This is a game,' said Terry Cooper, 'we cannot afford to lose.'

We are 1–0 up and reasonably comfortable. I get a back pass and there's a bloke running to close me down. It's a little tight, so I should just put it into touch; instead I try to do a stepover and I slip. He's going to score and all I can do is reach out and grab the ball. We're outside the penalty area and the referee sends me off. This time I'm no hero. Trevor Morgan, the assistant manager who plays up front, pushes me off the pitch. The fans are spitting at me as I walk towards the tunnel and it's bedlam. From there

Colchester come back, get an equalizer and win the game with a goal in the last minute. I cool down; they don't.

Terry Cooper walks into the dressing room. 'Well played everyone, brilliant. I can't ask any more of you. The reason you lost is because of that fucking idiot there.'

Welcome to the lower leagues. But, being me, I have an answer. 'Hold on Gaff,' I say, 'I'm not being funny here but when I was sent off we was winning 1–0. It ain't me that's cost us.'

I've said some dumb things in my life but this is one of the dumbest. My stupid attempt to defuse the bomb only detonates it. Terry Cooper goes mental, as you would. 'That's the most ridiculous thing I've ever heard. Go on, get out of my sight, have two weeks off. I'm fining you two weeks' wages. Go home and get out of my sight.'

The evening's train journey back to London is the pits, miserable. I ring Dad to explain. 'It went horribly wrong. I hate this life. It's over for me and I'm packing it in.' He slaughters me for talking of quitting. So I ring Anna, tell her how badly it has gone and that it's finished. I can't take any more. She slaughters me for being pathetic.

Two red cards in seven days; I am the reason cash-strapped Exeter are out of the FA Cup. I am now suspended by my own club and about to get a seven-match ban from the FA. Through the Christmas period, I sit at home and brood. No one from the club calls. Do I exist?

And as for the future, do I have one?

Gareth

I could tell from the phone calls that Woody was finding it tough at Exeter. We were back in the Premiership with Palace, the squad he had been part of the season before, and he was a long way from home with a struggling and penniless Division Three club. At one point he sounded so low I decided to go down and talk with him. We met at his digs, which were awful. Three of them shared a room and my visit meant four of us slept in it.

He had a game the next day and I went to pick up my ticket from the lady at the Exeter ticket counter. 'Alroight, my luvver?' she said. Exactly the expression we had used to wind up West Country boy Nigel Martyn in our dressing room at Palace.

Her greeting had me bent double with laughter. 'My God, Woody,' I thought to myself, 'this is not what you're used to.'

That evening we ate at the digs and it wasn't the kind of food you would want to eat every evening. The lady was nice, but either the club wasn't paying her enough to keep the lads or she wasn't spending the money on food. I felt for Woody. He was coming home from the football club every afternoon and didn't have anyone to moan to, have a laugh with and confide in. At a time in his life when he needed a mate close by, he didn't have one. For all his natural exuberance and confidence, he was a long way from home and not fitting in. He was also missing the security that Anna and her parents had given him; they had become like a second family to him. He needs to be around people who are on his side.

Over the years Woody's had his falling-outs with his dad, but when Woody went down to the West Country, he missed Colin too. Then, of course, there was footballer's insecurity, something most of us have. 'Wonder if I'll play? Do you think I could have done better with that goal?' The commonplace doubts. Those months in Exeter were the worst of his career and even though my own career was going well at the time, I felt I owed him. In the early years at Palace, when some of the boys were having a go at me because of the naff clothes, it was Woody who had put an arm around me and said, 'Look, don't worry, that's the way things are up here.' It would have been very easy for him to have joined in but he hadn't.

Andy

I heard nothing for a couple of weeks. Then the phone rang. It was Terry Cooper. 'Look, come back, you've got no problems here. No problem with me, no problem with Trevor Morgan. We just want you to do well, son. Come back, wipe the slate clean and go again.'

We met in his office and he was as good as gold, laughing, joking. Terry didn't hold grudges and was determined that we should start afresh. 'Forget everything that's gone on. I'm playing you in the Auto Windscreen Shield game against Shrewsbury tomorrow. Just go out there and enjoy it.'

On the way to the team coach, I picked up the local newspaper. The back-page headline read 'WOODMAN OWES US A CUP RUN'. The article started 'Exeter City's troubled goalkeeper Andy Woodman . . .' It quoted Terry Cooper as saying 'He regrets his mistakes but he owes us now and he's promised me he's going to do it.'

First minute of the game, a Shrewsbury guy beat me from 50 yards with a volley-lob that caught me off my line. We got it back to 1–1 and I then came flying out and a bloke lobs me again. 'Fucking hell,' I thought '*this* is the end.' In the dressing room Terry's son Mark, who played midfield for us, chipped in with his opinion, 'Fucking useless he is, Dad. He's fucking cost us again.'

This time there was no smart-aleck defence, no attempt to deflect the blame. All I wanted to do was to sort out Mark Cooper, but he was the manager's son, and even I'm not that daft. I stewed in the misery.

'Don't know where to go with you now, son,' said Cooper senior. 'I just don't know what to do with you.'

I had been given so many chances and it just wasn't working. Not long afterwards, the club went bust and the whole team was put up for sale. I didn't expect a stampede of managers calling round to Ros's place. One morning Terry Cooper pulled me to one side. 'A club has come in for you,' he said, 'they're interested in taking you on a couple of weeks' trial. I won't stand in your way, I don't want money for you. I'd be happy if you can get yourself sorted.'

The club was Northampton Town, then managed by Ian Atkins. He had come back for me. It would be the beginning of a long and occasionally turbulent affair.

The best thing about my seven months at Exeter was Gareth's visit. In one of our phone calls, I told him about wanting to give up. The club, the game and the place had got to me. In Exeter everyone spoke with an accent I couldn't understand, they ate bread all the time and to me they all seemed backward. The flip side of the coin was that I was young, cocky, ignorant and playing crap.

'I'm on the way down,' Gareth said. 'When I get to Junction 30, I'll call and you can give me directions.' An amazing thing, really. He was captain of a Premiership team at a time of the season when he was having two games most weeks and he was driving from London to cheer me up. He came to Ros's, she was delighted to meet him and have him stay at her house. We went down to Torquay that evening and deliberately didn't talk about my problems. Instead we had a few drinks and a lot of laughs, talking mostly about old times. Next day, before my match, we went and sat at a coffee shop by the quay. The weather was fine, the place seemed nice and it was good to see my mate.

9

Friendship among women is only a suspension of hostilities.
   Comte de Rivarol

Andy

It was the only place to go on a Wednesday night, the Bon Bonne, between Tulse Hill and Brixton – good music, fine collection of young women. We went there a lot of Wednesdays: Gareth, an old friend of mine called Clem Salmins and myself. It would be nice to tell stories of the girls we pulled but they wouldn't be true. Enthusiastic but mostly unsuccessful, we were. Anna says it was the way we used to dress. Gareth was captain of Crystal Palace but would never let on and being reserve goalkeeper at Palace didn't do much for my chances.

Ah well, even a blind squirrel occasionally finds an acorn and on this Wednesday night I spotted a tall, blue-eyed brunette who didn't stop dancing. Stan Collymore and Jamie Moralee from Palace were at the club that night and Jamie knew Emma, a friend of the girl I'd noticed. 'Come on, Jamie, sort me out here, introduce us to Emma's friend.' And so I met Anna Clifford. We exchanged pleasantries but, scared of making a prat of myself, I left it at that.

A few drinks for Dutch courage and my next move was to position myself between the dance floor and the ladies' loo. Eventually Anna came by and was innocently intercepted. A nervous, half-sensible conversation followed, but sooner than I realized the night was over. 'Could I take you out sometime?' I asked.

'Yeah, no problem,' she said.

There was the usual surge of people to get coats and then taxis. Giddy, a little hyper, I jumped in the car with my mates and waved to Anna, who was still waiting for a taxi. 'I'll be in touch,' I said, hoping she could lip-read. She had a funny look on her face, as if something wasn't quite right. 'Women are strange,' I thought.

'How soon are you two going to be getting together?' one of the lads asked a few minutes later.

'Oh shit,' I said. I hadn't asked her for her telephone number. What an idiot.

Palace left for a tour to Miami that weekend, and without any way of contacting Anna, I'd let her down. While I was away, she was on my mind a lot, and three days after arriving back, Gareth, Clem and I were back at the Bon Bonne. I wore my maroon cords from Benetton, Gareth had on the New York Yankees baseball shirt he'd bought in Miami. Maybe Anna was right about the way we dressed. That night I wasn't looking to pull, just wanted to meet that girl again.

She was there – across the floor, dancing in what must have been her usual spot.

I shouted and waved. 'Hi, you all right?'

She blanked me. Wouldn't even look my way. Eventually she came to the bar and I kind of ambled up to her. 'Can we have a quiet word?' She tried to look uninterested as I turned on the sincerity and explained that without her number, there had been no way for me to get in touch. Three hours it took me to make up for lost ground. Every scrap of charm was dredged up and eventually the lady relented. Even started asking me questions. 'What car do you drive?'

Good question, I thought. 'Actually, an XR3i Convertible.'

'Oh, no, not the common one, the white one with the black roof?'

I was gutted. White with a black roof, my car exactly. Common. Trying to think of an escape, I said, 'Yeah, yeah, but mine's different,' but couldn't tell her what the difference was. Two weeks and I still hadn't got her number; two minutes and she had mine. After that we got on okay. She wouldn't let me kiss her that night. She agreed to a date, though, provided I would call round to her house and meet her parents.

I'll never forget that first visit. It was Knotts Landing where she lived: beautiful big house with a swimming pool. Her dad opened the door. I'd done my homework: John Clifford liked greyhounds. 'How're the dogs?' I said. 'My granddad used to have a book-makers' pitch at Hove dog track.'

I struck the right chord. He took to me straight away and in no time we were talking about his greyhound. He asked if I would like to see a video recording of the dog's races. What could I say? 'Terrific, Mr Clifford, that would be terrific.' All I wanted to do was take his daughter out for a drink. Instead, we sat and watched the entire racing career of Lizmore Rocket. On my dying bed you can ask me the name of that dog. Never to be forgotten. Bored the shit out of me that afternoon, but it's okay now. John and I laugh about it. 'Stick the video in, John; let's watch Lizmore Rocket one more time.'

To be fair to John, he was very serious about whom his daughter went out with. There were two, maybe three, boyfriends before me. Anna described them to John and got the thumbs down. They weren't even invited to the house. If John didn't approve, there was no point: Anna ditched the guy and moved on. John likes you or he doesn't like you, very rarely is it anywhere in between. No one was going to be good enough for his Anna, but I just scraped in and I mean just. That day Anna's mum, Beryl, a really nice lady, pulled me aside: 'If you hurt my daughter you'll have hell to pay.' I didn't want to say it but Mr Clifford had already taken care of that. It became very clear to me Anna was part of an extremely tight-knit family. Her granddad and nan lived with her parents and they were all very close. Still are.

Eventually the greyhound tape ran out and Anna and I escaped to a quiet pub, the White Lion, not far from where we now live. We ordered drinks, took them out to the garden and things blossomed. I was allowed to kiss her that evening.

Gareth

That Wednesday night in the Bon Bonne, Woody was some mate. Left me with Clem as he zoomed in on this girl. I can still see him, standing over her, his arm stretched out against a wall, penning her in. She seemed to be quite taken by him. That was no surprise. Woody has a way with people, always has had. When Palace went to play that sensational Cup semi-final against Liverpool in 1990, Steve Coppell took Woody as part of the squad, even though he wasn't actually going to be involved; Steve loved having him in the dressing room. The way Woody was talking with Anna, you could tell he didn't want us intruding. I was curious about this girl and, as Woody and I were so close, he had to introduce me.

At the time I was seeing a girl from Southampton. She would come up to London on odd weekends and we would go out as a foursome. My relationship didn't last and the four became three. Anna, Woody and me. Around that time I bought a flat in White Leaf, reasonably close to Crystal Palace and about twenty minutes' drive from my parents' home in Crawley. Anna's mum and dad, John and Beryl, lived at the top of the hill, less than a mile away from the flat and if Woody was calling round to see Anna, he brought me along. We all became close.

I was close to Woody's dad, too. He and I would go to

Palace's reserve matches together to watch Woody play. Colin was hard on his son because he desperately wanted him to do well. We would go back to the house after the games and Colin would hammer him, 'What were you doing that time?' It made me think of my dad and the worst thing he ever said to me after a game: 'It didn't happen for you today, son, did it?' So I would say to Colin, 'You're being a bit hard.'

'Nah! Nonsense!'

Woody used to get so worked up about what his dad said. Sometimes in a game, if he made a mistake, he would look across to where Colin was sitting.

In the summer of 1992, Woody, myself, Colin and a few of Colin's friends went on a golfing holiday to Portugal. Colin's friends became our friends. I had found myself two new families in South London, Anna's and Woody's. Anna must have had the patience of a saint but, after a while, I think she enjoyed having me around. She even started to look out for me and became like an older sister; a little territorial, you could say. This was something that Alison, when she came along, would discover.

Andy

More dates, more time spent getting to know each other; Anna and I were up and running. A few months after that first meeting in the Bon Bonne I went to Bognor Regis to stay in my nan's caravan. Anna and her friend came to Bognor as well and we had a terrific time. Riverside Caravan Park, Bognor Regis; one of the great holiday destinations!

Gareth came along on many of my dates with Anna. If Anna's parents were having a party, Gareth would be one of the first people invited. John and Beryl had a tradition of asking the family round for a get-together on Christmas Eve and Gareth and I would be included. After a few beers, we sang 'The Twelve Days of Christmas' and different people would each take a day and play the part. Gareth used to be the partridge in the pear tree, which was the toughest of the twelve. That's a side of Gareth that people have rarely seen and one that I treasure.

One evening I was due to meet Anna at six o'clock to arrange the cars for our wedding. Women attach a lot of importance to the smallest details of the big day, and it's safe to say I let Anna down. And even that, of course, doesn't tell the full story. Meeting my agent at the Hilton hotel in Purley at two o'clock that afternoon, I noticed three of the Palace boys having a drink in the bar. Paul Stewart, who had come to us on loan from Liverpool, was with Chris Coleman and Darren Patterson. I decided to join them for one. Mistake. The hours passed. At five I was worried about being late for Anna, at six I was panicking but by seven, I was totally cool about it. And pretty pissed too. We were having a ball. Around eight o'clock, Chris and Paul decided to have a mud fight on the front lawn of the hotel.

They came back to the packed bar covered in mud and proceeded to pour pints over each other. In our drunken state, we thought it hilarious. The hotel staff and guests saw it differently. Back at her house, Anna was losing her mind. Knowing the trouble I was in, Anna's mum Beryl rang Gareth and asked him to find me. Gareth traced me to the Hilton but when he arrived, all hell was breaking loose in the bar. He got me out of there as quickly as he could and brought me home to face the music. It was loud.

There were more recriminations at Palace's training ground the next morning. Alan Smith said he wanted Paul, Chris, Darren, Gareth and myself in his office. On such occasions, Alan had a way of getting his point across.

'What the fuck do you lot think you're playing at? We're trying to get into the Premier League and I'm receiving complaints about Crystal Palace players being drunk and making a nuisance of themselves on a Tuesday afternoon. Paul, you've come on loan and you're doing brilliantly. Chris, you've got in the first team and you're having a great season. Darren, you're close to the first team and you're doing bloody marvellous. Gareth, you're my bloody captain. You've all let the club down, you've let me down and you've let yourselves down. As for you, Woody, you're just fucking Woody.'

Gareth had been in the hotel for a couple of minutes, he hadn't had a drink. All he did was get me out of there. Not many guys would have quietly taken the slaughtering he got from Alan and said nothing. But that's Gareth all over. He was prepared to be one of us, even when he wasn't.

When I decided to ask Anna to marry me, Gareth was the first person I told. We talked about it and decided to go to Lyons, a jewellers in Croydon.

The guy in the shop showed us the most expensive rings, of course. 'How about these? Impressive stones, as you can see.'

'Yeah, they are nice,' I said.

'Andy, are you sure about this? You really want to go through with it?' The salesman hadn't a clue Gareth was winding him up.

'Yeah, I think so, mate,' I replied.

'It's a lot of money to spend on a girl who might still say no,' said Gareth.

The shop assistant wasn't sure how to take it. Did we want a ring or not? After what seemed an age, we came to a joint decision about which ring Anna would like best. Both of us knew her well enough to know she'd love it.

Gareth

Some people are born to rebel, others to conform; I was a conformist. Trouble was something to be avoided. Sport in general and football in particular were the things I was passionate about and, with supportive parents, my childhood was as straightforward as could be. Girls were out there, somewhere in the future. As a committed young footballer full of dreams, I had neither the time nor the inclination. My lack of enthusiasm also stemmed from a natural shyness and a fear of rejection – if you didn't ask, you didn't get turned down.

During my two apprentice years at Palace, nothing much changed, and I was perfectly happy to tag along with Woody and Anna; it made things simple. But the time came when I did want my own girl.

On the way to training, I had to walk through Croydon to get to East Croydon station. It was on that walk that I first saw Alison. She worked in Benetton. Actually, Woody saw her first. 'There's this girl that works in Benetton, you should see her.' So I'd go into the shop and buy jumpers I didn't want, in the hope of being served by her.

Woody and I were friendly with Giovanni Gonzales, who owned a Spanish restaurant in Croydon. I knew Giovanni had got to know Alison because she sometimes ate at the restaurant and I got talking to him about her. But there wasn't much any of us could do; she had a boyfriend she was living with. About a year after I'd first noticed her, we were in the restaurant and Giovanni brought up the subject. 'That girl, Alison, she was in the other day. I think she likes you.'

That was all it took and my interest was revived. 'But what's the situation?'

'She's still living with that guy,' he said.

A few months later, Giovanni had an update. 'She's been in here with her boyfriend. She's not happy in that relationship. Go to her shop and ask her out. She works in French Connection in Bromley.'

'Are you sure?' I asked.

'Yes, you've got to do it.'

For me, it was a nightmare. This was a girl I didn't know but was keen on. I had to go to the shop in Bromley but the prospect unnerved me. Being captain of Crystal Palace and playing in the Premiership was easy compared to this. We had reached the FA Cup semi-final and would play Manchester United a couple of weeks later. I could handle that but the prospect of asking Alison out was a different story. No bottle at all. Pathetic, I know.

I drove to Bromley, parked the car and went into a couple of other shops while I tried to pluck up the courage to go into French Connection. Alison was serving someone when I walked in and as I waited, I wasn't certain she had seen me. She then disappeared out the back. I started picking up all sorts of jumpers and shirts, hoping she would return. I imagined she had seen me and deliberately made herself scarce.

More time looking at shirts and jumpers. Still no Alison. 'I'll take this shirt and these trousers,' I said to one of the other girls, buying clothes that I didn't want. 'Thanks, Giovanni, thanks a lot.' Then I thought, 'Gareth, be logical, you haven't even spoken to this girl. Maybe she genuinely had to go to the back of the shop and got tied up on a long phone call. You could be totally misreading the situation.'

I walked aimlessly through other shops in Bromley, churning things over in my mind. Eventually it was back to French Connection and another hour hovering around its door. I felt like a stalker or, at the very least, a 24-year-old with a sixteen-year-old's confidence. Should I go in there? 'No,' I thought, 'the other girls are going to be looking at me, thinking, "We know why you're here, you must have it bad."' More agonizing, until I just couldn't take it. 'Come on, get on with it.' I walked straight back in. Alison was folding jumpers.

'Hi, how are you?' I said.

'Fine.'

'Look, I'll be honest. I was talking to Giovanni. He said you'd spoken to him. Was wondering if you fancy going out for a drink sometime?'

'I'm afraid I'm seeing someone at the moment. So I can't.'

'Oh, I didn't realize. No problem! Fine! Okay!'

I got out of there. Fast.

Concerned that her suitor might still be loitering in the vicinity, Alison sent one of the girls outside to check that I had really gone. She was still seeing this other guy and it wasn't right for her to be even talking to me.

That weekend Woody, Anna and I were back at Giovanni's. Alison and her boyfriend were also there. She went to the bathroom and a few minutes later I got up to go myself. We met on the stairs. 'I'm sorry about the other day. I don't really know at the moment,' she said.

I sensed her confusion and gave her my telephone number. You don't play professional football for eight years without picking up some of the habits.

That night Alison and her boyfriend left the restaurant in a taxi. As it pulled away she looked out and our eyes met – it was one of those *Love Story* moments. She was obviously unhappy.

Anna noticed the frisson between Alison and I. 'What's going on with you and that girl?'

There was tension already. When Alison worked at

Benetton in Croydon, Anna worked in Next nearby and they had known each other slightly. For no particular reason, they hadn't hit it off.

'She's seeing someone. What's going on between you two?' Anna insisted.

'Nothing Anna, nothing at all.'

Woody jumped in and backed me, said it was Anna's imagination, but she saw beyond our bluffing. And because Alison had a boyfriend she didn't like it.

That night Alison had a row with her boyfriend and tried to ring me from a public booth. As she dialled, her boyfriend asked, 'Who are you calling?' and she put the phone down. She moved out the next day and rang me.

Excited, I called Woody.

'Are you sure it's over? Are you sure she won't be going back?' he asked.

'Well, Woody,' I said, 'she's gone round to her mum's. And she's taken her cats.'

On the following Thursday night Alison and I had dinner at Giovanni's. Three days before our FA Cup semi-final against Manchester United and, amazingly, the buzz wasn't just from football. Alison wasn't comfortable as she had just split with her boyfriend and didn't want to be seen so soon with someone else, but that night in Giovanni's convinced me I'd found my partner.

For our second date we decided to have lunch in Wimbledon village but to avoid being noticed, we agreed to meet at the Tesco car park in Purley and head on to Wimbledon from there. An injury in training that morning needed immediate attention and I had to spend time in an oxygen chamber which was then a very popular treatment. The fads, of course, come and go and the oxygen chamber has more or less disappeared from football. That morning, it was almost my ruination. I was looking at my watch. How much longer in here?

I flew back to the flat to change and, of course, the phone was ringing. 'Did we say one or half past?' Alison asked.

'Half past,' I lied.

Alison wasn't pleased. There may be good places to leave a girl waiting but the Tesco car park in Purley is definitely not one of them. It wouldn't be the last time I have been late for Alison, in fact it has been a recurring theme throughout our marriage. Yet it is extremely rare for me to be late for work. We eventually got to Wimbledon that afternoon, had lunch and gradually Alison's mood improved.

Two months later Palace were relegated and I was on my way to Aston Villa. Birmingham would be home and for Alison and I, it was decision time. At first I thought of going up there on my own and returning when possible to see her. 'Won't work,' Alison said. 'Either I come with you or we forget about it.' At least one of us was decisive. At twenty-four, I'd learned a lot about football but I was only now learning about life outside it. Before Alison, there hadn't been many girlfriends and I hadn't been involved in a relationship that ever looked like going the distance. All was about to change.

For the first three months at Villa, I stayed in a hotel, then a rented house and soon afterwards Alison moved up. While I was house-hunting in Birmingham, she moved into my flat in London and that was a kind of halfway house before the bigger move to the Midlands. It all happened quickly and Mum and Dad met Alison only once before we began to live together. They didn't mind that, but they were a little taken aback when, a year or so later, I told them we were going to get married. They found it hard to believe that a son who all through his life had been methodical, logical and weighed up everything a hundred times was suddenly getting married. And, of course, Mum didn't see me as a 25-year-old. I was her little boy, who needed to be looked after. I was waiting for them to say, 'Congratulations, son, that's brilliant, let's have a glass of champagne.' That's not Mum and Dad.

'Oh! Well, good luck, if you're sure it's the right thing . . .'

'But aren't you happy?' I said.

'Well, as long as you're happy, that's all that matters.'

Not to Alison.

'What did your mum and dad say?' she asked me later.

'They were fine.'

'No, what did they *say*?'

'Well, actually . . .'

It was difficult for Alison because, at first, she didn't feel she was welcomed with open arms. In their quiet and reserved way, Mum and Dad were saying, 'Son, we don't really know your future wife.' Things improved greatly as they got to know each other but Mum fits into that category of mother for whom no girl is good enough for her boy. Do you love your mum more or less for that? More, probably.

If there was a slight unease over how my parents felt about Alison and I, it was nothing compared to the problem of how Anna felt about Alison. That night at Giovanni's, Anna had seen Alison with her boyfriend and thought it was outrageous that she and I were exchanging glances. God knows what she would have said if she had known that I'd given Alison my telephone number.

The following day Woody and I were invited to lunch by Anna's parents. The subject had to come up. Anna felt Alison and I were going to start seeing each other while she was still with her boyfriend and that it would be an affair. That wasn't going to happen, but Anna didn't realize that.

Anna and Alison will hate me for bringing this up but

there was one classic moment during that lunch at Anna's parents. 'I'll tell you something now – there's no way that girl will ever sit at this dinner table,' Anna said.

Woody looked at me, sort of uncomfortable, and then turned to Anna. 'You're out of order, Anna. Gareth can go out with whoever he wants.'

Anna's mum, Beryl, then said: 'Anna, you can't say that.'

Anna is not a woman who backs down. 'Well I don't care. *That girl will never sit at this table.*'

So now, whenever we go on holidays together or meet up at weekends, Anna and Alison will be saying goodbye to each other, embracing, kissing and crying. Quietly but audibly, Woody and I will chime: '*That-girl-will-never-sit-at-this-table . . .*'

In harmony the girls say: 'You two can fuck off.'

10

We take different paths in life, but no matter where we go, we take a
little of each other everywhere.

Tim McGraw

Gareth

The guy at the newsstand outside Victoria station in London
knew who I was. It was the early summer of 1995, and I was
not often recognized. But this guy knew his football. 'Best
of luck in the Endsleigh next season,' he said.

Palace had been relegated from the Premiership, Endsleigh
then sponsored the Football League and you could tell he
was a Chelsea supporter. Something in the way he sneered.
He didn't know I was on my way to see Bernie Hoffman,
my accountant, followed by a trip to Birmingham and a
meeting with Doug Ellis and Brian Little, chairman and
manager of Aston Villa. If everything went okay, I would be
a Villa player the following day. The transfer and the personal
terms had been agreed, but not signed. Brian Little wanted
to wait until his chairman returned from holiday in Majorca.
Doug was due back that morning and we would rendezvous
at Villa Park.

We are already there when the chairman arrives. He bowls
in, looking resplendent in a Hawaiian shirt. He shakes my
hand and throws me an Aston Villa pin. This is the first

play in his attempt to sell the club to me; the tradition, the ambition, the plans. It is unnecessary, because the reason I am saying yes to Villa is because it is one of the truly big clubs in English football. But we listen because the chairman is . . . well, the chairman. Brian informs Doug that John Major has just resigned as leader of the Conservative Party. There is a hint of surprise in Doug's reaction, but it soon gives way to a knowing nod. Doug regales us with stories from some of his encounters with the PM. Bernie and I are waiting for Doug to start trying to reduce the terms we have agreed, but he seems in a good mood.

Eventually, he turns his attention to the contract and scans it in silence. I quietly tell myself that the amounts I have asked for are not extortionate. Doug peers over his glasses, focusing on both Bernie and me. 'It's a very good contract, you know. We're going to make you a very rich young man, Mr Southgate.'

Though I am grateful for the job and the wage, it is a shame I have no cap to doff. Doug looks towards his manager. 'Well, Brian, do you really want this young man?'

Brian quickly winks at me, reassuring me this is a formality. 'Yes, chairman, I do.'

Doug picks up his fountain pen. 'Very well, then,' he says, and signs the contract. Handshakes follow, everyone's happy. That's it.

But it isn't. Deadly Doug has one trick he has yet to perform. He says he must ring Ron Noades, the Palace chairman, to inform him about the deal.

DOUG: Hello, Ron.
RON: Oh, Doug.
DOUG: I have your Mr Southgate here.
RON: Oh yes, Gareth.

DOUG: Well, Ron, he seems a nice enough chap, but his demands
are a bit high.

My jaw drops and, alarmingly for me, so too does Brian
Little's.

RON: Look, Doug, if you're not happy, send him back to us.
He can rot in the reserves.
DOUG: Now, Ron, calm down.

Brian looks very uneasy while this is going on, I'm getting
desperate and Bernie doesn't know what to think. We know
Ron is furious and, all the while, Doug is as cool as a cucumber.

DOUG: Look, Ron, knock £100,000 off the fee and we have a
deal.

Ron's voice gets louder.

DOUG: Now, Ron, come on, don't be like that. Let's do a deal
here.

They continue to haggle. Ron won't consider knocking
£100,000 off the transfer fee and wants Doug to send me
back. At this point, I have completely forgotten the contract
has already been signed.

DOUG: Come on, Ron, £50,000 then. Fifty grand off and we
have a deal. It's a good deal for you, you know that.
RON: This is ridiculous.
DOUG: Okay, Ron, £50,000. We're both in agreement. We
have a deal.
RON: Okay.

The phone is put down. From Brian, Bernie and myself there is a collective sigh of relief. Doug purrs like a Cheshire cat. He has clearly enjoyed his duel with Ron Noades. The £50,000 wasn't bad either.

I got back to London that afternoon and the Chelsea fan was at his station selling the *Evening Standard*. Alongside him, the billboard now read: 'PALACE CAPTAIN TO VILLA IN 2.5M MOVE'. On that particular afternoon, it was a pleasure to buy the *Standard*. I winked at him as he handed me the change. Poor fellow, he wasn't to know his story was fifty grand out.

It cost Ron Noades £50,000 to spend five minutes on the telephone with Doug; what did it cost me to spend six seasons at Villa Park? In some respects they were good years. I played with a number of outstanding footballers: Paul McGrath, David James, Paul Merson, Dwight Yorke and talented young players like Gareth Barry and Lee Hendrie. The team always finished in the Premiership's top ten; we were once fourth and twice fifth. We won the League Cup, got to an FA Cup final and played in Europe regularly. Yet, in my time, Villa was a nearly club, a monument to underachievement. We could have been up there with the biggest guns but it didn't happen and it wasn't going to happen. Through my last two seasons, I couldn't wait to get out.

Two photographs tell the story of what I thought was wrong at Aston Villa. One is of Villa's 1982 European Cup-winning side, stuck on the wall over my peg at the training ground in Bodymoor Heath. It stood for the Villa I joined, the club Doug had spoken of before getting on to the business of saving the club £50,000. The other was a photograph of our team, taken early in the 1998–99 season after a victory over Southampton at the Dell. It represented what Villa had become, a great club gone wrong. A club where it seemed mediocrity was accepted. Villa, I felt, didn't act like a big club.

Through my friendship with the England physio Gary Lewin, I once visited Arsenal's training ground. Photographs decorate the walls; in almost every picture there is a trophy. It is like the club telling you, 'This is Arsenal Football Club, this is what we're about.' But Arsenal had not won the European Cup; Villa had. And yet at Villa Park there were photographs of our squad, of the team that won the League Cup, but it was almost impossible to find a picture of the side that beat Bayern Munich 1–0 to win that European Cup. I found that staggering. Some of those lads are still around: Gordon Cowans and Gary Shaw are coaches. But the side that achieved that victory has not been properly recognized at Villa Park. People said the reason for this was that Doug was not at the club in the European Cup-winning year.

John Greenfield, who used to run the merchandising department, had a painting in his office of the European Cup-winning side. Otherwise, you were hard-pressed to find evidence of that success. It rankled with me. Long afternoons were spent with the first-team coach Steve Harrison and Jim Walker, who was much more than a physio at the club, and in our collective attempt to see a better future for Villa I would hold up the '82 team as the benchmark. I discussed this once with a man who had come to do a job at our house, lamenting how that team had been forgotten, and the following day he brought me a photograph of the side that beat Bayern. That was the photo I pinned on to the wall over my peg at the training ground. It was a statement to both myself and the rest of the lads: forget everything else, this is the team we have to emulate. This is the target. The lads would rib me about it because, I suppose, some felt it was a slight on our lack of achievement. They were right.

Those old Villa players should be highly visible on match days. You go to Liverpool or Manchester United and the former greats are everywhere. They're there, some of them in person, every one of them in photographs. Villa have never been interested in saying, 'We are a European Cup-winning club. We expect.' Gary Shaw and Peter Withe played up front on that team. There were four in midfield, Gordon Cowans, Des Bremner, Denis Mortimer and Tony Morley. Alun Evans and Ken McNaught were the centre-halves. And even though I spent six years at Villa, I struggle to name the full-backs. Did John Gidman play on that team, or was it a guy called Gary Williams? Peter Withe scored the winner. But the game is best remembered for Jimmy Rimmer going off injured after ten or fifteen minutes and Nigel Spink coming on. I was twelve and remember watching the game with my auntie. When Spink came on, she said, 'Oh, that poor young lad, having to take over in a European Cup final.' The picture above the peg was tolerated until the summer I put in a written transfer request. When I came back for pre-season training a month or so later, it was gone. I had lost my right to remind the club of its past.

The second photograph shows the other side of life at Villa. It was taken early in the first full season, 1998–99, that John Gregory managed the team. John had coached us during Brian Little's reign and we'd had a bad run immediately after he left. At boardroom level, it was believed we were missing John's coaching. None of the players felt that.

From the beginning I wasn't sure about John. Having worked under him for a year during his coaching days, I felt he was an okay coach. No better. He came in for the last eleven matches of that season. We beat Liverpool 2–1 in his first game; Stan Collymore scored both goals and it seemed John might be able to get something from Stan. In those eleven games we lost just twice, pulled ourselves up to a place in Europe and John was regarded as a bit of a saviour.

We continued in the same form at the beginning of the following season. Unbeaten for the first twelve games, we were top of the table until December and there was talk of John being the next England manager. When things are going well, people are apt to get carried away. John was unproven and we were not as good as the results suggested. The key to our little run was that we had avoided injuries. Dwight Yorke had been sold to United and as the season went on we brought in Dion Dublin and Paul Merson. We kept churning out results.

Then there was the game in Southampton. Still unbeaten at that point, we went to the Dell in search of a victory that would give us the club's best ever start to a season. We won well and as we were coming off the field, John came to meet us. 'Come on, we're having a photograph.'

'We're what?' I said.

'We're having a photo of the team that has made the best ever start to a season by Villa.'

I couldn't believe it. What planet did this guy come from? We got into position in the corner of the Dell with our fans behind us. If you ever see a copy of that photograph, I am the guy at the end of the row looking confused. *Why are we doing this?* One of my regrets is that I didn't raise hell when we returned to the dressing room. People sometimes find it hard to accept Roy Keane's fury when he feels things aren't right at Man United. A lot of the time I find myself agreeing with Roy and lamenting that I had not been more outspoken. That photograph was a perfect example. Villa had won the European Cup. How could we celebrate a good start to the season? What medals do you get for a record start?

The photo was shown on that night's *Match of the Day* and printed in a couple of newspapers. We got grief from players at other clubs and we deserved to. Alan Shearer brought it up with me when England came together for their next match. 'Team photo, eh?' That was all Al said but we both knew what he meant: 'What the fuck was that all about?'

That photo was taken at a time when John's star was high and when I hoped he could take us places. It was an eye-opener. Was this what we were under John Gregory: a team that photographed itself after 'a record start to the season'?

Andy

Another picture.

A photograph of a penalty saved at Wembley in the 1998 Division Two play-off final between Northampton and Grimsby. The fact that we lost the game would spoil the memory for many players, but not for me. Possibly it was the best moment of my career. We were 1–0 down when the penalty was awarded seventy-seven minutes into the match. At such times a lot of things flash through your mind: this is your chance; can you produce a big save when it's most needed? It was into the same Wembley goal that my best mate had missed his famous penalty two years before and an opportunity for me to have a different experience.

Two days before, Northants 96.6FM radio interviewed Kevin Wade and myself on Terry Doyle's show. Kevin was a spiritualist and why they put us on together was a mystery, but I suppose that's Kevin's line of business. At the beginning of the show, I didn't think much of Kevin's psychic powers. In football dressing rooms, you deal in the here and now. But soon it started to get scary. People rang in and Kevin told them stuff about a long-lost relative or a recently departed loved one and everything seemed to be true. He told them things about pets they had lost. This was no hoax and everyone around the studio was transfixed. This guy had some kind of power. Then Terry asked Kevin what would happen to Andy Woodman in Saturday's game. Kevin consulted with the other side and started to talk about a save I would make, not an ordinary save but one I would remember for the rest of my life. 'Please God you're right,' I thought.

We trained the next day at Sixfields and I worked with Tony Godden, Northampton's goalkeeping coach. We had been together for over two years and, more than anyone in football, Tony made me a goalkeeper. He knew how to get the best out of me and allowed me to constantly pick his brains about the art of goalkeeping. At the end of our Friday session Tony asked me to walk with him to the other end of the pitch. We talked about Wembley and then he said. 'If they get a penalty, Kevin Donovan will take it and he will place it to your left at a saveable height.' Oh no, not another psychic. He then started taking penalties, trying to put them precisely where Donovan put them. On the tenth or eleventh attempt, he hit it precisely where he wanted. 'That's it,' he said, 'that's where he'll put it.'

'Hey, you been doin' some homework or what?'

Tony's look just said 'trust me'.

Right on cue, the next day Grimsby were awarded a penalty. As Kevin Donovan placed the ball doubts ran through my mind. 'I have a hunch he's going to put it to my right, not where Tony said.'

'*No, trust Tony, he knows . . .*'

'Make your own decision. Go right, make the save, you'll be a hero . . .'

'*Don't go against Tony, don't be mad . . .*'

At the last second, I committed myself to Tony. Kevin Donovan struck the penalty exactly as Tony had said he would. The save was Tony's; the glory was mine.

There haven't been too many penalty saves at Wembley in open play but I have one of them. Behind that goal was Pete Norton, a photographer from Northampton. Tony must have told him where Kevin Donovan would put the penalty because Pete caught it perfectly as well. Whenever he got a good action photograph, he would print up a copy and pass it on to the player in the shot. Pete was excited about this particular photograph as he gave it to me because he could see what it meant.

'Woody, if you'd like any copies for your family, it's no problem.' Pete printed copies for my dad and my brother. As always, he refused money for them.

A framed copy of the picture hangs in my brother's dining room. He is proud of what it says: his kid brother plays professional football and actually saved a penalty at Wembley. My dad's copy is in the study, a room he has turned into a shrine to Peter and me and our poor mum. I imagine Dad in private moments looking at the photograph and remembering the ups and downs of my career. Dad was never one for praising me but he was proud of what I'd achieved and in those early days, when I needed someone to drive me to Exeter or Northampton, he was there. In his own way, he showed how pleased he was and maybe that was as good as telling me. Scrapbooks and videos never interested me, but Dad kept a scrapbook of newspaper reports and articles in which I featured and any time I did a television interview he recorded it.

One Friday evening recently he called round with all the videotapes and the scrapbook. We were due to take Freddie to training at Selsdon Juniors, the schoolboy club Gareth and I had played for twenty years earlier. Before leaving he handed Freddie the collection of videos and the scrapbook. It had never struck me why Dad recorded the matches and kept the cuttings but he had always planned to do this. He didn't make a big fuss – he wouldn't – yet it was obvious he wanted Freddie to understand he had inherited something important.

By now, Freddie has watched all of the videos and the questions are endless. 'Where is Wembley? Why do they not play there any more? How did you know which way to dive? Why didn't you win that game?'

The photograph of the penalty save also hangs in the hallway of our own home, alongside the jersey and programme from that losing day. People have asked why I framed the loser's shirt, not the winning one from the year before. That shirt found a better home.

Shortly after we had won the Division Three final, a man called Southwell came to see the players and told us about his son, Patrick. He had been a devoted fan of the team, and of me in particular, so much so that he had called his dog 'Woody'. A few days earlier Patrick had been fatally knocked down in an accident and his dad wondered if it would be possible to get a Cobblers jersey so that it could be laid in the coffin beside him. We were numbed. It was easy to tell this was a lovely kid who was passionate about his football. What was winning at Wembley compared to such a tragedy and the enormity of the loss to Patrick's family? That afternoon Anna and I talked about it and decided the players should sign my shirt and we would give it to Patrick's dad. It was such a small, pathetic gesture but it was all we could do. The family was appreciative and said it was what Patrick would have wanted. The team attended the funeral and Patrick was laid to rest in my jersey. That shirt is now with someone who is special to my memory of that Wembley victory.

Gareth

My career at Villa began encouragingly. They paid £2.45m for me, the most the club had paid up till then for any player. Though they had been just one place above relegation at the end of the 1994–95 season, I still saw them as a big club and was impressed that Brian Little had paid so much to get me. That first season went well. We finished fourth in the Premiership and had a good side. Mark Bosnich was goal-keeper; the back three were Ugo Ehiogu, Paul McGrath and myself; Gary Charles and Alan Wright were the wing-backs; Mark Draper, Ian Taylor and Andy Townsend were in midfield; Savo Milosevic and Dwight Yorke played up front. Paul McGrath had problems with his knees and, by that stage, he didn't have great spring but he still powered through people and won everything in the air. It was an honour to play with him and though he had alcohol-related problems, you wouldn't have heard a bad word about Paul in the Villa dressing room. He was a softly spoken gentleman, a player we all thought the world of.

In those early seasons, Villa had a lot of strong characters: Townsend, Staunton, Taylor, Yorke and Bosnich were big men who expected to win when they played. We knew how close we were to being a real force, but the more we tried to make that final leap, the further away we seemed to be. Alex Ferguson said Villa was the team he could see coming through. Within the dressing room there was a debate about how good Savo was. Most of us felt he struggled, not quite top-notch in the Premiership. We reckoned if the club could find a twenty-goal-a-season striker to play alongside Yorkie, we would be right up there. It was an important call for Brian Little. By finishing fourth, he had earned the trust of the board and the right to buy players. Bring in the right players and fourth could become third or higher.

Brian paid £4m for Sasa Curcic from Bolton. Curcic was a ball-playing midfielder who could operate in the hole behind the strikers. Having done well at Bolton, Curcic seemed a reasonable buy. He turned out to be a waste of time and money. Character and attitude matter as much as talent and Curcic, it seemed, had no particular desire to be successful at Aston Villa. What he wanted more was a lively social life and he had that. He had come to England from his native Yugoslavia, was earning far more than he could back home and he couldn't handle it. He was out all the time, his lifestyle was horrific and his contribution to our team was negligible. What I most remember about Sasa is the time he failed to appear for a few days and we were all pissed off, then when he did show up we were even more annoyed. 'Where have you been?' we asked.

'I had an operation on my nose.'

'You didn't break your nose.'

'No, it was something to improve the shape.'

He couldn't play on the Saturday because he had plastic surgery on his nose. We had paid £4m for this. I would love to have had improvements made to my nose. I probably needed them more than Sasa, but in mid-season?

Halfway through the 1996–97 season, things had not progressed. The club wanted me to extend my contract and I wondered about the plans for improving the squad. 'Look,' I said to Brian Little, 'before we get down to talking about a new contract, I'd like to know what we're doing to strengthen the squad.'

'Well,' said Brian, 'you know people say we need a striker and I'd probably agree with that.'

'Have you got anybody in mind?'

'One or two.'

'I've heard a lot of talk about Stan Collymore. I played with Stan at Palace and he's a very complex lad. For me, he's not the one for us.'

'Well, to be honest,' said Brian, 'he's not really one I'm looking at.'

That tallied. Whenever I had heard Brian talk about Stan, he said he wasn't sure about him. Brian's view was that Stan hadn't dealt well with success. I signed a new contract, the team finished fifth in the Premiership and we all went away for our summer break. It was then that the news broke: Villa had signed Stan Collymore for a club record fee of £7m.

If you spoke to the guys in the Villa dressing room, they would say I didn't like Stan. It wasn't that. As a person, Stan wasn't a bad lad. As a footballer, I felt he seriously underachieved. With so much talent, he could have been a huge asset for Villa, but he never was.

Inside a dressing room you judge people on how they perform on the park. How they measure up as members of society is secondary. When Stan was signed, I felt it was a mistake and waited for it to go wrong. It went back to when he was at Palace. Almost every weekend he would return home to Cannock in the Black Country, as if unable to get on with his life in London. Neither was he comfortable with the banter and wind-ups that are part of the football culture. Wally Downes, the reserve-team coach at Palace, and Stan came to blows one day solely because Stan couldn't take the criticism that Wally dished out to everyone.

At Palace, we had played in the reserves together. Stan scored twenty goals and it was obvious he had incredible talent. The younger pros got on well with him and thought him a decent lad. Older fellows were wary; there was something about him they didn't warm to. He was deep, probably insecure, the guy who needed an arm around him. At Palace, there wasn't much room for a player like that. Ian Wright and Mark Bright had fought for everything they'd got. They had been hammered on the way up but it didn't get them down. Stan's mentality was different and he didn't fit at Palace. I felt he would have problems at Villa as well.

When he signed, he joined the lads on an end-of-season tour and everyone thought him a good guy. I didn't think it would last. Wait, I thought, until the days when Stan doesn't turn up for training and no one knows why he is missing. When he was at Forest, Stuart Pearce used to say, 'If he's scoring goals for us I don't care what he does.' I found that strange from Pearcey. At Villa, he never produced. We lost the first four matches after he came. I felt he wasn't trying hard enough, simple as that.

I had a go at him after a couple of games. People see me as being quiet but I can be hot-tempered in dressing rooms, generally not to an individual, but if I feel something needs to be said, I say it. More than most, Stan had a way of bringing out my fiery streak. After a European game in Bordeaux, I was incensed at how he had played. 'Stan, you were a fucking disgrace tonight,' I said. He had a go back, Brian Little tried to calm it down but what I said was what everyone else was thinking.

Later on in his Villa career, Stan booked himself into a clinic to have treatment for clinical depression. That meant he couldn't train with us; he would arrive from the clinic on Friday to play with us on Saturday. Naturally, he didn't play well and would then return to the clinic on Monday. There were stories about him socializing in London during the time he was in treatment. The other players were asking. 'What's going on with Stan?' and I raised it in the dressing room. It wound me up, to a point where it affected how I played. There was a banner at the Holte End of Villa Park, a Collymore banner. One of the lads said it was his family who put it there. I used to run out for the warm-up and think, 'Fucking hell, that banner! He's in the clinic for depression and the way he's playing is depressing me.'

I didn't deal with Stan in a compassionate way and had no understanding of what clinical depression meant. Maybe a more sympathetic approach would have kept him onside and got more out of him. All I could see was Villa stagnating. Everything I felt about Stan related to him as a footballer. Nowadays, he is on the radio, comes across well and I'm reminded of what a nice lad he can be. Back then he was Brian Little's most expensive mistake. To blame Brian for buying Stan would be a little unfair, because we were never sure how much pressure there was from Doug Ellis; it seemed the chairman played a significant part. Stan was seen as a Villa fan and there were a lot of supporters who thought him the solution to our goalscoring problem. He was a lot of things in those days, but a solution he was not.

Andy

Stan Collymore. There's a guy I really did like. He and another Palace player, Jamie Moralee, introduced me to Anna, so I've always had a soft spot for him. He had such talent and he was an intelligent lad. A character, too, a terrific character, always out clubbing. He was addicted to womanizing. Every day he would come into training with stories from the night before. Over the years I would hear people say Stan was a problem in the dressing room. I could never understand that. A little naïve, maybe, but great fun. If he had a problem it was with the winding-up that went on. He couldn't take it and Wally Downes went too far with him.

Still, the day he walked into Crystal Palace was a good day in the life of Andrew J. Woodman.

Before Stan's arrival, I had been Wally Downes's favourite target. Wally was a character. He had come from Wimbledon, a hard school, and he was totally ruthless. He called me 'No-Eyes' – it was a cruel name to give a goalkeeper but it stuck. Boy, did it stick. Guys that I haven't met since we were at Palace twelve years ago will see me today and say, 'Ah, No-Eyes'. Not surprisingly, the name didn't fill me with joy. It got to the stage where I dreaded seeing Wally. 'He's going to slaughter me again. Please, Wal, give us a break here.' But Wally didn't listen to pleas for sympathy. Then Stan walked through the door and Wally had a new target. No-Eyes could sit back and watch someone else get a caning.

Not just that, but Stan was in the market for a car and I had one to sell. It was a Vauxhall Belmont, like an Astra except with a boot. It had a very good stereo and it was in pristine condition – the stereo that is. The car was a C-reg and Stan could have bought a newer E-reg Belmont for £2,900. That meant my car was worth around £2,500, maybe less. But Stan had just got his first signing-on fee. Some said it was £5,000, others said £10,000 and I just thought, 'Hold on a minute, he has money and he wants a car. Hallelujah!'

'I'm selling mine, Stan,' I said.

He said he'd like to have a look at it. But me, being me, had a plan. 'Nah, why don't you take the car for a couple of days, get the feel of it?'

Everyone loves their first car. It's the power, the freedom of having your own wheels. Human nature. Stan was going to love my car. He didn't say if he had a driving licence and I didn't ask.

When he came back two days later, he had fallen in love. 'How much do you want for it?'

'Four thousand seven hundred and fifty pounds.'

'That might be okay.'

'But, Stan, I'm taking the stereo out. That stereo's cost me bundles. Couldn't possibly let it go with the car.'

I had to keep the deal hush-hush. Just me and Stan, because Andy Gray, one of the older pros, would want to sell whatever he could to Stan. We did the deal. Stan gave me £4,500, with £250 to be paid up later. I took out the stereo. Once Stan got the car and I got his money, the word was out and inside the changing room I was bad news.

'Woody's stitched up Stan. Four thousand seven hundred and fifty pounds for that old car.'

'You can't be serious?'

Andy Gray and a few of the lads gave me a terrible time. 'You took a liberty with that kid,' Andy said.

'You've taken him to the cleaners,' someone else said.

Realizing that the new love of his life had cost far more than it should have, Stan was gutted. It was wrong, I shouldn't have done it, but it was how things worked in the real world. Especially in the world I came from. If Stan was prepared to pay £4,750 for the car, that's how much it was worth. The lads kept giving me grief – Andy Gray, Mark Bright, Ian Wright – but with Mark and Ian, I could tell their real target was Stan. They were getting at him by having a go at me. When they found out I had taken the stereo as well, they were flabbergasted. 'Can't be true. Even you, Woody, wouldn't do that.'

One afternoon Andy Gray had a real go at me in front of the boys. Called me a spiv and meant it. Being a bit cocky and not prepared to be belittled by an older pro, I faced up to Andy. 'Hey, look who's calling the kettle black.'

Sometimes in life you know you've said the wrong thing as

soon as it's out of your mouth. I knew it. Before I could back off or try to defuse the situation, Andy had me by the throat over a pool table. Gareth immediately stepped in: 'Con e on Andy, there's no need for that.' Andy didn't end my life there and then. I speak with him now and it would be nice to say we laugh and joke about that little incident, but we don't. I stepped over a dangerous line that day.

We got to the end of the season and Stan still hadn't paid the outstanding £250. He felt £4,500 was more than enough and, to be honest, most everyone agreed with him. I saw it differently of course. A deal was a deal. I waited until Stan went away on his summer holidays and rang his home. His mum – God bless her, an extremely nice lady – answered.

'Mrs Collymore, is Stanley there?' I asked. I knew Stan's mum called him Stanley.

'No, Stanley's gone away on holiday I'm afraid.'

'Oh you're joking, Mrs Collymore! This is Andy Woodman from Palace. I sold him his Vauxhall Belmont and Stanley promised to send me a cheque for the £250 he still owes me. I can't go on my summer holidays without that money.'

'That's terrible, Andy,' she said. 'Tell you what I'll do, I'll send you a cheque for £250 and when Stanley comes back from holiday, he can give it to me.'

'That would be great, Mrs Collymore. Here's my address . . .'

The cheque arrived two days later; I cashed it. Now the deal was properly closed: £4,750 for the car and I still had the stereo.

First day back at pre-season training, Stan went for me. 'You're a joke, you are,' he said.

'Look, mate, a deal's a deal. Got to settle your debts.'

Ian Wright and Mark Bright loved it. It was funny at the time, but it was robbery. Stan was a little bit green and it was easy to imagine how he would struggle later on. Me, I was glad to have the old Vauxhall Belmont off my hands and Wally Downes off my back.

A good few years later I was playing for Brentford when Wally Downes was taken on as a coach. All through the summer before his arrival, I talked it over with Gareth: 'What should I do if he starts calling me No-Eyes?'

Gareth said I had to stand up to him, couldn't let it start all over again. I agreed. 'If he starts, Gareth, I'm going to knock him out. I'm a grown man now, no longer am I taking the shit.'

So the very first day, Wally walked into the changing room and said, 'No-Eyes – how're you keeping?' I swallowed that – once was okay – but he came for me again on the training ground. 'Come on, No-Eyes, a bit sharper.'

'Wal,' I said, 'I'm twenty-eight now, not a kid any more. No more am I going to be the butt of your fucking jokes.'

Wally understood and was as good as gold after that. From that day on, he would joke with me, never at me. Someone else would be his victim.

11

I don't need a friend who changes when I change and who nods when I nod; my shadow does that much better.

  Plutarch

Gareth

Earlier this year Alan Hansen interviewed me for a pro-gramme the BBC were doing on the issue of club versus country in football. Afterwards we spoke off camera about the things footballers and ex-footballers talk about. Was I enjoying it as much as ever? Sort of. For how long would I keep playing? As long as I was still good enough to play at the highest level. Did he feel he had got out at the right time? I was interested in why he had retired at thirty-six when, with his slim build and majestic style, it seemed he could have gone on longer. Was it the training? No, he loved training up to the day he stopped. Was it the wear and tear to his body? No, physically he could have kept going. What got to Alan in the end was playing matches; he stopped enjoying the games. He recalled lying in bed on a Wednes-day night, thinking that if his team, Liverpool, could beat Tottenham on Saturday and Everton lost at Leeds, then they would be just three points off the top. Tossing around the possibilities in his mind, he struggled to get to sleep. Anxiety started to take away from his enjoyment of the matches.

Eventually, he had started wondering what it was all for. He had won everything the game offered at club level, he didn't need the stress, and so he packed it in. What he missed was the camaraderie of the dressing room and the banter of the training ground. To some it will be a surprise that Alan lost his enthusiasm for the matches themselves. Not to me. You do lie awake at night and mull over bad results. A few seasons ago I decided Alison and Mia would not suffer because my team happened to lose a football game. Why should they? On losing days I do not allow my disappointment to affect those around me, but once we've all gone to bed and everything is quiet, the tossing and turning begins. How can I pretend it doesn't matter when it does? I want to play in a successful team and to be involved in matches that seem 'life or death'. When it comes down to it, I want my life to be affected by what happens at my work on a Saturday afternoon.

Alan's reason for quitting struck a chord because there have been times in my career when the fun has gone out of playing. My last two years at Villa were frustrating and, even though I played well, it was miserable. I didn't rate our manager, John Gregory, and ended up disliking him. The club had stagnated and it was impossible to see it move forward again. I went to training without enthusiasm. 'What we need to do is paint the gates a different colour,' the goalkeeping coach, Paul Barron, used to say, 'because every time you come through those gates you're reminded of where you are.'

Everyone thinks the money is enough to keep us happy but for me it doesn't matter what the pay is if I feel my career is going down the drain. In the last years at Villa I felt nothing but resentment at being where I didn't want to be – stuck in a club that was going nowhere and controlled by people I didn't respect. In the second of two bad seasons, there were times when I sat in the hotel on the morning of a game, or even in the dressing room half an hour before kick-off, and thought, 'I just do not want to be here.' The malaise that afflicted the club was not going to be cured by one good result, so what was the point?

Even my dad who would normally be reluctant to suggest I should leave a club could see I needed to get away from Villa. Long before my move to Middlesbrough in the summer of 2001, he had been advocating a fresh start somewhere else. By then I'd figured Villa out; how it was run, where it saw itself and how it stopped believing it should be among the elite of British football. Though Dad recognized my need for change, it was partly because of his influence that the move didn't happen quickly. He has always done things by the book and that was how I was brought up. Laws obeyed, rules of decency observed. 'Son, you did sign that contract.' Nothing could be dishonest or underhand.

He worked as a facilities manager with IBM for most of his life and it was clear why he was so highly thought of: Clive Southgate could be relied upon, he did things correctly. He turned up on time, he faced up to his responsibilities, he treated people respectfully. You pick up on those things. Once he was in charge of our boys' team in Crawley, he made a point of not showing favouritism towards me. He tried not to praise me in front of others and if he had to criticize the players, he picked on me more than on anyone else. At first I didn't understand but later I was proud of him. Once during a game my hamstring went and I fell in a heap. Dad could have run on to the pitch to see how I was. Instead, he waited on the sideline because he never wanted to interfere.

It was a great upbringing and it made me the person I am. Did it prepare me for the cynicism that is part of professional football? Afraid not. The first three seasons at Villa were okay; Brian Little was manager, took the team into the Premiership's top six and got us into Europe. John Gregory replaced Brian and we hoped he could take us to the next level. He came to the club from Wycombe Wanderers late in the 1997–98 season and started well. He was keen to make a good impression, was highly focused and made a good appointment in Steve Harrison as first-team coach. This was reflected in our results and briefly there was hope that Villa could become a top-three team. Yet most of the senior pros had reservations: John had risen without trace. Nothing on his CV pointed to him becoming a top manager. What had he done? Coached us during Brian Little's reign and then gone on to manage Wycombe Wanderers.

Though I had doubts, my natural inclination was to support the new manager, believe in the future, remain loyal. Midway through John's first full season, I agreed a new five-year contract with Villa. It was my way of committing to the club and my team-mates; let's go with this, let's make things happen. Through the first eighteen games of that season, when we were top of the table, there was an edge to the side that made each match an intense experience. I loved it. Every game was a must-win game. Through my career, that pressure to perform has been what I have missed most.

No sooner had I put my name to the contract than there were misgivings. 'Don't know if I've done the right thing there.' A year later, I knew it was one of the biggest mistakes of my football life. Six months after that, I asked to leave the club. For a time, I tried to make it work and as team captain it was my duty to support the manager. John had changed things: brought in Dion Dublin and Paul Merson; afterwards Alan Thompson, Steve Stone, Steve Watson and George Boateng. There was the basis of a strong team, though not a Championship-winning one. It soon began to fall apart. The lads were unhappy with John because of his public criticism of individual players. He criticized Dwight after he left, rubbished Mark Bosnich after he too went to Man United and had no understanding of how that annoyed the lads in the Villa dressing room. Yorkie and Bos were gone but every player thinks, 'That could be me, he could be saying that about me.' And, of course, we were soon getting the same treatment from John. He said negative things to the press about players that he didn't say to their faces.

When the general disenchantment was first aired, I took John's side, 'Hey, hang on a minute, he signed you, he's given you the chance here. You've got to produce.' But the manager kept on treating players badly and the dressing room turned against him. Villa excited and energized John for a while, then it all went flat. Working with Doug Ellis exasperated him; the chairman wanted proper financial management, the manager wanted a striker and the chairman was boss. John talked to me about his frustration. 'The old man's doing my head in,' he would say. Immersed in the politics of the club and his worsening relationship with Doug, John couldn't see he was losing the dressing room. He never sensed my frustration.

Mark Bosnich came up with the idea of the players forming a huddle around him in the dressing room before each match whereupon he would then deliver a short team talk. Bos was unbelievable; whatever book he had just read, that was how life should be. One month he would eat only toast, twelve slices of toast for lunch. Next time you noticed, it was fish with olive oil. 'What happened to the toast, Bos?' 'No, son, no good, the toast.' Obviously now he had read a book on another sport where they had a huddle and so he would stand there, 'Believe in yourself, guys, BELIEVE IN YOURSELF.' When Bos was out of the team the manager wanted to carry on the dressing room huddle. 'Gareth, you can say the few words before each game.' This was at a time when I was finding it hard to motivate myself. 'Look lads, we are a big club, we deserve to be up there with the best teams, we've got to win games like this. So let's do it.' Saying stuff that I just didn't believe.

The huddle, though, wasn't the worst bit. Immediately after it, John performed a little ceremony where he handed the captain's armband to me. He stood by the dressing room door, put the band on my arm, looked me in the eye and then shook my hand. In his book he said this was his handing over responsibility of the team to his captain. It was a pre-match ritual that I hated. I looked John in the eye knowing it wasn't sincere. How could it be when I no longer respected him? As time went on and my futility increased, that ceremony began to get to me. 'I don't believe I'm still doing this,' I would say to the lads. The manager and I would not speak all week, I would find something wrong in everything he did and still we went through this charade as we left the dressing room. It was such bullshit.

By the middle of the 1999–2000 season, eighteen months before my eventual move to Middlesbrough, I wanted to get away from Villa. It was clear to everyone how demoralized I had become. 'They must be looking forward to playing us,' I said at breakfast in the team hotel on the morning of our game at Leicester. Steve Harrison, the first-team coach, wasn't impressed. He followed me up to my room. 'I don't care how you're feeling, once you go over that line, you're on your own and will be judged on that performance. So you'd better be ready for it.'

The challenge of getting my head right for the matches was tougher than the games themselves but remarkably, it was still possible to survive on the pitch and even play well. Like actors and singers, footballers are performers. It is better if you perform with passion but not impossible to play well without it. In my last season at Villa I was emotionally detached from the club and yet had no trouble playing well. Without my usual intensity, there was less fear. Mistakes didn't get to me. My wages were a factor: I was being paid good money to produce and there was the responsibility that came with that. It was also in my interests to play well: my place in England's squad depended upon it and if I wanted to interest the better clubs, I had to show I was still hungry.

The older pros at Villa understood my motivation. 'I had a couple of years at Manchester United,' said Dion Dublin. 'If you can go and do something like that, brilliant, go and do it.' Steve Staunton had left Villa for Liverpool before returning. 'I had to try it, had to get away. I know how you feel.' At times the thought that I had voluntarily signed a five-year contract preyed on my mind, but never for too long.

Football clubs use you and when the time comes, they abuse you. Doesn't matter who you are. Paul McGrath was one of the most magnificent players to wear the Villa shirt. Villa let him go when it suited them; a year or two too soon as it turned out. Unless there's an old boys' reunion, you don't hear Paul's name mentioned. No one asks, 'How's Paul getting on, is he okay, how are his family?' You're gone, you're history; that's the reality.

Andy

Gareth has always been too nice for his own good. I've told him on many occasions, 'There are times, mate, when you have to be a bastard. Situations where it pays to be cynical.' Might as well have been talking to the wall. When the Villa thing was going on, he should have been in to see the manager every day, saying his unhappiness at the club was putting a strain on his marriage, his wife was close to a breakdown, and not let up until he was told, 'Yes, you can go.' In these situations Gareth isn't ruthless enough. Everyone's mum wanted to hug him when he missed that penalty at Wembley. My nan wanted to kiss him. The only man who can miss a penalty for England and increase his popularity, that's Gareth Southgate. People felt genuinely sorry for him. But being nice is no help if you want to get away from a football club. That's why it took Gareth so long to get out of Aston Villa. If it had been me . . .

My time at Northampton Town was the backbone of my career in club football. I spent four great years there, our son Freddie was born in Northampton and we made many friends in the town. From a football point of view, they were also the best days. When Ian Atkins rescued me from Exeter, Northampton were second from bottom in Division Three. From there we achieved promotion to Division Two through the play-offs and got within ninety minutes of Division One before losing to Grimsby at Wembley. When we returned from Wembley after winning promotion to Division Two, 30,000 people lined the streets of Northampton for our parade on an open-top bus. And the following season I was chosen man-of-the-match when Northampton played West Ham in a Worthington Cup game televised live on Sky Sports. During my time with the Cobblers, I played as well as I've ever done. Northampton's fans took to me and their support gave me a terrific boost. Goalkeepers are closer to the crowd than outfield players and more affected by their relationship with the supporters.

The season after losing our Division Two play-off match to Grimsby, it all went wrong for me at Northampton. We started badly, a hangover from the near miss at Wembley and bringing in a couple of new players on higher wages than everyone else. That spoiled the atmosphere in the dressing room. My problems began at an away match at Colchester, a game with a bit of needle because Ian Atkins had managed there previously. As I was warming up out on the pitch, the Colchester groundsman, Dave Blacknall, asked me not to warm up in the goal area. In my pre-match routine, I go into the goal only to take a few crosses. He said he didn't want me to do even this and we argued. Why should I not be allowed to do my normal warm-up? 'You can't,' he said. 'Piss off,' I replied. Dave was not going to be bested and he got six or seven Colchester apprentices to cordon off the six-yard box; they stood like bodyguards along the six-yard line. 'If that's the way you want to play it,' I thought. I went in there and came crashing out into these poor kids before taking the cross. This was a half-hour before the game.

With three or four minutes remaining and the game at nil–nil, Colchester got a corner. In it came and their centre-half, Dave Greene, lost his marker, Ian Sampson, and powered a header into the roof of the net from six or seven yards. Gave me no chance. By the time I got to the dressing room the manager was already into Sammo. 'What were you doing?' It was all going off.

On the coach journey back from Colchester, a few of us sat at the back and, almost in a whisper, held our own inquest. Up towards the front, the steam was still rising from the gaffer's seat and everyone sensed there could be another row. Everyone except our new signing, 6ft 1in Aussie Dougie Hodgson. He reckoned the team spirit wasn't right and what we needed was a night out to boost the squad's morale. Dougie was big and strong and daft. 'Should I ask the manager to organize it?'

'Leave it, Dougie, leave it,' said the lads.

'What d'ya think, Woody?' he asked me.

'Yeah, good idea, Dougie. Good idea. Go for it.'

On the team coach Dougie changed into carpet slippers for comfort. Blue moccasin slippers. Away he went, as naïve a man as ever wore a pair of blue moccasins. We rolled about laughing and then tried desperately to straighten up as the moccasins made the return journey. 'The boss didn't think it was a good idea,' Dougie said. What he didn't say was that the boss had slaughtered him. He shrugged his shoulders, unable to understand why such a good idea was knocked.

At training two days later Tony Godden, the goalkeepers' coach, told me Ian felt I should have come for the corner. There was talk that the other goalkeeper, Billy Turley, was going to get a game against non-league Lancaster in the FA Cup on Saturday. 'What's this?' I asked Ian later. He said it was a chance to give Billy a run. The team beat Lancaster 2–1, an okay result after having a player sent off in the first five minutes. Ian gave the impression I would start against Reading in our next game, but there were no guarantees and you get a feeling in situations like this. It was easy to tell they were toying with the idea of playing Billy. The assistant manager, Kevin Wilson, wasn't a fan of mine and the animosity was mutual. Kevin would have wanted Billy.

Yet I still couldn't see myself being left out. The week before Colchester we had won 1–0 away to Macclesfield, before that I had saved David Ginola's penalty in our Worthington Cup tie against Spurs. For three and a half seasons I had been number one goalkeeper at Northampton. You don't go from there to being discarded.

The day of the Reading game, the manager read out the team in the dressing room: 'In goal Billy [Turley], right-back Gibby [Ali

Gibb], left-back Frainy [John Frain] . . .' Before he got to the fourth name, I had picked up my bag and walked out. It wasn't the brightest thing to do. As I drove away from the ground, fans recognized me and wondered what was happening. I turned off my phone and drove to London. It was unprofessional and immature, yet it was me; quick-tempered and hot-headed. To make a miserable day worse, Freddie fell and gashed his eye that afternoon in London.

Monday morning Garry Thompson, the reserve-team manager, pulled me aside: 'Gaffer wants to see you in his office now.'

Before I got inside the door, Ian fired his first rocket. 'Who the fuck do you think you are?'

'What you did to me on Saturday was bollocks.'

'I pick the team, you weren't playing well, you were left out.'

'What do you mean, ''weren't playing well . . .''?'

Ian was now up out of his chair, leaning over the table. Thinking he was going to punch me, I stood up ready to defend myself. We were shouting, neither of us prepared to listen. How could he say I hadn't been playing well?

'Doesn't matter what I mean, what you did when you walked out was totally unprofessional and totally unacceptable. I am probably going to fine you two weeks' wages.'

Shit, I couldn't afford to lose wages and needed an excuse. 'Look, gaffer, I've got to tell you I rushed away because Freddie fell and smashed his eye in London. Anna was hysterical.'

'Would you have rushed home if you were in the team?'

'I only called to tell Anna not to come to the game because I wasn't playing. If I hadn't made the call I wouldn't have known about Freddie.'

'Look, get the fuck out of my sight.'

That evening I got a copy of the local *Chronicle and Echo* at a shop near where we lived. 'Woodman in Showdown with Atkins' was the headline. The paper carried a report of our row that was almost word bloody perfect. Unknown to the gaffer and me, a young reporter from the local paper had been in a room alongside the manager's office and overheard every word. Just what I didn't need. In terms of getting back in the team, I was further away than ever.

Billy Turley did well in his first few games but then things started to go wrong for him. Everyone expected the manager to put me back in, especially our die-hard fans, but Ian Atkins felt I had tried to undermine his authority by walking out before the Reading match and wasn't having that. No one was going to pressurize him into making a decision.

My first game for the reserves was away at Colchester, a week or so after the row with their groundsman, Dave Blacknall. First person I saw when we arrived was Dave. We both apologized although I imagined he was laughing his socks off seeing me with the reserves. A couple of seasons later I signed for Colchester and Dave and I became good friends. In that reserve game we lost 3–2, the third goal was my fault and my performance was crap. Ian came into the dressing room after the match and had a go at one of the other lads. Never said a word to me. Feeling down, I rang Gareth that evening and we discussed my situation. Gareth helped sort out my head. By playing lousy, I was making it easy for Ian to leave me out. It was a lesson: every game is important, even when one doesn't seem important.

Because I was such a favourite with the fans, the problem got out of hand. When we played Arsenal's reserves at Northampton, 4,500 people turned up to watch. For a reserves game, that was unheard of. As I sat in the dug-out for the first-team's home games, the crowd would chant my name, but the manager became more determined than ever that he would not be bullied. Then the rumour started. First on the internet, then in a fanzine, before it ended up in the local paper: Woody had slept with the wife of one of the directors and that's why he wasn't in the team.

It was totally untrue and I would have dismissed it as ridiculous except so many people had heard it and wondered if it was true. There was a kind of 'well-it-would-explain-why-he's-not-in-the-team' feeling around the town.

'You'll never believe what is going on here,' I said to Anna. 'There's a rumour I slept with the wife of one of the directors, and that's why I'm not in the team.'

'Well, you haven't, have you?' said Anna.

'Don't be ridiculous.'

But it wouldn't go away. Anna and I would be out to dinner with friends and it would invariably crop up. What bothered me was the need to convince friends it was untrue. Even then, after explaining how the rumour originated, there was always the same question in my mind: do they believe me? By now Anna could see the funny side but it also had a serious side. The girl who babysat Freddie was the daughter of the people who gave me a sponsored car at Northampton and we were all good friends. At school she got into a fight with a boy who said, 'Andy Woodman is not playing because he slept with someone else's wife.' It was complete lunacy but it was affecting people's lives. Some said it was the director David Kerr's wife, others said no, it was the chairman Barry Stonhill's, other people thought it must be Ian Atkins'. One director's wife actually rang up Anna and said the rumour about her and me was untrue; Anna was great about it and said she knew that. If you wrote all this stuff for an episode of the TV series *Dream Team*, people would say 'too farfetched'.

So out of control had the whole thing become that I decided to speak with a reporter from the *Chronicle and Echo*. In the interview I explained how disappointing it was not to be in the team and that as for the ridiculous rumours circulating about me, they were complete lies. As laughable as they were, I said, they were affecting people's lives. I'd hoped that Ian would back me but he was still feeling sore about the pressure he was under to pick me for the team and our relationship was non-existent. I gave the club's Christmas dinner a miss because I just didn't feel like sitting alongside the directors and manager. It would only have made things worse. Instead I arranged a round of golf with Barry Stonhill, and explained my situation. He told me everything would be sorted, just to be patient. Another week passed, then another and without even a suggestion of getting my place back, I was at the end of my tether. Another argument with Ian ended with me saying I didn't want to play for him any more. 'Anna,' I said that evening, 'I've got to get away, move to another club.'

Once the decision was made, I felt better. At least something was being done. I approached Brentford who had shown an interest and after speaking with them, felt they would sign me. Back to the Northampton chairman and the difficult bit of having to tell Barry it was all over, I didn't want to play for the club any more. They didn't want to let me go. After taking a call from the chairman, Ian Atkins telephoned and said, 'Look, you're going to play on Saturday.'

'Doesn't matter now, I don't want to play for the club any more,' I said. They put pressure on me to stay, I put pressure on them to let me go; it became a battle. Anna rang the chairman. She was pregnant with Isobelle at the time and suffering a lot of morning sickness. It was a tough time for us. Anna cried on the phone, the hassle had taken its toll. I told them it was destroying our family life. Anna told them it was ruining our marriage. You've got to turn the screws in these situations. As I've said to Gareth, you've got to be a bastard. They eventually relented and agreed to my leaving. All that was left were the arguments over money.

When I had signed my deal with Northampton in March 1995, they had agreed to pay me a £25,000 signing-on fee but asked that it be deferred until January 1999. Foolishly, I agreed. The first payment of £4,000 was due on 31 January, this was 20 January and they told me I had to waive my right to the money. 'Otherwise you sit here and rot.' There was a 10 per cent sell-on clause in my contract that had to be waived as well. It didn't matter that my life at Northampton had become miserable when I wasn't in the team. 'If you want to go so badly, you won't mind forfeiting the money.'

I did mind but there was nothing to be done except stupidly trying to get my own back by doing an article in the local newspaper. 'Would you like to have your say?' It was the same reporter who had overheard the row with Ian and basically it was an offer to slam the manager and the directors. Feeling bitter, I couldn't resist. Typical me, the shooting came from the hip: Northampton lacked ambition, it had sold some of its better players after losing the Division Two play-off and the club was going nowhere. What did I know about the club's financial state? Nothing. Neither had I the right to criticize a manager who gave me a chance when I was at Exeter City and wanting to quit football. Doing that article was unlike me because I have always made a point of having my rows man-to-man, face-to-face. I just wish I hadn't done that interview.

In May 1999 Brentford went up as Division Three champions and Northampton were relegated. Maybe people thought that pleased me. Not at all. Never could I take pleasure in the misfortune of my beloved Northampton. The following season Ian Atkins got the sack and I was one of the first to ring him. It gutted me to see him fired because he had done such a good job there. Our row was forgotten, as it always is with Ian. He doesn't know how to hold a grudge.

Three years passed before I again played at Northampton. It was for Colchester and it was a big occasion for me; Anna came to the game, as did Gareth's Alison. In a different shirt, I wondered what kind of welcome there would be. It was terrific. The fans chanted 'Woody's a Northampton Fan', then they sang 'Northampton Till He Dies'. When I gave them the thumps-up, they came up with a new song that resurrected an old story:

'Was she worth it,
'Was she worth it,
'WAS-SHE-WORTH-IT-IN-THE-END?'

I nodded 'no' and they went crazy. My fear was that Anna was going crazy in the stand. 'Please God she can't make out what they're singing.'

When I went into the bar afterwards, people welcomed me back and when Anna couldn't hear them, they asked, 'Come on, Woody, did you really sleep with her?' It was nine-tenths joke, one-tenth serious. And even now as people read this account of my last season with the Cobblers, some will say, 'No smoke without fire'.

For the last time, there was smoke but there was no fire.

12

A real friend is someone who walks in when the rest of the world walks out.
  Walter Winchell

Gareth

It is the night of the 2000 FA Cup final, which Villa have lost to Chelsea, and there is a reception at the Grosvenor House hotel in London. Chatting with our goalkeeper David James, I tell him my mind is made up. 'I've done as much as I can here, time for me to move on.' It should be an evening of bitter disappointment, even devastation but it isn't. We have lost the Cup final to a better side. I think I've played well but as a team, we have not performed. The game turned out as I feared it would. Going into the match there were unresolved issues about Paul Merson's contract and Benito Carbone's future. Carbone is on loan and doesn't know where he stands. No one is talking to him about the club's intentions. Those things didn't help but maybe we wouldn't have been good enough anyway. David understands my desire to move on, he was at Liverpool and feels I could play at a higher level. Though he is relatively new to Villa, he is beginning to sense the club's politics; the tension between John Gregory and Doug Ellis.

John is devastated by the Cup final defeat. This was his shot at vindication at the end of a difficult season. His disappointment, though, I feel, is entirely for himself. The following day we have a parade through Birmingham in an open-top bus. John wears a suit, a crew-neck top and dark glasses and doesn't have any stomach for the banter that fans like after a bad defeat. Neither does he want to do any of the press or radio stuff. So it is left to his unsettled team captain to thank people for turning out and promise to come back and go one better the following season. What I resent about John's reaction is the thought that if we had won, he would have done every interview and shaken every hand. His desolation after Wembley contrasts with his reaction to bad results at other times. When we were going through a bad run earlier in the season, John and the band in which he plays released a record and did their song on television. The dressing room wasn't impressed.

For months before the Cup final, my frustration had increased. John was spending less time on the training ground and disillusionment was at an all-time high. How I needed the good guys at Villa! Jim Walker had become a confidant and in the afternoon we would sit with Kevin McDonald and Tony McAndrew, the reserve- and youth-team coaches, and right all the wrongs at one of Britain's bigger clubs. Sometimes Steve Harrison and the kit man, Jim Paul, would join in. For two or three hours we would decide what needed to be done and how it could be achieved. It struck me that even in my disgruntled phase, I was leaving the training ground far later than the manager. At home Alison would greet my five-o'clock arrival with the usual comment: 'How on earth do you lot think you are going to change anything?' She was, of course, right.

The Cup run papered over the cracks and as the captain, I couldn't bring myself to ask for a transfer as we reached the quarter- and then semi-final. But now it is over and I am determined to speak to John. The day after the final, he is still unapproachable. Better to wait, I think, give him time to get over the disappointment. A week later I call. 'Gaffer, you around this weekend? Something I've got to discuss. I need to come and see you.'

'No, I'm away, here and there, not around.'

'In that case can we talk?'

'Yeah, we can talk. No problem. You know we're back in on July . . .'

'Look, before you go any further, I've come to a decision. The frustrations you feel as a manager, I feel as a player. I have gone as far as I can at Villa and it's time for me to move. Other lads maybe don't have the drive to win things and time is running out on me.'

'I understand what you're saying. I'm disappointed and whoever is going to buy you, they're going to need a lot of money. I will try to find five players to replace you.'

That's how we leave it. It is a relief that he appears to accept the reasons for my decision. I wait a few days, then ring the chairman, but Doug Ellis is not around. So I call Mark Ansell, the chief executive. 'Mark, just a follow-up call to the one I had with John the other day.'

'What was that?'

'Hasn't John told you? You know I've asked to leave?'

'We don't know anything about this.'

I'm astonished. John Gregory, manager of Aston Villa which is a plc, has been told by the team captain he wants to leave the club but hasn't passed the information on to the chairman or the chief executive. Either John intends to try to soft-soap me into staying and isn't bothered to tell the board or he is actually not talking to the chairman and the chief executive.

I press on. 'Well, Mark, I feel it's time for me to move on.'

'Listen, Gareth, I'm very sorry to hear that but whatever happens, we'll do right by you. We'll conduct things properly. You've been brilliant for us.'

A few hours later the chairman rings. 'Now then, Gareth, I've been speaking to Mark. What is all this? Firstly, if you wish to discuss matters of this nature, you don't speak to Mark. You speak to me. I think we have a good enough relationship.'

'Chairman, I tried to speak to you but you weren't around. I assumed Mark, as chief executive of the plc, was high enough up in the organization. And I also assumed the manager would have informed you of the conversation I had with him where I told him about wanting to leave.'

'John's not spoken to me about that. But I will be speaking to John. Now listen, Gareth, what I mean to say is, have you been tapped up?'

'No, chairman.'

'Now, I hear what you're saying about wanting to move on but I'm not prepared to accept your transfer request. So, politely, I'm telling you to fuck off.'

'Oh, right.'

'Now, if you want to come and see me to discuss it . . .'

'No, I don't want to come and see you, chairman. I've made up my mind. I'm not happy. Doesn't matter what anyone says.'

'Well, if you want to come and see me, with the manager of course.' That was rich, John had given me the impression that he wouldn't want to be in the same building as Doug, let alone sit and talk with him. 'Anyway, I'm still more than happy to sit down and discuss things with you. But, once again, I'm politely telling you to fuck off. I know you will continue to give your all for the club.'

'Okay, chairman, we will be having that meeting.'

As I put the phone down, I am fuming. It is like, 'Good old Gareth. Leave this to me, I'll put him in his place. He'll get on with it. We'll deal with it.' After all I am nothing but a serf, a well-paid serf.

I talk things over with Dad, who again says I must get away from Villa. Another telephone call to Alan Smith and I tell Alan a written transfer request has to be the next step. Otherwise they won't take me seriously. If I am not formally on the transfer list, I will never know if teams are interested. Alan agrees and suggests I leak the story to a broadsheet newspaper. 'If you put in a written transfer request, the club isn't going to make that public,' Alan says. He knows Chris Davies at the *Daily Telegraph* and that's where the story appears. This is the evening before we depart with England for Euro 2000. Knowing the story will cause some waves, I go to Kevin Keegan's room at Burnham Beeches and tell him it will be in the following day's newspaper. 'Why?' asks Kevin. 'I need a greater challenge,' I reply. 'I can understand that,' he says. Next day Villa say they have not received a formal transfer request and so I fax it to the chairman's office. They then come clean: 'Regrettably, we have received a transfer request from Gareth Southgate.'

That was early June 2000 and it might have been expected that before the summer was over, a move would have been agreed, but a year would pass before I would eventually leave the club. The last season was tough because it was clear how much I wanted to go and it seemed there wasn't much interest from other clubs. Villa would say, 'Well, we've had no offers.' But it was more complex than that. Frustrated, I asked John what was the situation.

'You've just got to keep yourself ticking along,' he told me.

'No, what fee are you prepared to accept?'

'One that matches our valuation.'

The club's argument was that they weren't going to say £5m while there was a possibility of getting £6m. They wouldn't say £6m because someone might be prepared to pay £7m. It was obvious they weren't keen to sell. Through the final season my resentment festered. Basically, I felt the club was stringing me along. Chelsea and Deportivo La Coruña made definite bids but they got nowhere.

I spoke to John again. 'Has there been any interest from other clubs?' I asked.

'Nah,' he said, 'no bids.'

'What about Chelsea?'

'I am not selling you to Chelsea. I don't like them, Batesy and all that lot. Anyway what do you know about the Chelsea bid?'

'I've spoken to Dennis Wise.'

I was incensed that a potential transfer could be blocked because John Gregory didn't like 'Chelsea, Batesy and all that lot.' Worse was to follow when on the day before our game against Chelsea, John went public with his view that I needed to prove to my team-mates and the fans where my loyalties lay. To aggravate matters further, John told the press he knew I had been speaking with Dennis Wise. He knew because I had told him – in a private conversation. What if I told press people the things he had been saying privately to me about the chairman?

Towards the end of the season I watched Deportivo play in the quarter-finals of the Champions League and felt deeply frustrated. 'Could have been playing in that game,' I thought. But nobody else knew that and no one apart from a very small number of people cared. It hadn't affected Deportivo's season. It hadn't affected anyone other than Gareth Southgate.

Andy

There is a story Ron Noades tells about me as a kid at Crystal Palace. Ron was chairman at the time and I was playing for Palace's youths. It was a match against Wimbledon's youth team at a pitch near the Robin Hood roundabout in London. There was only a handful of people present but early in the first half a well-dressed man came down to my goal and leaned against one of the posts. He was trying to wind me up. I didn't know who he was but I wasn't having him lean against my post. Being the prat I am, I made a play on his middle-eastern appearance. 'Excuse me, mate, you can't set up a shop there' and then, louder, 'Hey, he's trying to set up a shop on the corner of my goalpost.' He was out of order, I was out of order but, at the same time, it was all done in a good-natured way. What I didn't know was that he was the chairman of Wimbledon, Sam Hammam. To give Sam his due, he laughed at my put-down and moved on. Ron Noades thought it was hilarious and would remind me of it over the years.

Then one day the opportunity presented itself for Ron to intro-duce me to Sam. 'Do you remember this boy?' he asked.

'Yeah,' said Sam, 'used to be at Palace, right.'

That was Ron's cue to relate the entire story all over again. That incident set me apart in Ron's eyes; I wasn't just another youth-team player, I was the guy who had the answer for Sam Hammam.

So when my career hit the rocks at Northampton in early 1999 and Ron, who was now manager of Brentford, said he wanted to take me to Griffin Park, I couldn't sign quickly enough. With signing-on fees, I would be on £75,000; not a bad wage by the standards of the Third Division. Joining Brentford also meant a move back to London which excited Anna and me. Both our families were there and that was important.

To make everything right, the change had to work out from a

football point of view as well, but in the first home game there were hints of what was to come. We were out doing our warm-up, the ground wasn't even a quarter full and a Brentford fan shouted, 'Why don't you eff off back to Northampton.' Startled, I turned and looked him in the eye. 'Give us a chance, mate. I haven't even touched the ball yet.'

It was a losing battle. I joined in January, we got promoted as Division Three champions in May and yet the fans didn't accept me. I was not playing as well as at Northampton and they were comparing me to Kevin Dearden, who had just spent six seasons at Brentford and been a big favourite. At the start there was no goalkeeping coach and that also made things difficult; I am not talented enough to get by without regular specialist coaching.

How I missed Tony Godden, Northampton's goalkeeping coach, who knew me inside out. Tony knew the goals I should have prevented and the goals with which I had no chance. On Monday morning he would say, 'You think you should have stopped their first?'

'Yeah, should have got to it,' I admitted.

'The manager doesn't think so, but I agree with you. You should have saved it. Now, let's talk about why you didn't and then we'll work on it.'

Tony was good because he wasn't going to run back to the manager and say, 'Woody admits he cocked up for the goal.' He knew how to build me up after an indifferent performance. It gets to a point where a coach like Tony becomes like a crutch; without it, you struggle to walk. Without him at Brentford, my form suffered. It wasn't just that. After moving back from Northampton, Anna and I moved in with Anna's parents while we searched for a new house. There was never any problem with John and Beryl, who have been great to us but it was unsettling. It was at this time that Isobelle was born and, in hindsight, maybe it wasn't surprising my form suffered.

After a season and a half at Brentford, I could see the beginning of the end. We'd had an okay season and were stuck in mid-table as the campaign petered out. Ron came to me and told me Barry Fry had lost a goalkeeper with a shoulder injury and needed someone on loan. 'Woody, I've got no problems with you going there on loan, we've got nothing to play for and it'll give me a chance to play the other keeper, help me to sell him on. Peterborough can still make the play-offs, maybe another Wembley appearance for you.'

I fell for this three-card trick. What a plum! Ron, who was chairman as well as manager of Brentford, sensed there wasn't going to be much return on his investment in the club and needed to trim costs. Mine was quite a big salary and if I was on loan, someone else would help to pay my wages. In football going on loan to another club is generally your club's first step in off-loading you. Blinded by Ron's logic, I agreed to go to Peterborough.

That evening Anna and I had my team-mate Lorenzo Pinamonte round for dinner. An Italian, Lorenzo accepted our invitation on condition that he could do the cooking. It was a lovely idea that ended up a complete disaster. I told Anna the news.

'What?' she said. 'You're what?'

'I said I am going on loan to Peterborough.'

'Andrew, you can't do this. It is stupid. They're trying to get you out, this is their way.'

'It'll be okay. Barry Fry's a good fellow. This could work out.'

'Oh, you idiot.'

We spent the evening screaming at each other. Lorenzo's food was delicious but we hardly gave ourselves a chance to taste it. Poor Lorenzo, ended up in the wrong house at the wrong time.

Next morning I walked into Barry Fry's office.

'Woody,' he said, beaming at me, 'you are the best person in the country for the situation you are coming into. I've been trying to get you for a while, so glad you've come.' Ten feet tall, I felt. This is Barry's brilliance, makes players feel good about themselves. 'Anna,' I thought, 'you should be here, listening to this.'

But then Barry continued, 'But for Saturday, I'm not going to play you. Better that you get to know the lads properly before I put you in the team.' My heart sank. The reason you go on loan is to play first-team games. I had not come to Peterborough to sit on the bench. Definitely not. 'Anna,' I thought, 'thank God you are not here.'

If I'd had the balls, I would have told Barry to forget it there and then. Just gone straight back to Brentford. Instead I hung in. Peterborough went away to Rotherham and drew, the keeper played well. For the next game I didn't even expect to be in the team and I wasn't. Anna had been so right. After the second match I said to the coach at Peterborough, 'Look, I'm coming back no more. I have totally messed up here. I've come to help you out, put my own position in jeopardy and all for nothing.'

Back at Brentford, there were just six matches left. Away at Stoke, I dropped a cross in the first few minutes, they scored and that was the game's only goal. After that mistake, it went really well for me, but the newspapers all concentrated on the same thing: 'Jittery Andy Woodman was at fault for the crucial goal.' On the day of the final game of the season, I was at home in bed suffering from viral meningitis. But things would get even worse.

On the afternoon of Brentford's Player-of-the-Year dinner, one of my team-mates, Andy Scott, rang my home, got Anna and told her Brentford had signed an Icelandic goalkeeper, Olafur Gottskalksson. Ron Noades had done well out of Icelandic players, especially by buying Hermann Hreidarsson and then selling him on to Wimbledon for £2.5m. It was supposed to be on Hermann's recommendation that Ron had bought Gottskalksson. Goal-keeper for the Icelandic national side – but then if he wasn't Iceland's number one you'd be worried. Signed from Hibernian in Scotland, he would join us in time for pre-season. Everyone knew he wasn't coming as a number two. The news gutted Anna and didn't do much for me either. Deep down, we both knew the score.

The Player-of-the-Year dinner was the last place I wanted to be, but Anna wouldn't hear of it. 'You go there, Andrew, keep your head up and remember you're number one goalkeeper at that football club.' So that evening I went to Brentford's end-of-season awards night. Given my mood at the time, it was not a good idea. At a nearby table a group of guys were drinking too much and spent the evening shouting funny and not-so-funny insults at me. Even the funny ones didn't do much for me. One bloke at that table was particularly obnoxious. At the best of times, my fuse is not the longest and a voice inside my head said, 'Go on, give him a good hiding.' Another voice told me to stay calm. I warned him to have manners. For a time, he quietened down.

There was a charity auction of the players' shirts, each player being called in turn while his shirt was auctioned. As I went up the compère, Peter Gilham, a nice man who worked at the club, let go of my shirt as he handed it to me. 'Oh no, that's another one he's dropped.' Everyone laughed, except me. Peter could see the disgust on my face. 'Come on, Woody, I was only joking.' Not to me.

The loudmouth who had had too much drink then started shouting, 'He should be paying us £60 to take that shirt off his hands.' Ha, ha, fucking ha! The lads at my table could tell this was turning into a disaster. So too could Ron and the first-team coach, Ray Lewington. The evening was a shambles, a return to the bad old days: 'You can't blame Woody, because Woody's just a . . .'

A couple of days later I went to see Ron, Ray and another coach, Terry Bullivant, about my future at the club.

'Is he coming here as number one?' I asked.

'We don't know,' said Ron, 'we haven't actually seen him play. We've only seen videos.'

'Okay, let's make a fair fight of this,' I said, not sure that chance would come.

Then we were off to Portugal, Anna, myself, Freddie and Isobelle with Gareth, Alison and Mia. The thought of getting away from football and being with my mate had never seemed so appealing.

Gareth

We've been away a lot together, Woody and I: first as single lads at Palace, then with Woody and his dad, and now with our two families. We shared rooms at Palace for four years and that was where the friendship was forged: the neverending chats about football, the overheard phone calls to home that led into more personal areas. It soon came to a point where there was nothing we didn't talk about. You wonder why we hit it off like we did. We were opposites in many respects and for years we have joked about he being the town mouse to my country mouse. A lot of truth in that, even today. People warm to Woody far more quickly than to me. He is an open book while I may appear closed. If he walked into a party and didn't know a soul, it would take him five minutes to be at the centre of things. No one makes conversation easier. And in that room, almost everyone would love him. And all the time, I would be edging my way forward from the perimeter.

He is by nature an optimist; I am a realist. He's down to his last tenner and he gambles to turn it into £20; I save my tenner and budget for the following week. Yet we are closer than I imagined possible between two men. Several years ago we started playing golf together and a rivalry developed that still exists today. When we're away on our family holidays Woody has the scruples of a cat. 'Tell me, Gareth, what were you thinking as you walked up for that penalty at Euro 96?' and I've got a four-foot putt to win the hole.

It's funny how I remember the things we said about each other's girlfriends. It was like each of us needed the other to approve of his choice. Then when our first-born children arrived, they came roughly around the same time and we shared all that; as if it was the two of us who had invented fatherhood. Many of the old songs I hear on the radio take me back to a time and a laugh shared with Woody. We're like some nauseating married couple whose lives are measured out in the things they did together. 'Remember where we were when they played that song . . . ?'

If ever I see the four letters GSOH in a lonely hearts' advertisement, I think of Woody. More than anyone, Woody's got a sense of humour. Regardless of my mood, he can make me laugh. An old story resurrected, a new one just told and we're off, laughing heartily and then convulsing with laughter. He has never allowed me to take myself too seriously and for that I will be for ever grateful. He has also accepted my success with tremendous generosity. It must have been hard for him to sit and watch big matches that he would have loved to play in. We started at the same point but ended going in very different directions. Yet he didn't begrudge me a thing and never showed even a hint of jealousy.

I can honestly say I took as much pleasure watching his successes as from anything I achieved. There was one Division Three play-off semi-final that I got to see at Northampton. It might have been the one against Cardiff. 'Why are you here?' lots of people asked and it gave me such pleasure to tell them, 'Oh, I'm just Woody's mate.' To be able to say that was brilliant. I was proud of him that day. England duty meant I missed his Wembley finals but I watched the games on television and when he saved a penalty in the goal where I had missed two years before it sent a shiver down my spine. It takes a bit to get me jumping around the living room but that save did. What pleased me most was the fact that even though Northampton lost, Woody would have a football memory for life.

Andy

At pre-season the lads wonder how the presence of the Icelandic goalkeeper will affect me. They watch me as I come through the door: will he be the Woody of old?

'Nice break then, lads?' I ask.

'Yeah, how about you, Woody?'

'Yeah, mate, it was good, me and Anna and the kids went with Gareth and Alison and their little girl . . . yeah, Portugal, fantastic weather . . . played a bit of golf . . . lazed around the pool . . . could have done with another week.'

All the time, I avoid looking at the new goalkeeper. No eye contact, no polite nod. Nothing. He has come to take my job and is not a mate. Childish maybe but at least it's honest. He feels the same and makes no effort to speak with me. He was Oli to his friends but never to me. Gareth had encouraged me to keep up my fitness in Portugal and I'm in good shape. I beat this guy in almost every running exercise we do.

First big pre-season game of the season is against Fulham, they pick him and he plays really well. My days at Brentford are more or less over.

In football, a lot of things can happen before you get what you want. Our first game of the season was away to Northampton and because of my four years there, this was as big as it gets. No way could I go back there, where the fans truly loved me, to sit on the bench. Yet it was clear from our training Brentford intended to start with him. On the Wednesday before the game, John Griffin, Brentford's chief scout, called me and said Southend would like to take me on loan and if things went well, they would sign me. John and I had known each other since my time at Palace and he had always been good to me. 'Alan Little, the Southend manager, will call in the next five minutes.'

'Andy, it's Alan Little. Do you fancy coming and playing football for a month? I want you to come, enjoy yourself and play like I know you can. If you play well in the month, there will be a deal. I know what you're on, it's just a case of my chairman seeing you in action and being convinced of what you're about.' Alan said things that hadn't been said since I was twelve years of age. 'Enjoy yourself, play like you can.' He was refreshing and genuine, qualities you don't always find in football. Peterborough and Barry Fry were still on my mind but Alan reassured me, 'No two ways about it, you'll be playing for the whole month, it doesn't matter how you play.'

Now it was my turn to take someone else's place. Mel Capleton was Southend's goalkeeper and in my seventeen years of professional football, there wasn't a more likeable rival for a goalkeeping position. Mel was a smashing man and very popular in the dressing room. He couldn't have been nicer to me although it was easy to pick up on the wariness of his team-mates. They were looking out for their mate. The only way for me to get their respect was to have a blinder in Saturday's opening match of the season. We were home to Brighton which, as anyone at Southend will tell you, is a big, big game for them.

Without a car that Saturday, I travelled in Anna's dad's truck.

John is a roofer and the ladders, the shovels and the tiles were a problem for the steward manning the players' car park. 'I'm sorry, mate, you can't park here.'

'Look, I'm not trying to be funny, but I am a player.'

'I've not seen you.'

'I know, today's my first game. Andy Woodman, goalkeeper.'

'Mate, just wait there. I'm gonna check this with my superior.' He spoke into a walkie-talkie. I could hear him describe John's truck. Eventually, he came back to me. 'Do you have any ID?'

For some reason, I enjoyed the fuss. Why should I have a flash car? My wages didn't entitle me to it. The truck made me feel down to earth, a man going out to do a day's work. It didn't hurt my performance either because we won 2–0, I had a really good game and the crowd took to me.

Things continued to go well. We drew 0–0 with Birmingham in a Worthington Cup first-round second-leg match and it was time to sign the contract. 'Look,' said Alan, 'I've been speaking to the chairman, we might have to extend your loan, give me a bit of leeway here and I will sort it out. I am going to sign you, just need to iron out one or two things.' Brentford were looking for a £50,000 fee. Alan was genuine, he wouldn't have known how to be anything else. He had a meeting with his chairman for Thursday afternoon and first thing on Friday the deal would be completed.

That evening I was driving home from the osteopath when one of the lads telephoned. 'You've got to be the unluckiest bastard in football,' he said. 'I've just seen on the teletext that Alan Little's been sacked at Southend.' The meeting to get my contract sorted was the meeting at which he was fired.

Rochdale on the following Saturday and, without a gaffer, we managed to win 1–0. Everyone said the new manager was in the crowd and I couldn't have played better. Rumour had it that Dave Webb was the new man and it sent tremors through the dressing room. Everyone had heard Dave Webb stories: not a man to get on the wrong side of, not a man to mess with. Danny O'Shea and Dave Martin, who had played under him at Southend previously, told a slightly different story. 'If he likes you, he likes you. If he doesn't, forget it.' A week later Dave Webb was announced as Southend's manager. 'See out the rest of your loan period. You'll be in the team, it's up to you,' he said to me. Scared to make the slightest mistake, I played well in every game under Dave. We got on well and it was easy to see he liked me. Still, you would never have crossed him.

Towards the end of the loan period, he came up with an offer. It was half the deal originally proposed by Alan Little and would have meant my taking a pay cut of £500 a week to move from Brentford to Southend. As much as I loved Southend, the club, the crowd, the team, the offer wasn't enough. Anna and I don't have an extravagant lifestyle but a £500-a-week paycut would have destroyed us. 'Can't accept it, Dave,' I said, hoping he would come back with an increased offer. Dave Webb doesn't operate like that. Take it or leave it. I left it. By the time it was clear there would be no deal, Dave Webb had left the ground. There were no goodbyes which was a pity, because I liked him. It's the way it happens in football.

Like a bad penny, I kept returning to Brentford. Two days back in the fold and Ron Noades said Colchester United wanted me to go on loan. They were offering first-team football but with no chance of a permanent move. It was better than playing second fiddle to the Icelander. I met my new team-mates on Saturday at a hotel before Colchester's game at Reading. No team had kept a clean sheet there, and Colchester were leaking goals away from home but, hey presto, my first match and we won 1–0. Next three games, three more clean sheets. After the second, the manager, Steve Whitton, spoke to me, 'It's going well but don't get your hopes up. You're only playing until the other keeper's fit.'

Then there was an FA Cup tie at Yeovil, and Ron Noades rang Colchester to say they weren't to pick me as he didn't want me Cup-tied. That Saturday afternoon was spent watching Sky's football programme and listening to the radio. Brentford lost 3–1 at home to Kingstonian and Colchester were hammered 5–1 at Yeovil. Seeing those results, I danced around the kitchen floor with Freddie. 'One of them is going to want me now, son.'

Colchester had played their first-choice keeper but his foot wasn't right and it affected his kicking. Thankfully for me, playing made his injury worse. I went back into the team, had another three clean sheets and this didn't make his foot any better. Steve Whitton was getting twitchy. 'You're making this difficult for me,' he said. Music to my ears. Soon he had come round to the idea of signing me. He offered me £50,000 a year, less than I was on at Brentford but not by much. If I included all my signing-on fees, there was a shortfall of £25,000. Ron Noades, I hoped, would be sympathetic. 'Look, Ron, I'm gonna lose out here,' I told him, but I didn't say how much Colchester were offering. Ron must have been anxious to see the back of me. He said he would pay me £200 a week over the rest of my contract and would let me have all of my signing-on fees, amounting to £26,000. I couldn't believe my luck. So I went back to Colchester and said, 'Look, Brentford have come up with nothing here.' Colchester upped their offer a little and for the first time in my football career I was taking with one hand and also taking with the other hand. It was too good to be true.

Couldn't make any slip-ups now. There was a sportsman's dinner in Colchester and players were expected to attend. Well dressed and on my best behaviour, I don't think I've ever put so much effort into a social occasion. Never touched a drink, spoke to all the right people; chairman, directors, directors' wives, everyone who mattered. Best night's work of my life. They loved me and couldn't sign me quick enough.

It was coming up to Christmas and the FA weren't working Christmas Day or Boxing Day. Ron wanted to get the deal signed and sealed. 'We're all done at this end, we'll cancel your contract.' But there was a game for Colchester on Boxing Day and if I got injured, they would back out. 'No, Ron, we better wait until the day after Boxing Day,' I said. 'Not a problem,' said Ron. We went to Millwall on Boxing Day. For the previous month, I'd had enough clean sheets to stock a laundry and then on the eve of my signing for Colchester, we got thumped 6–1. Anna rang two minutes after the game ended. 'What's gone wrong here, Andrew? Please talk to me.' Ten minutes later, Gareth, 'What's happening, mate, what's gone on there?' The truth was that after we'd looked good for twenty minutes, they scored and we collapsed. Not one of the goals was down to me, something Steve Whitton recognized. 'Don't think you had a prayer with any of them.' The deal was still on, thank God.

Day after Boxing Day, I shot over to Brentford's ground, Griffin Park, with Freddie in the back of the car. Only the secretary, Polly Kates, was in. Marie Parker was at the other end in Colchester. That morning there was a call from Jim Stannard, goalkeeping coach at Brentford, to say that Ray Lewington, who had taken over as manager after Ron stepped down, was thinking of bringing me back from Colchester as he wasn't convinced about Olafur Gottskalksson. By now, my mind was made up. Colchester's offer was okay, Ron's money made it good and now the possibility of Ray getting in touch and calling off the deal scared me. I signed the waiver, allowing Brentford to cancel my contract. Faxes had to be sent to Colchester, so we got those away. All Freddie wanted was a runabout on the pitch. After everything was signed and the last fax sent and received, I took him on to the field and we ran around like two little kids. He had age on his side and, at last, the gods were on my side.

For this deal, I decided against involving my agent, David

Mannasseh. He's a big player in the business with people like Kieron Dyer and Ashley Cole and Dean Richards on his books. That was part of the problem. I thought I was unlikely to be high on David's list of priorities. Anyway, I was twenty-nine years of age and knew what I should be getting from Colchester. Scott Fitzgerald, who was a good mate to me at Colchester, told me what he was on and that gave me a good idea. So, I didn't feel the need to have anyone representing me and am glad I had the confidence to do it on my own. I was happy with the deal, Anna was happy and I really hadn't needed an agent. Afterwards I spoke with David and he said my signing for Colchester showed my lack of ambition and sent out the wrong signals to other clubs. It showed, he said, that I was happy to play in the second division.

Too right I was. Colchester gave me a two-and-a-half-year contract on good money, a wage that would pay the mortgage and feed my family. I could have reminded Dave what it had been like going to Peterborough and meeting Barry Fry and how ruthlessly Alan Little had been treated at Southend. This can be a cruel game and the small guy gets trampled on. I would have liked him to know how hard I'd worked at Colchester to get my contract. I could have explained how clever I'd been in the negotiations with Ron over the money. But, to be honest, there wouldn't have been any point.

Gareth

The last season at Villa was just a waste. We weren't going anywhere and all I succeeded in doing was vindicating Doug Ellis's belief that even in an unhappy state, I wouldn't let the team down. I played as well as at any time in my career. Basically the Villa strategy worked. They expected that as I wanted to get away, I would withdraw from the public relations and community work that had been willingly undertaken in the past, but they gambled that my mood wouldn't affect my form. At an important time in the season, an ankle injury kept me out of the team and Villa lost a number of matches. It dropped us close to the relegation zone, but when I returned, we went undefeated until the last game of the season. It ate away at me that by playing well I was doing them a favour, proving they were right to screw me about.

It wasn't anything personal against me, they were just doing what was right for the club. My disenchantment became very public and was embarrassing. Eventually Doug decided we should meet and it was agreed we would sit down to discuss things while I was in La Manga with England preparing for our final World Cup qualifier against Greece. This was almost a year after I had submitted a written transfer request. Doug suggested we meet in his room. At the appointed hour, I knocked and he opened the door wearing only his swimming trunks.

'You wanted to see me, chairman?' I said.

Inside, I expected Doug to excuse himself while he dressed. He saw no need for that and just sat on the edge of the bed in his trunks. 'Now, come on then, what will it take to keep you at Aston Villa?' Poor Doug, he gets a lot of criticism but he has his good side. At Villa he takes an almost paternal interest in some of the players and he was always very good to me. 'Why do you want to leave?'

'Chairman, I don't believe enough of the players are ambitious enough. And I need a new challenge.'

'You don't know this, but I've made offers for two players. The combined value of the bids is £10m. One I am confident of getting, the other we probably won't.'

'Oh!'

I subsequently found out the two players were Frank Lampard and Freddie Kanoute. Frank went to Chelsea for £11m, so Doug's £10m bid for both was never going to get too far. He knew of my disgust with the club's failure to improve the training facilities, which had fallen way behind our rivals'. Our schoolboy players were changing in portakabins and we expected them to choose us over Manchester United and Arsenal. He said the club was in the process of buying a new site that would be developed in the near future.

'Regardless of what I do, chairman, the club needs to give the players the best possible facilities,' I told him. Two years on, Villa remain at their old training ground. Doug then started to offer me an improved contract but I interrupted him. 'Chairman, this is not about money. Surely you realize that.'

He asked for my opinion about the manager. I would have loved telling him about John but for some unexplained reason, I felt a certain loyalty towards the manager. He was still my boss. 'Chairman, it's not right for you to ask me that question.'

We parted amicably and agreed to remain friendly. Doug had tried to give me his vision of Villa's future. What I left with was a vision of Doug sitting there in his swimming trunks.

John and I drifted even further apart, if that was possible. He began to use Paul Merson as his link to the players even though I remained captain. That wasn't ideal either; as outstanding a player as Paul is, he likes training to be geared around his needs. He shone in eight-a-side games, so we played lots of eight-a-sides. Steve Harrison would come with a plan for training but the sessions were changed and even though everyone knew it wasn't right, there was a lot of apathy about and no one said anything. I felt sorry too for our physio, Jim Walker. He had learned so much from Brian Clough during his time at Derby County and was desperate to see things improve. Told by some of the players they were going for a round of golf, Jim would tell them about a phone call he'd had that morning. 'Tiger Woods was on, he wants to know when he can come in for a five-a-side?' Jim has so much to pass on, so much of Clough's wisdom that sadly fell on deaf ears at Villa. Jim would arrange for a fitness trainer to come in and test the players on the Monday and Tuesday of the following week only for John to subsequently decide we would have those days off. 'Yeah, well, we'll do them another time,' John would say.

My last match for the club was the final game of the 2000–01 season, a middle-of-the-table encounter at Newcastle. Two weeks before it, John had decided we should have ten days off following our penultimate match, in which we had sent Coventry down to the First Division after thirty-four years in the top flight. Trailing 2–0 at half-time, we came back to win 3–2 and doom the Sky Blues to relegation. 'Don't see the need for you to be here,' he said to us afterwards. With the Cup final the following weekend, we didn't have a game and John reckoned we might as well take the time off. I thought it an absolute joke. Would we take ten days off after the first game of the season? Why should we take ten days off before the last game? Would Manchester United do it?

Players were tired at the end of the season but training didn't have to be physically exhausting. What about working on technique? There are some good young players at Villa and it was terrible to see them developing in an environment where they could be given ten days off before the end of the season. Hopefully they realized that in the elite world of professional football, clubs weren't run that way. True to form, the squad reassembled on the Wednesday before the Newcastle game and John's first words were, 'I can't stress enough the importance of this last game. It's one we've got to win.' So important we were given ten days off to prepare for it!

Surprise, surprise, after this meticulous preparation we went up to St James' Park and lost 3–0. And so the curtain came down on my Villa career.

I have friends in overalls whose friendship I would not swap for the favour of the kings of the world.

Thomas A. Edison

Gareth

It was the day of the Germany game in Euro 96 and Woody was sure to ring. I told him to call because it wouldn't have been right to have left for the match without speaking. He would call, we would talk about the house he was doing up in south London and then move on to the match. Early in the afternoon, the call was put through to my room at England's hotel, Burnham Beeches.

'Mate,' said Woody, 'fifty million people will be watching you tonight. They'll be relying on you. I played with you. I wouldn't be so sure.'

We laughed; nervous laughter on my part. It was typical Woody. Sensing how I was feeling, he wanted to relieve the pressure. Did he detect the dread I felt? On the face of it, things had never been as good. I was in the England side, playing really well and the team was within two games of winning the European Championship at Wembley. My football life had never been this good, so good it led to the irrational fear that something was about to go wrong. That has always been the pattern in my football life. For each good experience, there is often a disappointing one and the greater the high, the more crushing the low that follows it.

Southampton made me happy when they took me on as a thirteen-year-old schoolboy and shattered me with their letter of rejection a year later. I kept the letter and have never forgotten what it said. Even when success came, it wasn't quite what it should have been. In an eight-day period in March 1996, I won the League Cup with Aston Villa, made my full England debut, lost an FA Cup semi-final and tore my knee ligaments. The story of my football life condensed into a week. So Woody's joke struck a nerve.

From almost nowhere, I had come into the team and played every minute of the four games that had taken England to the last four at Euro 96. After the quarter-final victory over Spain, their coach, Javier Clemente, singled me out as one of England's best performers. Bobby Charlton said I was 'world-class' and that I reminded him of Nobby Stiles. The general view was that I had been one of the successes of the England team. For me, it was a question of how long more it could last. The voices inside my head were familiar: '*You know what's going to happen here. You're setting yourself up for a fall.*' 'Actually, I don't believe that. I'm playing well and feel comfortable at this level.'

'*Don't think that's going to save you.*' Deep down, I knew it would turn. It always did. I prayed that the fall would come after the tournament ended.

Andy

Gareth, Anna and I were on a beach in Crete. This was before Gareth started going out with Alison, and though Anna was my girlfriend, she was very fond of Gareth. Anyway, the three of us were lying there and talking football. It was June 1994 and the previous day the Republic of Ireland had beaten Italy 1–0 at the World Cup finals in the US. One of our team-mates at Palace, Eddie McGoldrick, was in the Irish squad. Eddie was an okay player, but he was no Gareth.

'You got any Irish connection?' Anna asked Gareth.

'No.' Gareth was annoyed at the question. That got me going.

'Well, you could probably find one if you looked hard enough,' I said.

'I'm English. I want to play for England,' Gareth replied.

'Well, one Irish cap is better than no English cap.'

'I'm not qualified to play for Ireland, England is my country.'

'Oh "England is my country"; is it?' I said.

'Come off it, Gareth,' Anna said. 'Do you really believe you'll play for England?'

'Maybe I will.'

We weren't shouting, but Gareth was pissed off. We'd been at Palace for five years; he was then a central midfield player. Garry Thompson, one of the lads at Palace, used to say Gareth was a poor man's Bryan Robson and meant it as a compliment. Anna came to most of Palace's games and had her opinions about football. She didn't see Gareth as an England player. To be honest, neither of us did.

Gareth

Anna really got into my ribs that day. 'So you're telling me you would turn down the chance to play in a World Cup?' I said I would never play for another country. I was on my high horse. Anna kept on. 'If you had no chance to play with England and Ireland came along?'

'Anna, I don't have an Irish granddad.'

'I'm saying "if".'

My grandfather, Arthur George Toll, was a proud and patriotic Englishman. He served in the Royal Marines, supported the Arsenal and was mates with John Sewell, the man who maintained the clocks at Highbury. Granddad would have been appalled at the idea that I would consider playing for any country other than my own. Woody and Anna weren't to know I had dreamed of playing in the World Cup for England. At the age of twelve, I had the team kit, the old Admiral one from the 1982 World Cup in Spain. When I wore that I was Bryan Robson, captaining my country, winning the World Cup. As I got older and became an apprentice at Crystal Palace, the England team remained my greatest ambition. Burnham Beeches, the team's Buckinghamshire hotel, was a mystical place. You were somebody if you had stayed at Burnham Beeches.

It is the custom for the England backroom team to leave your training kit outside your bedroom door. First time it was there for me, I picked it up, brought it inside the room and closed the door. Standing in front of the mirror, I pulled on the different training tops. The three lions on my chest . . . Yes! It felt as good as I had imagined it would. When playing for England, I sing the national anthem heartily. That's Granddad's influence. If he's looking down from heaven, I want to be sure I'm singing.

Andy

You know you're late for a match at Wembley when the Hanger Lane roundabout is clear of traffic. It was the first game of the 1996 European Championship, against Switzerland, and we were dead late. My fault, of course. Always ducking and diving – it's one of the many differences between Gareth and me. I'd been late picking up Alison at her mum's and she and my brother Peter were panicking. 'It's okay,' I told them, 'I've allowed the usual thirty seconds if things go wrong.'

It was 2.35 when we got to Hanger Lane and there wasn't a car in sight. I was thinking we must have got the kick-off time wrong. From there to the stadium, we weren't held up once. We picked up the tickets Gareth had left and got to our seats just as the teams were walking on to the pitch. All we had missed was the opening ceremony. Perfect.

It finished 1–1, a nothing game, the kind you often get when teams play their first match in a major tournament. Gareth, though, made a great start, never put a foot wrong. We met him in the players' lounge afterwards. 'You played really well,' I said. They were given Saturday night off and Gareth came home with us. On the way we stopped for petrol and as I was filling up, I thought to myself, 'I've got my mate in the car, an England international who's just played a match in the biggest tournament in this country for thirty years and we're going for something to eat.'

That thought was the best part of my day.

Gareth

Terry Venables selected me for the England squad at the beginning of the 1995–96 season. For the first two games, I travelled with the squad but didn't get changed. That was okay because I was young and, having played midfield for Crystal Palace, was beginning a new life as a central defender at Aston Villa. Terry had a way of making you feel involved, even when you weren't playing. He would pull me to one side and enquire how I was enjoying my new role at Villa. These little chats gave you a sense of how he was thinking and were good for your morale. I liked Terry from the first day. He was an exceptional communicator with a nice, easy confidence. His quality as a coach was obvious and he was tremendously popular inside the dressing room.

The hardest opposition we faced at Euro 96 was Spain, who probably should have beaten us in the quarter-final. At half-time in that game, Terry wanted to change things round to counter the left-sided Sergio, who had caused us problems in the first half. We had started with a flat back four and Terry wanted to switch to a back three with Darren Anderton staying close to Sergio. Don Howe, Terry's assistant, shook his head and said, 'No, Terry, that's not right.'

Cool as anything, Terry said, 'Just give us a second, lads. Don and I need to have a quick chat.' They stood by the drawing board where Don drew the formation that he felt would work. Terry then turned back to us and said, 'Lads, Don's right.' We went to a back three, Gary Neville pushed on to Sergio and played as a right wing-back. The change worked well and a game that had been Spain's in the first half was much more even after that. I thought it was incredible that Terry didn't feel in the slightest undermined by Don pulling him up. To become one of Terry's first eleven was a huge boost to my confidence.

Andy

It was a bad buy, the house in Selsdon. Anna and I had bought a place that needed a lot of work. I'm game to try most things and I decided to do the renovations myself. So while Gareth was swanning around at Burnham Beeches, playing with and against the stars of Euro 96, I was up to my eyes in rubble and mortar. At coffee break, I would blow the dust off this old brown telephone that came with the house and call him.

One day I rang after a wall had fallen on top of me and I'd been lucky not to get hurt. 'Hey mate, want to know what it's like in the real world?' Our conversations never ended there; I wanted to know the England gossip. How much truth was there behind the tabloid headlines?

Gareth got us tickets, and Alison, Peter and I travelled together to the games. He seemed anxious the evening before the Holland match.

'How're you doin', mate, you all right?'

Something wasn't right. 'Nord,' I said, using his old Palace nickname, 'what's up?'

'I've got a problem with tickets for the game,' he said. 'My family are coming.'

'Look, Nord, it's not a problem. Your family are your family.'

'You're family as well. What I've done is I've bought you some tickets, but they're not in the section for the players' families, they're behind the goal with the England fans.' He seemed a bit choked, like he had let me down. Pete and I were happy to have any seats, being with the England fans wasn't a problem. In fact, we were looking forward to being able to shout and scream. Gareth said he was still able to get us tickets for the players' lounge afterwards. That, I told him, was the main thing.

We went in Pete's taxi, a Vauxhall Carlton from Gatwick Cars. Outside the stadium we had the usual commotion at the car park. Every time you went to a game at Wembley you had to pay £8 to park your car. Others could be ripped off, I'd grown tired of it. 'Eight pounds? It's a joke,' I said to Alison and Pete. 'We're not paying.' So we got to the gate and Peter said there wasn't time for messing around. Alison said, 'Oh, Woody, don't do it! Not now – just pay 'em the eight quid.' And I was saying, 'No chance, Ali.' Next thing, we were at the gate. I said, 'Excuse me, we've got to pick our tickets up from the tunnel, left by Gareth Southgate, England international. Our car-park pass is in the envelope with the tickets.'

The car-park attendant went through a right rigmarole. 'Park your car here, run up and get the pass, come back, put the pass in the window and re-park your car.'

I pretended not to hear him and drove on. He started running behind us, waving his arms. 'Hope he's fit,' I said to Pete and Ali, 'because he's going to have to run a long way to catch us.' 'I can't believe you're doing this,' said Pete. The guy seemed to be still chasing us. 'Just let me give him the tenner,' Alison said. And I said, 'No, no, no. Eight pounds? No way.' It was a bit of a thrill for me, trying to get away with it, beating the system. Because once you're in that huge car park, you're hard to find. Alison was afraid we would be clamped. I said, 'Alison, there's 60,000 cars here, they're never going to check all the windscreens.' Eventually the guy disappeared from my rear-view mirror. I was delighted. Got away with it. That was my little starter for the evening.

Gareth

I was nervous about fitting in. Not knowing most of the lads, I was afraid Gazza [Paul Gascoigne] wouldn't take to me but would see me as an altar-boy type. It couldn't have worked out better. On the team coach, Stuart Pearce sat alongside and we got talking. Pearcey's the British bulldog, the guy with tattoos, the lover of punk music and, if you didn't know him, you'd presume he was your typical English hardman. You'd be wrong. Over the years I would discover he was one of the team's most interesting blokes and its best tourist. Wherever Pearcey was, he wanted to see the places of interest. Museums, historical sights, the harbour; whatever, Pearcey made the effort. When it came to going out drinking he'd say, 'Nah, not when I'm away with England. Can do that at home.'

Stuart has a strong personality; you didn't want to cross him. In one of our early training games, we both went for a 50–50 ball, full-blooded. We ended up on the ground, the ball caught between us. I could tell what he was thinking, 'Ah, so you're not some fucking fanny merchant.' I had his respect.

Throughout Euro 96 we spent hours sitting in the reception area at Burnham Beeches. We had the hotel entirely to ourselves and Gazza would walk endlessly around in a white bathrobe and bare feet. 'Liberace', Pearcey called him. One afternoon while we were playing cards, we counted the number of times Gazza walked past us. Every time he came past, we put a tick after his name. It got close to forty.

'I'm going to play snooker,' he'd say.

'Who'll play snooker with Gazza?'

Different lads had to volunteer for different games. 'Anyone for badminton with Gazza?'

'Can't, I'm knackered, I've played table tennis with him for two hours.'

Gazza had the energy of a restless four-year-old. Tireless and irrepressible, he told the lads that if he scored against the Scots, the celebration would be a re-enactment of the 'dentist's chair', the drinking lark in Hong Kong that had got the lads into the tabloids a few weeks before the tournament began. Only Gazza would have contemplated that. The lads loved him. I found him a genuine guy with a big heart. Subsequently things came out about his battle with alcoholism and difficulties at home, but you couldn't imagine Gazza hurting anybody. He could sometimes be funny in an immature way, but footballers thrive on schoolboy humour. In a way, we've never left school. Just the classroom has changed.

Then there was Gazza on the pitch, the most complete footballer I have played with, gifted beyond anyone this country has produced for years and years. Maybe at the end of it all, what made us most love Gazza was his vulnerability. He was an open book and the press were on his case all the time. He didn't deserve that and it made us protective towards him. We knew the person and we saw the hurt.

Andy

Gareth is one of those players that you have to watch closely to know how good a job he is doing. Too often, what he does is overlooked. The key to his defensive play is his football intelligence and his brilliant reading of the game. I had watched how hard he worked at Crystal Palace. I would tell him he could be a very solid midfielder, but not a great one. He wasn't good enough on the ball. He spent hours improving his skill, making himself better. When he switched to defence at Aston Villa, the work he had done at Palace stood him in good stead. Still, I was surprised he got into the England team so quickly.

In every game during that European Championship, I watched Gareth first and the match second. He played brilliantly. He did a proper defensive job; nothing flashy, but faultless. It amazed me he was so comfortable at international level. Being with the England squad fazed him but when he was on the pitch he proved himself one of the players of the tournament. As for fitting in with the other guys, that was never going to be a problem. Gareth gives a certain impression, kind of educated and thoughtful. Not your typical footballer. But he mixes easily. I'm the best example of that. We are total opposites. He thinks about things, I act off-the-cuff. We've always done things differently. I wanted to buy a car on hire purchase; Gareth wouldn't have dreamt of borrowing. For me it had to be straight away; Gareth preferred to be patient. But for twelve years, we've been like brothers.

Apart from the Dutch match, Alison, Peter and I sat together in the section for players' families. I got to know Teddy Sheringham's parents, who were alongside us. The players' bar became a little like the Oscars: if you were somebody, you had to be there. Pete and I would engage in a star-spotting game.

'Isn't that Noel Gallagher?'

'Yeah. There's Mick Hucknall, he's got Gazza's England shirt.'

'Caprice is over there, Rod Stewart too.'

Then Gareth would come up after the game. 'Good bar tonight?'

'Brilliant.'

Unless you had a pass for the players' bar, you were stuck in the general bar with the FA people and the other hangers-on. Not the place to be. One night we walked through the downstairs bar and saw Liam Gallagher. He didn't have a pass for upstairs, otherwise he wouldn't have been where he was. We had a chuckle about that. Pete kept saying how he felt like a king when he was in the players' bar and I'd say, 'Nah, it's no big deal.' But of course I was thrilled to be among the big hitters.

Gareth

We beat Holland 4–1 and Spain on penalties. The band-wagon was rolling, but cocooned inside Burnham Beeches we knew very little about it. On the trips to Wembley we could sense the mood of the country because the number of people outside the hotel and along the route was growing for each match. They would come out of pubs to clap us, people would give us the thumbs-up and there was a real feeling of the country getting behind us. As we made the journey from the hotel on the day of the Germany game, it was hard not to think of how close we were. Two more wins and it would be our year. For me, it was an extraordinary experience. Tony Adams was on one side of me, Pearcey on the other; two giants, and I was doing okay, holding my end up.

At the time Alison and I had been seeing each other for a year and a half but we weren't married. So this tournament was everything to me; a single man without responsibilities totally absorbed in his football life. It was the most incredible experience. A more mature perspective would come when Alison and I got married and started a family but for those two weeks in the summer of 1996, the game was my life. On the last coach trip to Wembley, I thought of the hours of endless training, the eight-mile cross-country runs, the practice to improve my left foot, the years of yearning. This journey was fulfilment.

Woody understood what it meant to me. He knew where I'd come from. While he was doing up that house in Selsdon, he was living it with me.

Andy

I picked up Alison that evening, the evening of the Germany game. She was at her mum's in Addington, not far from where we were in Croydon. Outside the ground, inside the ground, the atmosphere was electric. Ali wasn't really a big football fan – she never has been – but when Gareth played for England, that did affect her a little. He played very well against the Germans, did a proper defensive job: no frills, no mistakes. Totally solid. It was on a knife-edge, we should have won it in normal time and because we didn't, I sensed it wasn't going to be our night.

Gareth

The final whistle came with a certain relief. One–one. We weren't through, we weren't out, but I had played well. It's strange. Because while you desperately want to play and be part of occasions like this, there is relief when the outcome is taken out of your hands. We had our penalty-takers. Whatever happened now, it wasn't down to me.

We gathered in a loose huddle around halfway; some standing, some sitting. Fellows patting each other on the back.

'Well done.'

'Well played.'

'Should have finished them off.'

'What about that chance at the far post?'

Pearcey moved among us, geeing us up: 'Come on, stay focused, it's not over.' It wasn't over for Pearcey and the other penalty-takers, but it was for me.

Terry Venables and Bryan Robson came towards me. 'Gareth, if it goes to six, will you take one?'

It hit me like a bolt from the blue. 'Yeah, if you want me to take one, I'll take one. No problem.'

They walked away, but about thirty seconds later Bryan returned. 'Gareth, have you taken one before?'

'Yeah, Robbo,' I said.

With the penalty shoot-out minutes away and tension mounting, Bryan didn't ask for details. Suited me. What could I have told him? As penalty-taker, my career had been brief. Three seasons earlier, Palace were drawing 2–2 at Ipswich in a Premiership game, when we got a penalty in the eighty-eighth minute. John Salako picked up the ball, ready to take it. Then our manager, Steve Coppell, shouted some instruction from the bench.

Lee Sinnott came running towards me.

'Nord, *you*, Nord! The gaffer says for *you* to take it!'

It was a surreal moment. 'What, me? *Me?* Why me?' I was trying not to speak too loudly. No footballer likes to betray doubt at key moments. I walked up, determined to smash the penalty into the net. Clive Baker, the Ipswich goalkeeper, changed my mind.

'Cor,' I thought, 'he's tiny. If I put it into the corner, he can't get to it.' So I changed my mind and side-footed the ball for the corner. It struck the post, rebounded and was cleared. I sulked all the way back to London.

That was it: the one chapter in my story as a penalty specialist. I reassured myself that the sixth man was rarely needed. 'Our guys,' I thought, 'are so good at this.' The Germans were equally good. When Christian Ziege beat David Seaman to make it 4–4, the uncertainty disappeared. This was coming down to me. 'Come on, Dave, save this one, just one save.' But I knew my fate; once it got to 4–3 and then 4–4, it was obvious the script had been written and I was part of it.

Stefan Kuntz made it 5–5 and the wait was over. I didn't look around, didn't speak to anyone. I was the sixth man. It was my turn, no one had forced me to volunteer. Inside my head, the struggle had already begun: 'You can deal with this, be definite, look confident, don't change your mind, don't look at the keeper, don't fall over.' I began to walk forward and suddenly there was an eerie quietness around the stadium. I sensed the reason for it.

'Who is it? Who is it?' the crowd was thinking.

Andy

'Gareth's walking up,' Pete said.

'Oh my God,' said Alison.

It was the first time Ali had ever shown emotion at a football match. I'll always remember that. They were both waiting for me to say something. 'He'll be fine, he'll hit it straight in the back of the net.'

I'd never discussed penalties with Gareth because there was never any chance he would have to take one. Just wasn't on the agenda. Would he have been my sixth man? No, but then I didn't know what other England players had been asked, which of them had already said no. Gareth was probably eighth or ninth choice. He just had the guts to say yes. At this point in his career, he wasn't a good enough striker of the dead ball and there was that miss at Ipswich. All he could have had in his locker was a smash straight down the middle. Jesus Christ, I felt for him. Time stands still when your best friend makes that walk from the centre of the pitch.

'Come on, mate, come on, you can do it. Bang it in the goal.'

Gareth

The walk seemed to take for ever. It struck me how dark the night had become. The crowd was trying to make me out.

'It's Southgate, the inexperienced lad.' I could feel what they were thinking. 'Oh awright. Come on. Let's get behind him. *Come on!*'

And I was waiting for their reaction. Halfway there, the clapping started. Nervous at first, then wholehearted. My senses were razor sharp. Behind the goal, the fans were clapping and I thought, 'Well, at least they're on my side.' All I wanted was the ball: put it on the spot, get it over and done with.

It wasn't that simple. Without looking up, I was aware of Andreas Kopke, the German goalkeeper, having the ball in his hands. He then threw it or kicked it and the ball ricocheted off the crossbar and rebounded to the far side of the penalty area. 'Why have you done that?' I thought. But I knew exactly what he was doing: he was trying to spook me, to string the whole thing out, to make me think. It worked. The walk to fetch the ball was nerve-racking.

'God, I could do without this. Don't stumble, don't trip over yourself, don't show any sign of nervousness.' The whole world was watching me and I felt it. The penalty would be side-footed to the left corner. Placing the ball on the spot, I stole a glance at the target and immediately sensed Kopke had noticed it. I then looked at the other corner, to give the impression I was going to put it there. But he had read my mind. Still, there could be no change; a side-foot to the left corner. I wanted it to be firmly struck but didn't want to hit it too hard and risk putting it over the bar or wide. A natural penalty-taker wouldn't have had these thoughts; the expert penalty-taker would not consider the possibility of missing. In trying to be precise, I hit a soft and badly placed penalty. All Kopke had to do was go the right way. He did and saved comfortably.

'What have I done?'

I put my arms over my head. That pose became the picture of England's exit from Euro 96. The thought of the lads on the halfway line made me despair. They were out of the European Championship because of me. Pearcey, typical Pearcey, came from halfway, put his arm round me and said: 'Come on, we're all in this together.' He dragged me back to the lads. There was still a chance that Dave Seaman could keep us in it by saving the Germans' sixth penalty but it wasn't going to happen. There are times in life when you know your fate. I knew before Andy Moller's shot hit the net.

At that second, everything seemed crystal clear. I was the person who had ended a nation's dream. England's loss was down to me. Straight away, I knew this would be a major issue for the rest of my life. It would stay with me, it would be what people remembered me by and I had to accept it.

Different players walked up to me: 'Look, you've had a fantastic tournament, don't blame yourself.' They were too late. I already had. Terry Venables came over, held my face in his hands and said, 'It's not your fault, you've been brilliant.' Jürgen Klinsmann was sympathetic, though I didn't really take in what he said.

At that point, I was no longer with them. The scene was being played out in front of me but I wasn't a participant. Spiritually, I had already departed. Physically, I couldn't wait to disappear. Tony Adams held me by the arm: 'Come on, we're doing a lap of honour.' Jogging around with the lads, I had the sense of everyone looking at me, everyone knowing I was the reason England had lost.

'There he is. Southgate. He's cost us.'

I clapped and waved because that's what you do but I would rather have been anywhere else at that moment.

Andy

Everything just went dead. People started crying around us. I hugged Alison, who was in tears. Ali, who was never interested in football. Then people started patting her and me on the back. They were really kind; Teddy Sheringham's parents, Gary Neville's dad. We were treated like the next of kin: 'Look, don't worry, it could have happened to any of us. Don't worry about it.' Other people came and sympathized but you wondered what they were really thinking: 'Poor Gareth, will he ever recover from this?'

My eyes followed him as he wandered, lost, around that pitch. Different players went and put an arm around him. I wanted to run down and hug him. I wanted to take him away from there. Make him laugh. Because I can always make him laugh. It was terrible to see him on that lap of honour, the other players having to push him along to get him round. He was that far gone. He needed to get to the dressing room, to have time to himself and get his head together. Seeing him like that was one of the toughest things. It broke my heart to watch him. I was thinking, 'Mate, you're lost out there.' It brought a lump to my throat.

Back at home Anna hid behind the settee when the penalty was being taken. She couldn't bear it. Then they were all crying: Anna, her mum and her dad. Anna said she just wanted to get inside the telly and cuddle him. Gareth was family to us all.

Alison was terrific. After shedding a few tears, she composed herself. 'Fucking football,' she said. 'It gets on my nerves.'

Gareth

Inside the dressing room heads were down; a few of the lads were overcome. I cried too. People held my shoulder and said it was okay, but I felt they were looking at me and thinking, 'Christ, he's cost us.' By the time I got to Wembley's old plunge bath, most of the lads had finished and it didn't take long to get washed and dressed. One of the FA people said the press wanted to speak with me. The funeral rites were about to begin.

I spoke to the journalists because it wouldn't have been right to walk away. Nobody else had missed a penalty. They were quite sympathetic and appreciated the honesty. How did it feel, they wanted to know.

'I feel I have let the entire country down.'

That sentence would be the following day's headline and it was how I felt. When the interview ended some of the journalists clapped and thanked me for talking to them.

By then the rest of the team had gone to the players' lounge. As I made my way round the pitch, the scene struck me as being just right: the stadium was empty, there was debris everywhere, the lights had been switched off. The party was over. Then it was down the Royal Tunnel and up towards the Royal Box before getting to the bar.

As I started up the stairs a familiar face breezed past. John Major, the Prime Minister. It wasn't the most opportune of times to meet him. He looked at me.

'Hi,' I said and continued walking.

On the next flight of stairs, someone was calling. 'Gareth, Gareth.' When I looked behind it was Mr Major running after me. 'Gareth, you mustn't blame yourself for this, it's been an incredible tournament for the country. You will feel terrible for a while, but it was not your fault.'

He spoke not as the Prime Minister but as a man; a human being, not the leader of the country. Because of that, I appreciated it all the more. Yet it couldn't change my mood. By the time I got to Alison and Andy in the players' bar, I was pretty down.

Andy

The players' bar was like a morgue. People looked at Alison and me, knowing we were there for Gareth. Alison was great that night, so strong. Gareth needed her to be like that. When he walked into the bar, it was obvious he was distraught. He hugged Alison and then I hugged him.

'Ah, crap penalty, Woody, crap penalty,' he whispered in my ear.

'I don't think it was that good, mate,' I agreed and we laughed a little. Then I said: 'Listen, you were brave enough to take it, that's the biggest thing, that's what you'll be remembered for.' Sometimes in life you've got to tell a little lie.

While we were talking, Stuart Pearce came over and gave him a hug. Tony Adams also did the same, then turned to Alison. 'Permission to have a drink tonight with your fiancé?'

'Do what you have to do with him,' Alison said.

The plan was for the players to go back to their hotel and spend their last night together. No partners, just the squad. I would drop Alison back to her mum's. It was a lonely and sad journey home.

Gareth

It was a long night. Alcohol and the company of the lads dulled the pain but couldn't make it go away. The last thing I wanted was the solitude of my room and the prospect of trying to sleep. So it was five or six in the morning by the time I got to the room. I lay on the bed wide awake, waited until 7 a.m. and headed straight down for breakfast. The previous night ran like a steam train through my head. We had met Andy Townsend downstairs. Since playing together at Villa, Andy and I have been good friends. 'I can't say, "Don't worry" or "Don't let it bother you",' he said, 'but I tell you, I've seen better players than you miss big penalties. Zico, Platini, Baggio.' It was true but, at that moment, sadly irrelevant. I was going to have to live with this.

On the coach ride back to Burnham Beeches, Pearcey announced to the lads that he was retiring from international football. How many others were there? Players whose last chance to win something had been destroyed by me. I still had my international career, but for some of the lads there wouldn't be another tournament. I went to my room at the hotel and there were already fifty or sixty messages waiting for me: John from Slough, Fred from Huddersfield, Michael from Lincoln. Mostly people I didn't know, although there was a kind note from Graeme Le Saux. For Public Enemy No. 1, I wasn't doing badly. It made me smile.

I rang my parents who had been at the game but not in the players' lounge.

'I thought you said if ever you had a penalty, you would just belt it,' Mum said.

'Yeah, but not really, Mum.'

Tony Adams saw me walking into the bar at Burnham Beeches. 'Boo, boo, boo!' he shouted and everyone laughed. The ice was broken. I sat beside Pearcey over dinner. 'Tell me what to expect,' I said and he recalled what it had been like for him after missing a penalty in the semi-final at Italia 90. Pearcey was great, but then all the lads were. Truly, we had been in it together. After dinner we returned to the bar, Pearcey set up his ghetto blaster and the mood became a lot more upbeat. Win or lose, you've got to get on with your life. Terry Venables came and spoke with me for some time. He quoted Friedrich Nietzsche: 'What doesn't kill you makes you stronger.'

There is another Nietzsche quote that, on reflection, might have been more appropriate. 'The thought of suicide is a great source of comfort: with it a calm passage is to be made across many a bad night.'

Andy

It was around one o'clock in the morning when I got home. The party had ended, the good times were over. No more phone calls from DIY Man in Selsdon to England International at Burnham Beeches. No more larking about with the car-park attendants at Wembley. The season of star-gazing in the players' bar had passed, too. What made me truly miserable was the thought that Gareth would be blamed. I feared for him.

Because we were doing up the house in Selsdon, we were staying with Anna's parents at the time. There was some left-over curry in the fridge and, starving, I put it on the cooker. Anna and I were sleeping in her old bedroom and I carried my plate of food with me when I went to see if she was asleep. Pregnant with Isobelle at the time, Anna was awakened and then sickened by the smell of the curry. 'How could you bring that into the room? No, first tell me how's Gareth?'

I started going through the evening and before getting too far we were both in tears. The magnitude of what Gareth would have to face really upset us. Soon the whole house was awake. Anna's parents joined us, then her grandparents, Les and Ivy, came from their room further down the hall. All we did was talk about Gareth. How he was, what the newspapers would say about him, how it would affect him. All of us in that room thought of Gareth as family. We spoke for ages and when there was no more to be said, we all went to bed.

Next morning I woke up early and felt terrible. First thing, I went down to Warlingham Green for the papers. I bought every one of them, sat in the car and read every line written about Gareth. Raymond Cooper, a policeman I know, tapped on the window. 'Did you speak to Gareth? How's he doing?'

I am a goalkeeper, I play in the lower divisions of the Nationwide League and, though professional and serious about my career, I don't think I had ever voluntarily gone for a run before that morning. When I got home with the papers, I changed into training gear and went for a run. Down Warlingham Green, along Limpsfield Road, up by Warlingham School, up Westhall Hill and home. It was maybe thirty minutes but I ran hard. Anger, defiance? I don't know.

14

A friend is someone who can see the truth and pain in you even when you are fooling everyone else.

Unknown

Gareth

It was the evening of 11 February, 1997. The day before England played Italy in a key World Cup qualifier at Wembley. As usual, we were staying at Burnham Beeches. 'Gareth, would you mind dropping in to my room,' said the manager, Glenn Hoddle. At the time I was a regular for England and it was obvious Glenn liked me as a player. 'I'm going to leave you out,' he said. 'I feel what happened with the penalty last summer has affected you.' I couldn't argue with that. 'I would like you to go and see Eileen. It could be good for you.' I was disappointed because it was the first time I had been left out of an England team. In fact it was the first time I had been left out of any team since breaking into the Crystal Palace side at the age of twenty. As for visiting his friend Eileen Drewery, my mind was open.

Though I was disappointed to be left out, there was also a feeling of release. Standing before Glenn all I could say was, 'Fair enough.' Tears began to well – not just from anguish but from relief. At last someone else had seen what I was going through.

The fuss had died down after Euro 96 and people had

generally been kind and sympathetic about the penalty. Theoretically I should have come out of it a tougher character: what doesn't kill me can only make me stronger. And I had established myself in the England side by playing the best football of my life. But the fall-out from the missed penalty overwhelmed everything. It wasn't rational but neither was it controllable. Glenn took over from Terry Venables and named me in the squad to travel to Moldova for a World Cup qualifier in September. Ideal match to ease back into international football but as soon as I linked up with England, it was obvious there was a problem. People wondered whether the penalty still affected me, not that they said anything but it was there. 'Ah, Gareth, good summer, how've you been?' In other words, does it still bother you?

I was still lacking experience, and it was getting to me. Usually I don't read newspaper reports and never need anyone to tell me whether I've played well or badly. But after the penalty miss, it was as if I needed to punish myself. I read the newspapers and seized upon negative comments about my performance. 'This guy thinks I haven't got over the penalty, how can he write that?' I would say to Alison.

Against Moldova I was petrified of making a mistake, which is a bit like playing in handcuffs. Not surprisingly, I didn't perform. Next game we had Poland at home and when they scored early on, I was partly at fault. The cross for the goal was just about reachable but I moved a fraction late and didn't get to it. We went on to win and after the goal, there was nothing wrong with my performance. I passed well, made a lot of interceptions and generally played confidently until going off with an ankle injury ten minutes from the end. The reports were predictable. 'A late injury compounded Southgate's nightmare return to Wembley.' When there is already doubt in your mind, it feeds on

23. Pursued by Christian Vieri of Italy during the World Cup qualifier in Rome, 1998. We drew 0–0 and qualified for the World Cup Finals.

24. Sweden 2 England 1, 1998 European Championship qualifier. Playing for England has always given me enormous pride.

25. Memories don't get better than this. Saving Kevin Donovan's penalty in the 1998 Division Two play-off final at Wembley.

26. Last home game at Brentford. We secured promotion to Division Two. Now we had to play Cambridge in the title decider.

27. Me and Danny Boxall. We beat Cambridge 1-0 and won the Division Three championship.

28. The loneliness of defeat. FA Cup final, 2000. Chelsea 1 Villa 0.

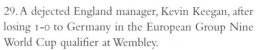

29. A dejected England manager, Kevin Keegan, after losing 1-0 to Germany in the European Group Nine World Cup qualifier at Wembley.

30. Saving a penalty during the Worthington Cup second round, Charlton v. Oxford, 2002.

31. The FA Cup third round, Chelsea v. Middlesbrough, 2003. Chelsea won 1-0.

32. Enjoying the hero headlines in 2003. Too many times the goalkeeper is painted as the villain.

33. Mia, Freddie and Isobelle. I hope they enjoy a friendship as close as mine and Nord's.

34. A proud godfather with his godson. In the Wembley players' bar after an England game with Freddie.

35. Feeding the two girls in Portugal. Look where we have ended up ten years on from our train-station conversation!

36. A few beers and a game of cards, followed by a long sleep and a hangover.

37, 38. Portugal 2002 with the two women in my life!

39. Holidaying in
Portugal, 2002.

40. With Anna and Isobelle relaxing in Portugal, 2002. We look forward to our holidays at the end of the season more than anything else.

41. A relaxing and well-deserved drink in Portugal.

42. Anna, my rock. Enjoying each other's company without having to talk or think about football.

43. Isobelle and Freddie. I hope that one day they will read this book and be as proud of their dad as I am of them.

44. Freddie enjoying a game of pool in Portugal with Gareth.

doubts expressed elsewhere. So many reports rubbished my performance against Poland that in my mind, perception became reality. How I wish that Bill Beswick, the sports psychologist who now works with Middlesbrough, had been around back then. I wish too I had been big enough to say, 'Look, I made a slight mistake, picked up an injury, these things happen, I'll bounce back.'

After Poland, we went to Georgia. My injury needed four to six weeks' rest but desperate to redeem myself, I rushed back in two weeks. This was inexperience in action. On the day before the game, the ankle actually felt wobbly on the uneven pitch in Georgia. The following night I was nervous, jittery, obsessed about not making a mistake and trying to forget about a dodgy ankle. Next day things were so bad I checked the player ratings in different newspapers: they gave me 5 out of 10, England's worst player in a solid 2–0 victory. This was another first because I'm never the worst player. It was a strange turnaround. Before linking up with England, I felt I'd handled the aftermath of Euro 96 really well. The attention had come and gone, my form with Aston Villa was good and Wembley on that summer evening seemed behind me. But a couple of days back with the England squad was all it took to make me realize my rehabilitation was an illusion.

Back in my room after the meeting with Glenn, the relief was more powerful than the disappointment. Fear is your biggest enemy in any game and I had become frightened of playing for England, incapable of performing to my best. It was something I daren't admit although Alison knew, as did Woody. There was no animosity towards Glenn for leaving me out and though I didn't admit it at the time, there was an appreciation of the fact that he had been able to see that it was going wrong. As for the solution to my loss of form for England, I didn't know where to begin. If Glenn thought I could benefit by speaking with the spiritualist Eileen Drewery, I was prepared to give it a try.

Eileen would become part of the story of Glenn's downfall as England manager. Her presence was interpreted as an attempt by the manager to impose her spiritualist beliefs on the players. FA Council members were reported to be furious that she had visited the team hotel a couple of times. It never bothered me and it wasn't something that was much discussed by the players. I went to her house with an England team-mate and we met Phil, her husband, who seemed a regular guy. He told us about the people who had come to Eileen with serious ailments and had left completely healed. I didn't have a strong view on faith-healers; didn't believe nor disbelieve. Just didn't know. Woody went to a faith-healer because of his bad back during our early days at Palace and swore by the lady. We were in the kitchen talking with Phil when Eileen walked in. 'Right,' she said matter of factly to my fellow England player, 'I'll see you first. You need to see me urgently.' Then she turned to me. 'You sit there and have a cup of tea with Phil.'

When Eileen and the player returned to the kitchen some time later, they were having a post-therapy conversation. 'You've taken drugs haven't you?' she said.

Taken aback, he replied, 'Well, I might have smoked the odd . . .'

'It's okay, there's no need to say. I know.'

Then Eileen explained to him what she had done. 'You had an evil guy in you that was screaming to get out and he's gone now. Gone on his way. I've sent him on his way.' Different things flashed through my mind. I thought of the many people Eileen had cured, thought again of the faith-healer that sorted Woody's back and perhaps this wasn't the most unbelievable thing I had ever heard. But at the same time it was the most unbelievable thing I had ever heard.

As I understood the philosophy, everybody has an aura around them. When something bad happens in their lives, this aura is breached. When things are going wrong in their lives people are vulnerable to bad influences. Eileen believes there are spirits that haven't moved on to heaven or to hell but are floating around on earth. These spirits are in a kind of limbo, a sort of living death. If you were in a bar, it would most likely be frequented by the spirits of those who hung out in bars during their lives. If you're very drunk or high on drugs, you open yourself up to these nasty spirits who get inside your aura and attach themselves to you. I hope I am doing justice to the philosophy as Eileen explained it. She also wrote some stuff down, drew a diagram and at the time it did make some sense to me. Who knows for sure what happens when we die? And people with too much drink can behave pretty irrationally. Being as open-minded as possible, I thought 'Well, maybe, there is something in this.'

Eileen's take on my situation was that the spirit of a lady, a timid and apologetic figure who felt sorry for me, had clung on to me. Eileen said I was now carrying this lady with me and she had become a burden. She put her hands on my shoulders and prayed. She then said the lady had been sent on her way and that I should be careful about the future. 'Have a couple of drinks,' she said, 'but if you get really drunk, you might open yourself up to these sort of things.' As I write this now, Eileen's warning looks daft, yet it didn't seem so at the time.

How did I feel walking away from Eileen's house? The funny thing about my visit to Eileen Drewery was that I felt better after seeing her. There was a little spring in my step leaving her house, a sense of having been cleansed.

Mind-games, you may say, another form of psychological manipulation. Maybe that's all it was. Given how tentative I had become playing for England, I was not bothered about who provided the solution or how it came about.

The next game was a friendly against Mexico, in which I played okay, a definite improvement on recent performances. After that it got better. We played South Africa in a friendly and Georgia and Poland in World Cup qualifiers and then went on to Le Tournoi in France that June. The team performed well there and I was the only player picked for every game. Many of the reports said I was our best player. Sol Campbell and I were the big pluses to come out of Le Tournoi. The new line on G. Southgate was, 'He's over-come his problems and he's back to his best.' I wasn't about to tell people that a visit to Eileen Drewery might have helped. There was still a lot of scepticism about her work. In some cases it was downright ridicule. Could you risk people thinking you were mad?

Later on I spoke to Paul Merson about Eileen and some time afterwards Merse went to see her and he thought it had been of some help to him. Among the lads, Eileen was never much of an issue. There was the story about the player who, when she laid her hands on his shoulders, is reputed to have said, 'Short back and sides, please.' Whoever said it, Ray Parlour has got the credit. But it always seemed to me that Eileen was much more of an issue outside the dressing room than inside it. Possibly there were a couple of players who weren't in the team and wondered if they would have improved their chances by visiting her. My feeling was Glenn sent her only those players who would have been open to Eileen's spiritualism in the first place. Or maybe it was a case of Eileen saying to Glenn, 'I've seen this guy and there is something there that has to be addressed.'

One evening Alison and I were out to dinner with another Villa player, Tony Daley, and his wife. Tony had suffered a lot through injury and after we had discussed my visit to Eileen, his wife wanted him to go and see if Eileen could help with his injury problems. It wasn't that I regarded the visit to Eileen as some kind of dark secret, not at all. With some people I was very open about it, but I did tend to choose my audience carefully.

Andy

As a fourteen- or fifteen-year-old, I had awful trouble with my back. The doctor said it was because my tall and spindly body wasn't strong enough to cope with all the football I was playing. He suggested a physiotherapist. After a few sessions of physiotherapy, it was still bothering me. I had tried conventional medicine and not got very far, so my mum and my nan Daphne, who believed in faith-healers, took me one Wednesday afternoon to a faith-healer who saw people in the church in West Norwood opposite the fire station. We sat in the foyer and through a small window I could see this old lady and a gentleman in white doctor-like coats seeing patients who were all quite old. A dear old lady came out to greet my mum and then took both mum and I through to the church.

The lady's name was Ella, she couldn't have been any more than 5ft 2in but she gave off this aura of warmth and calm. Before I said anything, she told me that she would heal the pain. She put her hands on my back and such was the heat, it felt like she had placed a hot-water bottle on my bare skin. Except that I had not taken off my clothes and it was amazing she could generate so much heat through her hands. As she held her hands there, she seemed lost in deep thought. It took ten or fifteen minutes. Mum asked if we could pay but was told that Ella would not accept anything but if we wished to make a little contribution to the church fund, that would be fine. Ella hugged me before I left. 'If you get any more pain in that area, just put your hand on the spot and call my name. That will take away the pain.' When I left the church, I wasn't sure what to think. Ella had seemed an extraordinary woman but the pain was still there.

When I woke up the next morning the pain had gone. Years later I told Gareth about this experience and he was sceptical. He just didn't believe a faith-healer could work. Then he told me about visiting Eileen Drewery. I laughed. 'Knew you'd come round, mate.'

Gareth

Things got better with England. I was again comfortable playing in an England shirt and became the central player in Glenn's back three. Following a straightforward defeat of Moldova at Wembley, in November we faced a crunch tie against Italy in Rome. We needed a draw to go through as Group winners. Tony Adams came back after injury, and was disappointed that Glenn left the captaincy with Paul Ince. It was an outstanding England performance, a nil–nil draw that will always be one of the fondest memories of my international career. The preparation for the match and the performance on the night were an insight into the complexity and coaching talent of Glenn. He took us to a training camp in Italy three days before the game, something that was almost unknown for an England team. But it was clever. We trained at a magnificent complex in perfect weather away from the hype that was building to its usual absurd level back home.

I had a slight strain and couldn't train until the day before the match. Alan Smith, the physio, passed me as 100 per cent okay after a tough fitness test. That evening we went to the Olympic Stadium in Rome for the customary eve-of-match run-out. On the way, Glenn said to me, 'Great, it's great you're fit. You're going to be playing tomorrow night but I don't want you to train when we get to the stadium this evening. I want to keep something up my sleeve.' I've seen myself in different lights but an ace up someone's sleeve? This was a first. If I was in the team, it was a small price to pay. 'Fine,' I said, 'no problem.' So I went through the charade of walking round the outside of the pitch with the physio and could imagine all the journalists coming to the obvious conclusion: 'Southgate didn't train, clearly he is not going to make it.' What was harder to imagine was the disquiet in the Italian camp, '*Mamma mia, Signore* Southgate, he may not play?' Glenn also asked David Beckham not to complete the training session and so create some doubt over his fitness. In terms of what the manager was trying to achieve, that made some sense.

Glenn could be sharp. He explained how the Italians liked to play. Their midfielders would press up on us, making it difficult for us to break forward and if we did pass their first line of defence, they would invariably foul us. This way they would prevent us from building up any momentum. The natural English response to such tactics is to get on with the game quickly but as we were playing away from home and only needed a draw, this was not the time for the natural English response. Instead Glenn encouraged us to play smart, accept the free-kick and regroup before taking it. That night the Italians fouled us precisely as Glenn said they would and the lads played it brilliantly. We didn't stay on our feet when they fouled us, we didn't jump back up to get on with it and the clock kept ticking. To our credit we played like Italians, used our heads and deservedly got the draw. Incey was off the field having his wound treated for what seemed about twenty minutes but we didn't let it affect us. I played solidly, didn't do a lot with the ball but gave nothing away. Glenn had read the game brilliantly. The feeling at the end was one of magnificent achievement.

The World Cup finals in France promised so much. Our first match against Tunisia went well and was another of the nights I shall remember from my England career. One side and one end of the Marseilles stadium were packed with England fans, at the other end were the Tunisian fans and finally there were the rows and rows of international media. What an occasion! England played solidly and Alan Shearer scored from a free-kick we had practised in training. Paul Scholes got a second and that was it: a positive start to our World Cup.

Next day the squad flew back to our base at La Baule in Brittany. Glenn Roeder took the lads who had played the previous day for a warm-down. Just a light jog around the pitch. Having had many ankle injuries in my time, I always use strapping in training. For this little run-out, I didn't bother. Everyone was buzzing and a few of the players got some balls. David Beckham kicked one fifty yards in the air, but without my ankle strapping my inclination was to stay clear of kicking or running. If I don't do things properly, things go wrong. But David Batty then kicked a ball into the air in my direction and jogging along, I could imagine Batts shaking his head, 'Typical Gate, got to do everything by the book.' To hell with it, I ran to control the ball and must have landed awkwardly because the pain just shot through my ankle.

There was no need for any scan or X-ray, I had torn ankle ligaments. One side of the pitch was packed with press and television, cameras everywhere and I couldn't go down.

Tony Adams shouted across at me, 'It's all right, no one's seen ya!' He was thinking it had been a clumsy stumble, something you didn't want on that evening's television news in England. French school kids waited for autographs by the side of the pitch and after throwing the ball back to the lads, I walked over to them. Couldn't be seen going to the doctor. Signing the autographs I glanced down at my sock and could see the golf ball protruding from where my ankle should be. 'Gary,' I said to our physio, Gary Lewin, 'just turned on my ankle.' He took the sock off; it was worse than I'd feared. I was devastated. Out of the World Cup because of the most stupid injury imaginable.

Gary got the team doctor, John Crane, to have a look. John is an old-school doctor, very well spoken, loved by the players for his eternal cheerfulness. 'Bloody good film tonight chaps, *GoldenEye*,' and you wanted to watch because of the way John built it up. For once, his smile vanished. 'Bloody hell, matey, what have you done here?' I knew exactly what I'd done: I'd blown my World Cup.

Distraught, I hobbled on to the team coach. Glenn followed soon after. 'What have you done? What have you done?'

'I've just gone over on my ankle.'

'Fucking hell. Fucking stu . . . What were you doing? *What-were-you-doing?*'

This injury was an old enemy, needing four or five weeks off. In my mind, the World Cup was over. I was already feeling so low and then, in front of every England player, the manager crucified me. Yes, it shouldn't have happened. Given the chance to turn back the clock there would be no running after that ball, no momentary lapse, but it was still an accident. For some reason it was meant to happen. All my life I had worked to get to the world stage, to prove I could do it at the highest level. This was my opportunity to change my international epitaph, to give the public something that might have stood alongside the penalty miss. And now it was gone.

All Glenn could think of was the hole in his side and the probability of having to go from a back three to a back four. At that moment he saw it only from the team's point of view. Totally understandable, I guess. He was in a fix; I was in a mess. The circumstances of the injury galled Glenn. They devastated me. The team got on with it but not as well as we had hoped. Losing to Romania meant a difficult route to the final and an earlier-than-ideal meeting with Argentina.

Andy

Ah, the summer of '98.

It began for me with a promotion play-off final for North-ampton against Grimsby at Wembley where the disappointment of losing the match was offset by my saving a penalty. Then as Gareth headed off to the World Cup, Anna, Freddie and I flew to the Caribbean on our family holiday. The time difference meant it was impossible for us to keep in touch but the matches were shown in the hotel where we stayed. For England's first game against Tunisia the atmosphere was electric. By sheer coincidence an ex-England player, Geoff Thomas, who had been with Gareth and me at Crystal Palace was holidaying in the same complex. Geoff and I met in the bar and watched the Tunisia game together.

When we got back from holiday, England were about to play Romania in their second Group match but by now Gareth was injured and it wasn't the same for me. I spoke with Alison on the phone and she said he was really down in the dumps. 'Call him, Woody,' she said, 'try to sort him out.' By the time I spoke with him, a week had passed and he hadn't been able to pick himself up. It was the way the injury happened, the realization that he probably wasn't going to play another game in the World Cup and the way Hoddle had a go at him afterwards. 'Try to stay in a good frame of mind,' I said, 'it could settle down quicker than you expect.' As is usually the case, I tried to make jokes about his situation but this was one of the few times when it was impossible to make him laugh. He was badly cut up and I sensed he was blaming himself. I felt he could have done with a more sympathetic response from Hoddle. We spoke about the Argie game, how tough it would be, and he felt there was a chance he would be fit to play but that it was unlikely the manager would put him straight back in.

A couple of days before the game, Gareth rang to say he had booked me on the FA's trip for friends and family. The arrangement was for me to go to a hotel in Luton early on the morning of the game and people from the FA would meet me there and sort out everything. All I needed was a passport. It was an early start, with everyone convening in the hotel at 7.30. Being on my own, I felt a little out of place until meeting Gareth's parents. They always make a fuss over me and that morning they made me feel totally at ease. Barbara took me to the lady from the FA and then introduced me to Tony Adams's mum and dad. Straight away, I hit it off with them. What bloody lovely people they were. 'One of our own,' as my mum used to say of south London people. The Adamses made sure I didn't feel out of it. From the hotel we boarded coaches that took us on the short journey to Luton Airport, but not to the check-in desks. Instead we were taken straight out to the aircraft. Ah, so this is how the England boys do it. I felt like royalty.

As we got on the plane, it was possible to start making out who was who. There was Michael Owen's family, the Beckhams over there, the Nevilles; some of the faces I knew from sitting in the families' section at Wembley during Euro 96. On the plane I sat alongside Barry Nevill who seemed a nice guy. He was Teddy Sheringham's agent and on the journey he was reading the manuscript for Teddy's autobiography. I supposed it was what agents did. 'Checked over the book, guv, it's fine.' To me, it was another world.

After arriving in St Etienne, we got on the coaches that were waiting to take us to the centre of the city. England flags were everywhere, the atmosphere was sensational and we were dropped off at this magnificent old building. It looked full of history and I was afraid it was a museum. Inside there was a big room with tables laid out for 200 people to have lunch. My relief was enormous. It was a five-course meal and my admiration for the Football Association was rising by the minute. Peter Taylor's family were alongside me during the meal, the red wine flowed and my only regret was that the Northampton lads could not see me as I lapped it all up.

On the coach journey to the stadium, I sat with Paul Merson's folks. It was fascinating to discover what kind of families the players had come from. What surprised me was how eager everyone was to be friendly and chatty. They were going out of their way to be pleasant and that added a lot to the experience. Dropped off about a mile or so from the stadium, I walked with Clive and Barbara and then with Tony Adams's mum and dad. Tony's dad had a problem with his breathing and didn't seem in the best of health. Every so often he would have to stop and he was always apologizing to me for the delay. We had loads of time, but no matter how much I told him there was no need to apologize, he would say, 'I'm sorry about this Andy.' Some time later I read that he passed away. We spoke for no more than half an hour that day but it was memorable.

In the stadium, I sat alongside Michael Owen's family. The tension was unbelievable, and even though England's fans vastly outnumbered Argentina's, I will never forget how much noise the Argies made. They were mostly below us and to our left. It was a brilliant match and while it will always be remembered for Owen's goal, what sticks in my mind was his reaction to scoring. After rifling the ball into the roof of the net, he turned and sprinted straight to where his parents were sitting. Getting close enough to make eye contact, he pointed to them and then raised his arms in the air. Like he was saying, 'It's for you, Mum, for you, Dad.' It was a class moment. His family were in tears, a lot of people around us felt the same. We had just witnessed the most extraordinary goal from a player who was just a kid.

Gareth came on midway through the second half. I knew how much that would mean and was thrilled for him. It was such an even game but I just wanted Gareth not to make a mistake. He was his usual faultless self. Of all the top centre-backs, he's the one who makes the least mistakes. When the game went to penalties, my fear was he would have to take one. 'Please, Gareth, don't volunteer. Don't feel you have to make up for 96.' He couldn't win by taking one. The tension was almost unbearable and my eyes never left Gareth, hoping he would stay in the centre circle while others made the long walk to the penalty area. Bizarre as it sounds, when Batty missed and England were out I felt a little relief. I had worked it out that if Batty had scored, Gareth would probably have taken the following one. Thankfully, it never got to that.

The FA arranged for us to see the players for ten minutes in the car park. They were all so dejected. Beckham looked totally distraught. His family, who seem such decent people, were just about holding back the tears. Two years before it had been my mate who had felt responsible for England going out, so I could sense how they felt. Gareth was gutted by the defeat but pleased to have played. He reached into his bag, pulled out his shorts and socks and gave them to me for Freddie. He said he would get his shirt signed by the rest of the team. True to his word, he did and wrote 'To Freddie' before adding his own signature to the others. The 'To Freddie' bit was so I couldn't sell it. The shirt is now framed, along with the match programme and my match ticket, and hangs on the wall beside Freddie's bed. We said our goodbyes to Gareth and headed for the airport. The Beckhams sat in front of me on the flight home. Not a word was spoken. It was 5 a.m. when I got back to London, close to twenty-four hours after I had left.

Four hours later I was on the training ground at Northampton; it was our first day of pre-season training. I wore Gareth's shorts, still carrying the grass marks of St Etienne. The boys were well pissed off. First thing we did at training was a bleep test: shuttle runs at ever increasing speeds to test our basic fitness. The fit guys can get to level fifteen or sixteen. Three hours' sleep and a lot of travelling the day before – I was fucked. Cramp set in at level two in the blip test. 'Woody,' screamed the manager, Ian Atkins, 'no one ever drops out at level two.' He slaughtered me.

Gareth

I react well to adversity. There were three-times-a-day sessions with the physios, Gary Lewin and Alan Smith, and long hours in the swimming pool as we tried to repair the damaged ligaments. Gary and Alan were my crutches for those two weeks. Without them I couldn't have got near the team. We achieved miraculous progress and over the weekend before Monday evening's game at St Etienne, we realized the ankle would stand up to a game. As managers do with injured players, Glenn had written me out of the script and we hardly spoke during my recovery.

Two days before the match, I declared myself fit to play,

but by then Glenn was sticking with the eleven who had beaten Colombia in the previous game. That was understandable, but it would have been nice if he had said, 'Look, I don't think I can risk you,' or something along those lines. He just named his side and I didn't even get a chance to train.

Glenn is a complex man. Deep down, I believe, he is a decent person but he doesn't communicate well with people and he has a way of rubbing players up the wrong way. It was clear Glenn rated me; he picked me to play twenty-two times for England and showed faith in me through the bad times after Euro 96. His one and oft-repeated criticism of me was that I didn't use the ball well enough. He felt I was uptight and not prepared to be really positive in my distribution. His view was that a good centre-back should be able to play through midfield and see different sorts of passes. He had played sweeper in a back three at Swindon and started many of the team's attacks from that position. He wanted me to lean a little towards that kind of game. I couldn't be the player he was.

He was impatient with the poor technical ability of the players he had to coach. In our coaching drills, the strikers would finish crosses. Everyone noticed it was Glenn and not one of the lads who supplied the crosses and to be fair, his ability to cross the ball had not diminished with time. It was almost a case of 'see, I can still do this'. On the day before the Argentina game, we practised set-pieces and he had one particular free-kick ploy he wanted Paul Scholes and David Beckham to practise. The idea was for Paul to flick the ball up for David who would take it on his thigh and volley it over the wall. They tried a couple of times but couldn't pull it off. In our previous match David had scored with a cracking free-kick against Colombia and was confident. But Glenn just said to him, 'There's no point, you're not going to be able to do this, we'll have to do something different,' and walked away. You could see David's anger. He muttered something half under his breath. I felt Glenn lost Becks at that moment. The following evening David was sent off. Who knows whether or not there was a connection.

It was typical Glenn, though. A few days earlier the lads were preparing for the Colombia game and those who weren't in the starting eleven were watching from the side as the team rehearsed its set-pieces. Obviously the second string should pay attention and make a note of the different hand signals for corners but players don't always do as they should. That day Glenn called the back-up team on to the pitch and decided to practise a near-post corner. 'Macca, can you take it?' he said to Steve McManaman. Steve hadn't a clue what the signal was and to make light of his difficulty, he put one hand up, then the other, he then put his hands on his head, shook the flag and we all had a welcome laugh. Except Glenn. He gathered us round him, asked someone else the signal for near-post corners and drew another blank.

'Right, the starting eleven, off you go.' He kept the rest of us there. He couldn't deal with situations like that sensitively. Instead of saying, 'Look guys, you are as important as the eleven that are playing, any one of you could end up playing a big part in this tournament,' he was just plain angry. He didn't seem to realize he was speaking to eleven blokes who felt they were bit-part players, watching from a distance as the World Cup passed them by. They needed encouragement, not chiding. But the bad vibes were there from after the Tunisia game when Glenn slaughtered them for their poor attitude in one training session. That just demoralized guys who felt they weren't going to be in the team anyway.

After England went out on penalties to Argentina, Glenn

A Football Friendship 217

spoke about us having given it everything. The feeling about Becks was that he had been a little silly but the sending-off was unjustified. One of those diabolical refereeing decisions you sometimes get in football. I didn't speak with David afterwards because I was more conscious of what David Batty was going through. Having missed my penalty just two years before and being closer to Batts than Becks, I imagined he was the one who would need geeing up. Little did I know Batts. His view was that he had missed a penalty he would have preferred to score, but it was over and done with. Not able to change it, not in a position to wind back the clock, he was going to get on with it. His take-it-on-the-chin attitude was a reminder of how different my reaction had been after Wembley. He wasn't going to beat himself up over a missed penalty and I couldn't blame him.

Glenn had sides to him. He played games that were hard to fathom. After I had turned my ankle in La Baule, he asked me to do a press conference saying the ankle was okay and there wouldn't be a problem for the game against Romania. Within the squad everyone knew there was no chance of my being fit and Tony Adams almost lost it when he heard what Glenn told me to do. 'Why is he asking you to go there and lie, putting you in that position?'

'Well, if it helps the team, I don't have a problem.'

'He shouldn't be asking you to tell a lie. That's wrong.'

Of course, the obvious question was how could it help the side? Were the Romanians going to change their plans because I was okay? Yet he was a good coach and when he worked on one aspect of our game, you could bet on it reaping a dividend for the next game. He seemed to know how to hurt the opposition. We had prepared for having a man sent off and being down to ten men against the Argentinians. Everyone in the squad knew we would switch from a back three to a flat back four and because it was something that had been planned for, it was easy to implement. Four years later with an extra man against Brazil in Japan, we didn't know how best to exploit our numerical advantage because it was not something we had worked on. Terry Venables and Steve McClaren are the best coaches I've worked with and Glenn would come next.

But it was downhill for Glenn after France 98. And his book didn't help. I remember thinking Paul Gascoigne's not going to like this. The impact made by the serialization left him open to the accusation that he was cashing in on his infamous fall-out with Gazza. There were other problems. Many of the journalists who covered England seemed to have grown tired of Glenn. Not enough ill-feeling to start a campaign against him but a lot of guys who were once his friends weren't disappointed to see him go. He had started to pick and choose whom he would speak to in the press and that's often the beginning of the end.

When the article in *The Times* reporting his views on reincarnation appeared, it was obvious there would be major fall-out. I was up in Newcastle with Villa and showed the piece to our coach Steve Harrison. 'What do you think?'

'That's him finished,' said Steve. 'Rightly or wrongly, he will go on the strength of that.'

I thought it was wrong. He had expressed personal views on something that had nothing to do with football. But, typical of Glenn, he expressed himself tactlessly. If there hadn't already been antagonism towards him before that interview, it wouldn't have been used against him the way it was. It wasn't right for the Prime Minister, Tony Blair, to get involved, but once he rowed in against Glenn, you could see which way the wind was blowing. England would be looking for a new manager.

15

The meeting of two personalities is like the contact of two chemical substances: if there is a reaction, both are transformed.
  Carl Jung

Andy

Managers influence footballers' lives to a ridiculous degree. It all boils down to one thing: does he fancy me? Our happiness is in their hands. If you don't get on with the manager, life is terrible. Gareth had this with John Gregory at Aston Villa and the only solution for him was to get away. I've experienced so many different managers I would have to think when listing them all. Most of them were good blokes, not too many of them were good managers. But that's players; in our eyes, the manager is always a prat. One of them, Ian Atkins, has had a huge impact on my life. Without him, there is no knowing where my career would have gone but one thing is certain, it wouldn't have gone as far. I played for five years under Ian at Northampton Town and he's been my manager at Oxford United for the last two years. I've had seven years of work from him and that's what it matters in the lower leagues. Will the guy give me a contract? It might be an unglamorous way of seeing my career but that's how it is.

Ian's an unusual man. The phone rang the other night at about 10.15. Ian was on his way home from Blackpool reserves against Preston reserves where he had seen a player he had liked. 'You know the guy, Woody, you played with him at Colchester. What's he like? Does he have the right mentality? Would he be good for us?'

What an absolute lunatic, I thought to myself. If it wasn't Blackpool's reserves, it would have been Grimsby's or Norwich's. How many evenings does Karen Atkins see her husband? Karen's a lovely woman, comes to the games and knows her stuff. But it's a three-way marriage; Ian, Karen and football and not necessarily in that order. I'm sure it's the same for many managers but Ian is still an outstanding example of a man who gives everything.

More than any manager I've worked with, Ian appreciates what I can bring to the dressing room. I know when guys need to be picked up and how to bring in the young lads who are being excluded from the group. For the team spirit to be right, everyone has to feel involved. Ian lets me get on with this stuff; finding the balance between fun and work and making sure the lads don't forget that, in the end, only results matter. I don't kid myself, the manager took me as much for my personality as my goalkeeping.

He first saw me play for Bognor Regis against Woking. That was back in the early nineties when I was sent from Crystal Palace on loan to the non-leaguers. God knows why he was at the game but you could say that about him most nights of the week. The fact that he was at Bognor Regis that evening was a major event in the career of Andy Woodman. When Ian became manager of Doncaster Rovers and needed a goalkeeper, I was in the frame. Palace released me at the end of the 1993–94 season and Exeter City led the chase for my signature. It wasn't exactly a stampede. Doncaster were the only rivals. Ian rang me and pleaded with me not to sign for Exeter. He told me Doncaster was a great city with a fantastic nightlife. Typical Ian, he didn't mention the club to me because it was run-down, with an old ground that had one stand that could not have seated more than 500 people. 'Anna,' I said, 'I have an offer from Doncaster Rovers.

Meant to be a great city with a fantastic nightlife.' So I joined Exeter.

Exeter offered a one-year contract, which seemed a lot at the time. When it turned out to be a disastrous move and all went horribly wrong, Ian still wanted me. By then he had moved on to Northampton and he had not forgotten what he saw in that Bognor versus Woking game. At first it was a contract for the ten remaining games of that 1994–95 season. They take no chances in the lower leagues; ten games to prove you're worth £400 a week. The trial period went well and at the end of it, I signed a two-year deal. My career as a professional footballer was up and running, thanks to Ian Atkins.

He knows me inside out, something that isn't always to my advantage. But deep down he believes in me and that overrides everything. In return, I give him loyalty. We've had our fall-outs but with two fiery people, that's to be expected. The only rule is that he must win the argument. Leaving Northampton, I blamed him for messing things up for me but the anger disappeared quickly. Not all the guys warm to him and you can understand their lack of enthusiasm. He lives and sleeps football and demands the same commitment from them that he gives as manager. But if they gave that, they wouldn't be playing Division Three football. So I try to keep the peace: 'Look, lads, life is simple here: the gaffer loves us when we win, despises us when we lose. Monday to Friday, he is a top man. Saturday afternoon, he's manic. Completely sane if the result is right, impossible bastard when it's not.' And when we lose, I think to myself, 'Wouldn't have happened if we had his passion.'

When Freddie, our first child, was born, poor Anna's labour lasted for ever. It began on Sunday evening and continued for thirty hours until she delivered Freddie into the world at 4 o'clock. on Tuesday morning, 4 March. All through the labour, Ian called me regularly. After asking the obligatory question about how

Anna was doing, Ian got round to what was on his mind: 'Have you told her we've got a huge game against Brighton tomorrow evening?' After the delivery, I held Freddie for half an hour, went home, had three hours' sleep and rang Ian. 'Gaffer, baby son arrived this morning, three hours ago. Freddie.'

'Great, Woody, that's great.'

'I was wondering if it would be better for me to get some proper sleep and head straight from London to Brighton for the game. Only takes forty-five minutes from here.'

'No, Woody, I want you to come up to Northampton. You know the rules, everyone travels together.'

'But, gaffer, in the circumstances . . .'

'No. You got to be here.'

There is no arguing with Ian. It took me over two hours to get to Northampton, another two hours on the team coach to Brighton and at that point, I was knackered. We lost 2–1 and I played badly.

The next morning I was on my way to the hospital to see mum and baby when the mobile rang. It was the secretary at Northampton. 'I'm sorry, Woody, but the manager says you have to report to Stevenage for this evening's reserve game. He reckons it will do you good to get last night's game out of your system. You've got to be in Stevenage by six o'clock.'

'Tell Ian to shove the reserve game up his arse. I want to see my boy.'

A little later, the secretary rang back. 'The manager says it's okay, you needn't be there until 6.30.'

'I'm not gonna be there.'

'Woody, I'm only the messenger. He says you have to be.'

I phoned Ian and told him he would have to make other arrangements because I wasn't travelling. In my eyes it was ridiculous sending me off to play with the reserves two days after our son was born. On Saturday we were away to Hereford and he left me out of the team. Disciplinary measure because I had refused to go to Stevenage. This was too daft to be true. We exchanged more than a few unkind words but it got me nowhere. He was the boss and any player who challenged him lost. I served my one-match ban and got back in for the following weekend's game. That was it, over and done with. He and I were quickly back to where we were before Freddie's arrival.

Gareth

It was the Thursday night before what would be the last game ever played at the old Wembley. As fate would have it, this was also to be Kevin Keegan's final match as coach to the national side: England against Germany, October 2000. The stakes were high as it was the first game in our World Cup qualifying campaign, and when he said he would like to see me in his room, I had a good idea of what to expect. While he knew about my good form at Villa, he was going with Martin Keown and Tony Adams in the middle of the defence. There would be no complaints from me. Since Kevin had taken over from Glenn, I had not been first choice. We got on well on a personal level. He was a warm, passionate man who made people feel good about playing for England; a man I wanted to play for. What worked against me was the fact that I had rarely played well against Newcastle while he was manager at St James' Park. Now he was doing the decent thing and telling me it would be Martin and Tony.

'Gareth,' he said, 'I'm going to play you. I want you to sit in front of the back four and pick up Mehmet Scholl.' Germany had been playing two strikers with Scholl sitting in just behind them. 'Kevin,' I thought, 'you're going to get hammered for this.'

Other thoughts came to mind. How were Paul Ince and Dennis Wise going to feel about a centre-back playing midfield while they sat on the bench? Neither was playing well at the time but it was still hard for them to take. My overriding feeling was a desire to make it work because Kevin was going out on a limb. I don't know why he went with me in midfield. Something in the back of my mind suggested it was a loyalty thing: he was repaying the loyalty I had shown him. For me, it was simply a question of liking him as a man. We trained the next day at Bisham Abbey and he told the players the team. Everyone looked around, trying to catch the other guy's reaction and it was obvious people were taken aback. 'Gareth in midfield?' About five minutes were spent training with the formation we intended to use against the Germans.

Then came the usual rigmarole with England: training ends, players receive telephone calls from their agents, the team is passed on and the agents speak with their journalist contacts. The team is leaked. The following morning Kevin was crucified for his decision to play me in midfield and before a ball was kicked, I became the fall guy.

On the night before the game the journalists on Sky's *Hold The Back Page* knew the starting line-up and tore Kevin to pieces. As much as they kept saying 'Let's get this right, we're not having a go at Gareth here,' they actually were. They were castigating Kevin for picking me to play a midfield role they didn't think I was up to. Which is not what you want to hear the evening before a game. Of course I should have switched it off but there's a morbid fascination in hearing what people say when they are publicly knocking you. It bugs you and yet you want to hear it. The morning papers weren't to be outdone either. They ridiculed Kevin and were dismissive of my chances of making a success of the role. 'No disrespect to Southgate *but . . .*'

The most disappointing aspect of this was its stupidity. In allowing the side to become public knowledge, we invited all the criticism on ourselves and offered Germany the opportunity to change their formation if they chose to. In my eyes, that was unprofessional.

I started the match with the brief to man-mark Scholl but Germany opted to play with just one striker, Scholl sitting just behind him. Martin Keown and Tony Adams should have taken care of Scholl but as I had been picked solely for the purpose of marking him, I was reluctant to desert him. With me playing deep on Scholl, we were outnumbered in midfield and they were able to keep the ball for long periods. Like it was a game of pontoon and we didn't know whether to stick or twist. I wasn't experienced enough as a midfielder to be able to say, 'Hold on here, we need to reorganize.' Because they changed their formation, we had been outmanoeuvred. Kevin changed it at half-time, went with a back three in the second half, and playing on the left side, I did very well. But Dietmar Hamann had already scored and the damage was done.

The 1–0 defeat was desperately disappointing and the end for Kevin. As he walked from the field, with the crowd's boos ringing in his ears, you saw his mind was already made up. All he said in the dressing room was, 'That's it for me, lads, I think I've taken it as far as I can. It's time for someone else to come in.'

It was a sad exit. I so much wanted it to work, to be able to turn to people and say, 'Look, he put me in there, he knew what he was doing.' More than anything it hurt me because he is such a decent man. I don't think he rated me as much as Glenn had and he certainly didn't put me in the side as often as Glenn did but we still got on really well. He was easier to talk to and as time went on, his opinion of me as a player rose and he appreciated what I brought to the squad, whether or not I was in the team.

A lot of nonsense was subsequently written about England under Kevin. It was said that he liked a bet and that during his reign race-nights and card schools flourished. The accusation was totally unfair. For as long as I have been an international, cards and gambling have been a part of the England scene. There were race-nights during the 1986 World Cup in Mexico and we had them under Terry Venables and Glenn Hoddle. Generally one or two of the lads ran the book, we would get a list of the horses, place our bets and then watch a video tape of the race. We all tried to fleece the bookies. My bet was £10 or £20, others would put down £50 or £100; it was never that big a deal. One night Kevin played bookie and gave us ridiculously good odds, trying to make sure he lost. That was the kind of man he was. Race-nights were optional but they were popular with the older lads and I felt they were good for team bonding. As for the infamous card schools, it was a bit of a storm in a teacup. The stakes could be high but no higher than you see at club level.

In a tactical sense, Kevin erred on the side of giving too much credit to players. If you play international football, you've got to be able to adapt to the ebb and flow of games. So he didn't spend a lot of time working on team pattern and rehearsing different formations. I think it was a mistake because there are very few players, even at the highest level, who are tactically aware. Far better to start out believing players understand little about tactics and work from there.

Team spirit was Kevin's strong point. His side played with passion. During his reign the atmosphere was excellent. Maybe my judgement is clouded by how much I liked the man but the guy has the ability to inspire people. We saw that at Newcastle, we're still seeing it at Manchester City.

Euro 2000 was a wash-out, both for me and the team. I played just ten minutes, and that was in the final, disastrous match against Romania. I might have had three touches, not more than that. We didn't have the ability to change our approach as the match unfolded, a weakness that would again hurt us during the 2002 World Cup campaign in Japan. The Euro 2000 side did not play well. Some of the senior players felt that in tactical terms, we lacked flexibility. Strategy was not Kevin's thing. 'This is the way he is,' one of his backroom team would tell you, 'and he's had tremendous success operating this way.' And even though I liked him more than any England manager I have played for, I couldn't argue with his own brutally honest assessment that, tactically, he came up short.

After the calamitous loss to the Germans at Wembley, the FA allowed the players to disperse on that Saturday evening as had originally been planned. We would return the following evening to prepare for the midweek game against Finland in Helsinki. Howard Wilkinson would be in charge. After the loss to Germany and Kevin's resignation, there was an empty feeling within the team. When players don't perform and the manager resigns, the dressing room is like a mortuary. Many felt for Kevin and there would have been some guilt in there too.

Howard's reputation as a dour coach didn't do much to lift the morale. As people left on Saturday evening, you knew there would be absences on the trip to Helsinki. Guys carrying injuries would not play and Howard's first job would be to cobble together some kind of team. We went to Helsinki and got a nil–nil draw, denied victory by the referee and linesman failing to see Ray Parlour's shot was a foot over the goal-line. It was a horrible evening for football – a near-gale force wind made conditions extremely difficult –

but England did well. David Seaman had just one save to make and we played with a lot of spirit after the dejection of the previous Saturday. What happened afterwards? Howard was pilloried and nil–nil was described as a 'disastrous result'. There are times when journalists see things as they want to see them. Because Howard was considered not to be up to the task, he was rubbished.

Did anyone notice that no one in our group won in Helsinki and that the Germans could not beat the Finns at home or away? Who remembered our Helsinki performance when, under Sven-Goran Eriksson, England needed David Seaman to pull off a magnificent save from Jari Litmanen to hold on to a 2–1 victory over Finland at Anfield? I liked Howard's approach. He has a wit so dry that if he coughs, you expect chalk dust to fly. Some lads didn't know how to take him, but I found him funny. 'I am playing people in their club positions,' he said, 'except for Emile [Heskey] but to be fair to Emile, I don't think he knows what his best position is.' I try to think now of the eleven who played in Helsinki: Seaman; Phil Neville, Keown, Southgate, Barry; Parlour, Wise, Scholes, Heskey; Cole and Sheringham. He had to go without Gary Neville, Tony Adams, Graeme Le Saux, David Beckham and Nick Barmby from the side that had played the previous Saturday and he left out Michael Owen because he wanted to play the Manchester United strikers, Cole and Sheringham, together.

His time as England's head coach was always going to be brief, but he got no credit for his contribution. For that result in Helsinki though, I say, 'Well done, Howard.'

16

True friendship is when two friends can walk in opposite directions, yet remain side by side.

Unknown

Andy

It's a funny thing about being taken on as an apprentice at a professional football club: you think you've arrived. Your mates envy you, other people say, 'Congrats, make the best of it and don't forget us when you get there' and it is all about the glamour of being a pro footballer. 'He's training with the Palace first team.' Sounds great. It bears no relation to reality. What I found at the training ground was a ladder and directions to the bottom rung. Beside the ladder was a mop to clean the floors and toilets, barrow loads of sand to spread on the training pitch and endless boots to clean.

At Crystal Palace, they gave me Ian Wright's, Gary O'Reilly's, Alan Pardew's and Mark Hone's. A barrel of water at the back of the changing room was our washing machine and on cold winter days, first man in broke the ice to get at the freezing water. Wrighty used two, three or even four pairs of boots during a training session, Gary was injured a lot so the workload there was light, while Mark didn't mind if his boots weren't spick and span. Christmas was a good time for an apprentice because the pros looked after their boot boys. One Christmas Wrighty gave me £40, Pards £20 and I got another score from Mark. For a sixteen-year-old earning £27.50-a-week, it was terrific money.

Gary, who hadn't given me anything, bumped into me one day coming up to Christmas. 'Woody, I haven't given you your Christmas box, have I?'

'No, but not to worry, mate.' What a lie.

He lined up five one-pound coins on the pool table. 'Merry Christmas,' he said. 'Have a good one.'

'Thanks, mate,' I said with a smile and thought, 'Tight fucking bastard.'

It was all part of your apprenticeship: the misery that comes before the good times. The ambition was to play in Palace's first team and to end up driving to training in flash cars like Wrighty and Mark Bright drove. After becoming Palace's reserve keeper, I trained and travelled with the first team and got a glimpse of what it was like for the big boys. Boots, kit and towel all laid out when you turned up for training, water bottles on the perimeter of the pitches. After training you stepped out of the sweaty and muddied gear, left everything on the floor; the apprentices gathered it up while you headed for the canteen. By two o'clock you had trained, washed and eaten. The rest of the day was yours. A game of snooker, a round of golf – this was the life.

Then, one morning, Alan Smith called me into his office and ended the good life. Said it was one of the hardest things he had ever had to do. If I'd known what life in the lower leagues was like, I would have thrown myself at Alan's feet. I went from a Premiership club to Division Three, the kind of journey you have to experience to know what it is really like.

First day of pre-season at Exeter each player was handed a bag with two sets of training kit. They were yours for the season and they could be washed or allowed to stink. The choice was yours because there were no apprentices. And so it was that I learned the realities of football away from the Premiership's bright lights.

Good men exist in the basement, blokes who love the game so much they could put up with unbelievable shit. Terry Cooper, the former England international full-back, was my manager at Exeter and a classic case. He went about his work with an enthusiasm you wouldn't believe. Our training ground was a pitch with a hut for a changing room. There was no heating, and if you weren't first in from training, you missed the hot shower. On the wettest and dirtiest day, the keenest man on the training ground was Terry. He had won leagues and cups with Leeds United and played twenty times for England in an era when international caps meant something. At the 1970 World Cup in Mexico, he marked Jairzinho in Guadalajara when the greatest team of all beat England 1–0 and Gordon Banks made that great save from Pelé. Jairzinho actually went past Terry before putting in the cross that led to Banks's save.

'Bloody hell, gaffer,' I said to Terry one miserable day at training, 'did no one tell you that you've got to stay on your feet when Jairzinho is running at you?'

'Fuck me, Woody, I don't seem to remember your last game against Brazil.'

How right. The only good game I played in my season at Exeter was when we won 1–0 at Preston. I remember not so much the performance but the journey from Exeter to Preston. We met at the Toby pub in the centre of the city at six o'clock on Saturday morning and began our journey north. Somewhere on the M6, Terry asked if anyone wanted something to eat. We all did. In one bag he had a selection of microwave dinners; in another, sandwich rolls. Terry never told us but I suspected his wife, Rose, made the rolls. As you identified your choice, Terry served it up. If it was a microwave dinner, he would heat it for two or three minutes. This man was a legend and here he was cooking for us, treating us as if we were his own kids. Could you imagine any of today's England players doing the same twenty years from now? One thing is sure, their glamorous wives won't be making the rolls.

Most of all Terry brought a smile to our little team. Top man he was and it was a terrible disappointment for me to have played rubbish for him.

Part of the reason I was so bad was that I didn't settle. A London boy, I missed family and friends and would try to get home after a Saturday afternoon game. Getting back to Exeter for Monday morning training was an ordeal. Anna would call me at 4.15 a.m., drop me into Paddington for the 5.15 to Penzance, changing at Didcot Parkway. After arriving at Exeter St David's station, I would take a taxi to the ground. The journey took slightly less than six hours.

Gareth

Even by the standards of the Premiership, our training facilities at Middlesbrough are high quality. A professional sportsman could not wish for a better environment. There are about seven training pitches, a luxury that means no pitch is overused. If you've got an injury, you go to one of the three physiotherapists. For rehabilitation, you see one of the masseurs. Should the injury be serious, local hospitals will fit you in at a moment's notice and if someone needs surgery, the question is always, 'Who is the best surgeon in the world?' If the player is deemed to be sufficiently important, that's the surgeon we use. Anything technical, you talk with one of the three coaches and if you need specialist fitness training, there are two full-time sports scientists who can work one-on-one with you. For those who find it hard to control their weight, there is a nutritionist, and each week a chiropodist and a chiropractor visit the club. Sometimes, though, the problem is in your head and the club caters for that too; Bill Beswick is assistant manager and resident sports psychologist.

Our changing room is the size of a five-a-side pitch and each player's locker is big enough to walk into, shuffle about and still not crease the clothes that hang there. When we come in after training, we leave our muddy boots outside and our sweaty training shorts and tops are collected from us and taken away. Where once apprentices cleaned up after the first eleven, now a team of industrial cleaners sweeps through our changing room each afternoon and when we return in the morning it is shining clean. The gymnasium is like what you see at an exclusive health club except it is bigger and better equipped. Of course we've got our sauna, steam room and jacuzzi and it is easy to forget that not every professional footballer enjoys these facilities. Upstairs there is the restaurant that we still call 'the canteen'. It serves breakfast and lunch and overlooks the training pitches. Boro's academy players have their own changing room and their own canteen. The young guys must earn the right to sit at the same table as their elders.

One weekend I spoke with Woody on the phone, the Oxford lads had just eaten breakfast at their team hotel on the morning of the game. He told me each player had to pay for his own breakfast. That same weekend we flew from Teesside to London for a match against Chelsea. We stayed at the Royal Garden hotel in Kensington, had dinner, breakfast and pre-match snack, overlooking Kensington Gardens. Everything was, of course, taken care of by the club. We then flew home after the game.

Andy

Saturday, 8 February 2003

We are on the team coach, moving out of Rochdale with a three-hour journey back to Oxford. After that I will have a two-hour drive to London. If I can't wriggle out of this, it will be the early hours of Sunday before I'm home. But, of course, I've got a plan. My cousin is driving behind the team bus, knowing we will stop at motorway services for a bite to eat, and I'm hoping the manager, Ian Atkins, will allow me to switch from the coach to my cousin's car. If he does, I'll get home well before midnight. It has been an awful day. We couldn't afford to lose at Rochdale and at 1–1 with time almost up, we had the point we needed. They got down the flank, crossed, our centre-back slipped and their midfielder had a free header. It spun off his head, looped high into the air, and as I was a few yards off my line, it flew over my hands and into the roof of the net. It was one of those goals. Not for a second did I feel it was my fault.

Ian saw it differently and had a right go in the dressing room afterwards. Thirty-one years of age now, I've taken a lot over the years. From Alan Smith and Wally Downes at Crystal Palace and quite a few others on the way. But that day's gone and no longer do I take the shit. When Ian had a go, I told him I wasn't having it. Maybe it wasn't the cleverest way to deal with the situation but being me I don't back down if someone wrongly accuses me. When we lost at home to Wrexham the previous Tuesday, he blamed me for one of the goals and did so in front of the lads. Now it's happened for the second time in five days and I feel like every time we lose, it's my fault. It makes me paranoid. Is he losing faith in me? Is this the end? I want to nip this in the bud and piss him off. The frustrating thing was that I made four good saves today and thought I did okay. Their keeper hardly had a save but because we lost, I'm the problem. Leaving the dressing room, I asked if it would be okay for me to travel home with my cousin and get back to London three hours sooner. No, he said, he wanted me on the coach.

I tell my cousin to hang in behind the coach because we'll be stopping at a motorway services for something to eat. Ever so politely, I ask Ian again if it would be possible to switch to my cousin's car. He agrees this time and I am on the road to London.

Gareth

You have been picked to play for England. So what happens next?

You are picked up from your home and taken to the team hotel in a chauffeur-driven car. By the time you arrive, someone from the FA has already checked you into your room. If you are going to a World Cup finals or European Championships, an array of sponsors' gifts awaits you. Lots of free leisure wear, maybe a set of TaylorMade golf clubs to ensure you don't have to hire a set on the team's rest day. A laptop computer to while away the free hours, lots of CDs and other stuff. On the day of travel you check in for your flight at the team hotel, walk to the team coach and enjoy a police escort to the airport. Usually we are driven directly on to the runway and dropped at the stairs leading to our business-class seats. If forced to undergo the indignity of check-in at the terminal, we are rushed through with minimal delay. For afternoon tea on the plane we are served a scone with clotted cream and I confess that has always been a personal favourite.

At the other end of our journey we walk off our flight and on to the coach that takes us to our team hotel. Immigration, luggage carousels – they are for ordinary passengers. Our luggage is delivered to our rooms about twenty minutes after our arrival; any longer and the boys get restless. Same smooth arrangements for the return journey and often the same chauffeur-driven car to taxi you home. On an early trip with the England team, a golf day was organized. We got to the club and I was about to pay the green fee when someone said, 'Don't be ridiculous.' At first, it staggered me. Being on England duty meant you got a good match fee, a cheque from the players' pool for being in the squad, a bonus from your boot sponsor for representing your country and Aston Villa, my club at the time, continued to pay my wages. While you're away with England, everything is paid for. Food, phone bills and laundry; 'Just sign here, sir.' And what's that in my room? An envelope with £60 in it! A little something to cover out-of-pocket expenses. When wages rocketed, the FA discontinued the £60 payment but we've borne the loss stoically.

Two years before I played for England, my wages at Crystal Palace were £700 a week. Then I went away with England and felt like the most pampered sportsman on the planet. That first time, I laughed and laughed. Not smugly, not boastfully, just at the ridiculousness of it all.

Andy

I have travelled more miles than an Eddie Stobart truck.

After Northampton Town signed me from Exeter City (with Exeter's administrators cheering in the background), it took me two and a half hours each morning to travel from my home in south London to Northampton. Along the way I would pick up our player–coach Danny O'Shea. For the journey home Danny contributed a flask of tea and biscuits, I brought the sandwiches. Later on Anna and I moved to Northampton and training was just fifteen minutes down the road. That was bliss. After I moved to Brentford in 1999, we bought a house in south London and have been there ever since. Clubs in the lower leagues can't afford to pay relocation expenses and given the insecurity of the footballer's life, it would be madness to move house every time you moved club.

When I went on loan to Southend three years ago, we had only one car and I couldn't very well ask Anna to get buses and trains to work. Instead I walked into an exchange market in Caterham and bought a mountain bike. Ninety pounds, the guy wanted. I haggled and got him down to £75. I then travelled to Southend by mountain bike and train. The journey was not what you associate with the life of a footballer. Out of bed at 6.30, on the bike at 7 a.m. to make my way down the unbelievably steep hill to Warlingham station. The station master at Warlingham was a Grimsby fan and every morning he reminded me of the 1998 Division Two play-off at Wembley when Grimsby beat North-ampton. It seemed to brighten his morning. The train pulled in at 7.25 and the trick was to be close to where the baggage and freight carriage would arrive. Get the bike on board and from there to London Bridge. The train would chug along, getting more packed at each station. Young guys in their classy suits, earning big bucks in the City, but I wouldn't have swapped with them. If we had to trade places, I reckon I would have done better in their jobs than they would have done in mine. From London Bridge I cycled to Liverpool Street and took the train to Southend. That was always a quiet train and a pleasant journey. From the station in Southend, I rode to Roots Hall stadium. The bike was hidden away in one of the youth-team offices as the boys would have found inflated tyres too great a temptation.

The return journey was tougher as it came after training and ended with the steep climb up the hill from Warlingham station. At the end of a loan period that lasted almost three months, Southend decided they didn't have the money to take me on. And I was on my bike again, this time on loan to Colchester.

The following season things improved. Signed by Colchester, I got together with Scott Fitzgerald, Bobby Bowry and Anthony Allman and became part of a car pool. Each of us drove for a week and then had three weeks off. Anna and I bought a second car, a Ford Ka because it was the cheapest new car on the market and repayments were minimal. Late in 2001, it was actually my late mum's birthday, 18 December, I picked up Scott and Bobby in Warlingham, Anthony at Dartford. At the Dartford Tunnel, I missed the lane for the auto toll and ended up in a longer queue. 'Fuckin' hell, Woody, asleep, mate, you were fucking asleep.' Eventually they calmed down and between Junctions 30 and 29 on the M25, we were bombing along in the outside lane in my little Ka when a Sainsbury truck jack-knifed and careered across the road towards us. It was one of those dreadful split-second decisions: accelerate and try to get past or brake and hope it misses? I put my foot to the floor but the car hit the central reservation and spun out of control. Not made to take on trucks, the Ka disintegrated. The truck buried itself in the central reservation.

Facing the wrong way now, there was a deathly silence in our car as we waited for oncoming vehicles to plough into us. But the Sainsbury lorry, which was spread across the road, shielded us. We got out of the car and Fitzy chirped that there wouldn't have been a problem if it hadn't been for me missing the auto toll back at the Dartford Tunnel. All Woody's fault, again. The M25 was immediately closed between Junctions 29 and 30, the traffic backed up for ten miles, the police turned up and when we went to look at the debris, we realized how fortunate we had been. An instant after we got through, a second articulated lorry ploughed into the Sainsbury lorry and we had come within half a second of being wiped out. Four more names on the M25 death roll.

Anna and I had booked to see *The Lion King* that evening and though she wanted me to give it a miss, I thought it wouldn't be a problem. But at the theatre I began to shiver. Delayed shock, I think they call it. It had been that close. That night I hugged Freddie and Isobelle in their sleep and thanked God I was there to do it.

The driving is one part; the scrimping and saving is another. Playing in Division Three affects every aspect of our lives. I played for Exeter City, Northampton Town, Brentford, Southend United, Colchester United and now Oxford United. At every club between Palace and Oxford, I washed my own training kit. No big deal you think. Well, you're not the one doing the washing. Unlike an outfield player, a goalkeeper can not train without being covered in mud or in finer weather picking up the green stains that are even harder to remove. Anna would not tolerate my leaving dirty kit for her. So I divide my kit into two loads and get everything done in two washes. It takes its toll on the washing machine as the grit and the grime clog up the filter. Next thing you notice, Anna's white blouse isn't coming out white any more and it's war. 'Andrew, the washing machine is being destroyed by your stuff.'

'What am I supposed to do? It's got to be washed.'

'What am I supposed to do when the kids' school shirts don't come out white?'

'We'll have to get a new machine.'

If we didn't divorce over washing machines, we won't over anything else.

We get on with it easily enough because Anna has no illusions about life in the lower leagues. Oxford has been one of my better experiences. They wash our training gear but they too have their moments. One day we complained there was no orange squash to flavour the water for a first-team game. We were told it was part of the club's cost-cutting. How much is a bottle of squash? Two quid? When we play away from home, the deal is that if you had a microwave dinner on the way to the game, you can't have one on the journey home. The club pays for just one microwave dinner per player. Boots and gloves are, of course, your responsibility.

Yet in this league, nothing bothers me except the thought that it will end pretty soon. That night coming from Rochdale, still down about the manager blaming me for the opposition's winning goal and waiting for the right moment to ask if I could jump into my cousin's car, I felt utterly miserable. And the thought did strike me: 'Wouldn't it be better to work in a job that brought more money and less grief?' The answer is no. Nothing out there has the same buzz, the same feeling of living life to the full. Even after a terrible day in Rochdale, I could see that. The money hasn't been a problem and nothing will stop me from playing except injury or, far more likely, someone deciding I'm no longer good enough. That'll be hard because there will not be any nest egg to fall back on and my football pension won't keep the wolves from the door. But as I say to Anna, something always turns up. I have never begrudged the Premiership player a penny of his £40,000-a-week wages. Clubs have always exploited players and now the big players are able to turn the tables on clubs.

One thing the game has taught me is that loyalty means nothing. You are a lump of meat, to be off-loaded as soon as you reach your sell-by date. If there is one bee in my bonnet, it is the Premiership player who thinks he's got it tough. What he needs is three or four hours' travelling to training every day and then to come home and wash his own kit. There was a story in the newspaper the other evening about the Newcastle player Kieron

Dyer asking the team coach to stop because he had left his diamond earring in the changing room at Villa Park.

He would have had a long walk if he had tried that one on us.

Gareth

Footballers at the highest level are frequently recognized and constantly fussed over. It is something they are used to. Despite what you may believe, it isn't always as joyous a life as you might imagine. If you missed *that* penalty against Germany in Euro 96, your face becomes a reminder of a dismal night in England's football history. Not easy. Yeah, I tell myself, time has moved on, people aren't bothered about that any more and then you are inside the hotel lobby and a girl turns to her boyfriend and says, 'I think that's the guy that missed the penalty'. 'Shssh,' he says but too late. It brings a smile to my face now, along with the thought that it is a small price to pay for the privileges we enjoy. They pay top footballers like they pay rock stars, movie stars and . . . actually, I can't think of any other profession that is as well paid.

I have been in this league for twelve years and played over fifty times for my country. Middlesbrough football club pay me the going rate for a player with my credentials. I don't speak about my wages because it feels to me like I am rubbing people's noses in it, but it is worth bearing in mind that thirty-five years ago Clive, my dad, was offered an opportunity to become a professional footballer with Luton Town but the pay was not sufficient to tempt him to give up his job with IBM. We earn money our fathers couldn't have dreamt of.

It is wrong, it is obscene even. An insult to social workers, firemen and school teachers for sure. But football is now part of the entertainment industry and a major player in television's ratings wars. Players have been the beneficiaries. Clubs spend too much of their income on player wages but that's their lookout. Am I going to say, 'Hang on a minute here, pay me a little less and get your house in order'? Hello! And why is it that those who complain about footballers' lavish earnings never question the rewards given to the stars of rock and film? Is it that footballers, most of whom come from lower-income families, are seen as less deserving? Maybe it's just that music and acting seem out of reach while everyone's got a bit of football inside them. I don't know.

When I returned to Aston Villa as a Middlesbrough player in the November of the 2001–02 season, the Villa fans sang 'There's Only One Greedy Bastard', as fans do when players return to a club they have recently left. It annoyed me because money has never been the motivating factor in my career. Middlesbrough was the only club with whom I discussed money and after I agreed to accept their offer, there was a call from West Ham. 'Have you signed?' they asked.

'No, I haven't but I have given . . .'

'We'd be prepared to pay you more than Middlesbrough.'

They didn't ask what had been agreed with Boro but were still willing to pay more. My word to the Middlesbrough chairman was my word though. I have never haggled with a club over money and don't suppose I ever will. Football allows me to help my family or Alison's family if either needs help. It has enabled me to provide for the future of our family and at thirty-two, I appreciate how fortunate we are in this respect. Since the wages escalated, I try to keep a grip on reality. Teddy Sheringham, Stuart Pearce, Tony Adams and I played a game of hearts when on England duty, a fiver a game, and it was fought for tooth and nail. There are many England players with the same outlook, you just don't hear about us. Dull blokes, maybe. The first really nice car I had was a Jaguar XK8 bought in my early years at Aston Villa. It cost close to £50,000 and seemed so indulgent. I hummed and hahed for ages because it was hard to justify spending that amount on a car. The Jaguar was a nicer car than the cheaper Mercedes diesel I now drive but being in the Jaguar didn't make me any happier.

I struggle with the celebrity thing even more. When going out for an evening with Alison, she will sometimes ask, 'For God's sake, Gareth, put on a baseball cap and a pair of dark glasses, I'm fed up with people coming up to you.' But it's just not me. Sorry, I've got to do it my way. People do approach me and make conversation but generally they're friendly and move on quickly enough. One night with Woody and Anna in London we decided to go to the Ivy restaurant but didn't have a reservation. Of course, the restaurant said they couldn't fit us in. Woody got straight on the phone. 'Good evening. I'm Gareth Southgate's agent, Gareth and I and our wives were wondering if we could get a nice table this evening.' And, of course, it wasn't a problem. I couldn't pull a stunt like that. Woody reasons he would have been unbearable if he had become well-known. But you've got to recognize the falseness for what it is and try to be taken for who you are rather than what you are. Woody's selling himself short. He knows the difference.

There is so much bullshit, though. You will be in a shop buying clothes and the assistant attending you tips off his manager that you are a well-known footballer. The manager comes along, makes a fuss and offers you a good discount. I am thinking, 'In actual fact, I'm maybe the one person in this shop who should have to pay the full price. I can afford it.' You take the discount because the shop is still making a good profit but it still seems ludicrous.

When we have gone on holidays with Woody, Anna, Freddie and Isobelle, money is an issue but one we don't speak about. I might pay for a few of the bigger expenses but then we go halves when we eat out. There is a temptation to think, 'Well, I earn so much more than him, I should pay for everything,' but that's not right. People have their pride and it wouldn't be a proper friendship if one person paid for everything. I can hear Woody saying, 'Okay, let's settle for an improper one then,' but he wouldn't mean it. We mostly eat in restaurants that are not ridiculously expensive and if we go to a golf course with exorbitant greens fees, I will pay. It is a question of balance; not being tight but always keeping our friendship on a sound footing.

I don't want to abuse the privileges and that was why I agonized before agreeing to do the Pizza Hut ad after Euro 96. Newspapers and magazines all offered good money if I would pour out my heart about the penalty miss. But it was too close to the event and I turned them down. Months passed, the furore died down and the Pizza Hut ad seemed to me an opportunity to poke a little fun at myself and at the same time show people I had moved on. Stuart Pearce and Chris Waddle, who would co-star in the ad, were keen for me to do it. We were offered £40,000 each and their fees depended upon my involvement. 'Come on,' said Pearcey, 'are we doing this ad or not?' We went down to a studio in London and Stuart and Chris did their parts in no time. Long after they were gone, I was still there trying to get it right. It was nine o'clock at night before they got something that was usable.

Some people were upset: 'You've cashed in on your failure with the England team.' I could see where they were coming from but I'm afraid I saw it differently. If the experience of missing that penalty taught me anything, it was that football is only a game. Many of those who wrote to me after Euro 96 had suffered real loss in their lives. Need I say any more? In my first season at Middlesbrough, one of the good guys in our dressing room, Colin Cooper, lost his son Finlay in a freak accident. That shocked us all and when I think of Colin and of his little boy, everything becomes pretty insignificant.

There is something I've learned in my football career and that is that you are wasting your time if you think you can avoid criticism. Most of the time I'm portrayed as an okay if pretty dull bloke. Then when I stick a paper bag over my head on national television and make an idiot of myself, people hammer me for not taking things seriously enough. You can't win!

17

I don't like to commit myself about heaven and hell — you see, I have friends in both places.

  Mark Twain

Gareth

He went without saying goodbye. Alen Boksic. Croatia's finest. One day he was there: tall, aloof, unconcerned. The next day, gone. There were rumours about a move to Spurs, another about an injury that could keep him out for some time. We were his team-mates; how would we know? Then one morning at training someone asked, 'Where's Alen?' No one knew, but Michael Ricketts, our new signing from Bolton Wanderers, was told to change in the locker over there. Alen's locker. For two and a half years, Alen had played at Middlesbrough. Lived in a village near Darlington, the house rented for him by the club. Did his own thing. What did Middlesbrough mean to him? Was there sadness for him in leaving? To whom did he say goodbye? From his yacht on the Dalmatian coast, will he follow Boro's results? Alas poor Alen, we didn't know him well.

Steve McClaren sat me down in the summer of 2001. I was his first signing as Middlesbrough manager. 'These are the guys you will be playing alongside this season,' he said. He went through the players individually, indicated those he felt he could depend on and those who might be useful in the short term. Things would change over the course of the season as Steve got to know people better but Alen Boksic was always meant to play a key role. Steve reckoned that when Boro dropped into the relegation zone the previous season and Terry Venables was brought in to help Bryan Robson, the team simply tightened at the back and relied upon Alen for goals. Put those goals together, make a little video of them and the montage would be spellbinding. Alen's goals tended to be a reflection of his own character. They were imperious. I remembered him from his time with Lazio and Juventus and looked forward to playing on the same side as a striker who was clearly one of the best of our generation.

Some doubts tempered my enthusiasm though. Against Villa the previous season, Alen had been quiet. Injured, I watched from the stand and noticed that when he was substituted with twenty minutes to go, Alen waved to the Boro supporters and jogged straight down the tunnel. Boro were deep in a relegation battle and I wondered how concerned he was about the team's plight. Might he not have watched the closing minutes from the substitutes' bench? There was also the rumour that he was earning twice as much as the majority of his team-mates and that raised other questions. Was it purely money that brought him to and kept him at Middlesbrough?

From the first few days of pre-season training, it was obvious Alen was not prepared to go with the new regime. In Steve McClaren's vision for Boro, everyone works together and no one seeks or receives special treatment. There can be big characters but no prima donnas. It is what Steve saw at Old Trafford when he was Alex Ferguson's assistant and what he believed to be right.

Steve's right-hand man, Bill Beswick, is a keen follower of the NBA and often draws from professional basketball when making a point to us. Bill told us about the multi-millionaire stars of basketball Michael Jordan and others, who had no difficulty making personal sacrifices for the good of the team. As a Croat, Alen would have been a basketball fan but he didn't conform. In fact, I have taken quite a liberty in using the words 'Alen' and 'conform' in the same sentence. They were complete strangers.

It takes just two or three days to sense the mood in any dressing room; to know the players who are respected, those who are not. There will be leaders and followers, honest professionals and shirkers. Alen was none of these: he was simply himself, a one-off. I sensed the lads didn't like him and it was easy to understand why. Pre-season training is tough; they run you till you drop and then some more. You get through it as a group, one lad encouraging another, dragging each other through the last 800m or the last set of abdominal exercises. Alen didn't see it like this. When he felt he had done enough, he walked away from the group and began his warming-down exercises. The remarkable part was the complete lack of embarrassment, the refusal to excuse himself. We would plough through the last 400m while he did his own thing on the other side of the pitch. This was new to me, as was the fact that no one challenged him. There were two sets of rules at Boro: rules for Alen and rules for the rest.

Intrigued, I asked questions of the other players. What was Alen's problem? 'Would you be bothered for sixty grand a week?' someone said. Well, yes actually, I would. In fact for that money any normal player would feel a particular responsibility to the club. Alen wasn't any normal player. At first it seemed to me he was a shirker, the kind of guy who would sleep on the floor if lying in bed was work. But that was not the case. One evening I was at the training ground at four o'clock and Alen turned up to train on his own. He would work with Chris Barnes, head of Sports Science at Middlesbrough, and it was something he did quite often. He pushed himself but not when he was with the group. He was more complex than people realized, and having been unsympathetic in my dealings with another complex centre-forward, Stan Collymore, I was determined to do better with Alen. Strikers, particularly the better ones, tend to have big egos and a natural selfishness. Tools of the trade perhaps. Alen, I admit, interested me.

Conversation, though, was not easy. My first attempts were greeted with a distinctly eastern European distrust. 'Why do you want to be friends with me?' his expression said. Other players had tried to get to know him but been put off by his wariness. Nothing was going to deter me, though. I asked him about some of the guys he had played with at Lazio and Juventus and felt that as an England inter-national, I had some credibility with him. He was like that; there were lots of players he didn't rate and when some of the lads had the ball, he would not bother making a run because he didn't think they would be able to make the pass. He was no chaser of lost causes.

I persisted where others had been put off: 'Did you enjoy playing with him?', 'What was Zidane like?', 'Did you get on well with Lippi?' Robbie Mustoe, one of the Premier-ship's most honest pros, used to inquire about my progress. Was I getting anywhere? Robbie had played at Boro for ten years and seen the foreign stars come and go. He told me about Emerson, Branco and Marco Branca; players who came for the big wages and often went missing, on and off the field. Players, ultimately, that cost Middlesbrough as much in dressing-room harmony as in extravagant wages.

Andy

Alen Boksic a bit different? Where I come from he wouldn't get in the top ten.

I bumped into Dave Martin, who played with us at North-ampton, in the bar one evening after a home game. Unable to play because of injury, Dave was already there with a couple of mates and well into a little session when I arrived. They were loud and Dave was drifting into Crazy-Gang mode. He had been at Wimbledon during the wild years and claimed full membership of the Crazy Gang. As we stood around talking, a waitress offered us a plate of mixed vegetables. 'If she comes this way again, I'm going to tip those vegetables over her head,' Dave said. 'Yeah, sure, Dave,' I said, 'you were just the tea boy for Vinny Jones and the other big hitters in the Crazy Gang. I know Wally Downes, Wally was real Crazy Gang. He would do things, not just talk about them.'

The bull had seen the red rag. Four or five minutes later, the waitress came with another plate of vegetables. As she weaved her way through the lounge it was obvious what was going to happen and I felt unbelievable guilt. Dave was wound up and determined to prove himself. She was about forty, a pleasant woman about to have a seriously unpleasant experience. A couple of feet from Dave she stopped and he took the silver platter out of her hands and tipped the lot over her head. Shocked, the poor woman stood motionless in the silent room. Dave then proceeded to rub the vegetables into her permed hair. It was a dreadful incident and something that only a lunatic would do. With a few drinks inside him, Dave was close to that. She stormed out of the room. Not realizing just how out of order he had been, Dave kept saying, 'The Crazy Gang lives on.' The embarrassment was enormous and the humiliation of the waitress was disgusting.

On Monday morning Ian Atkins hauled him in, tore him to pieces and made him write a letter of apology to the woman. But he didn't kick Dave out of the club because football is a winning business and those players who help the team to be successful get away with things off the field. Dave had a fantastic will to win and he could be almost heroic on the pitch. The madness was a factor there too because he put the fear of God into the opposition. Often he scared me and I was on his team.

Dave was a typical cockney lad who had played for Millwall, Wimbledon, Bristol City, Southend, Leyton Orient, Brighton and many others. I tell a lie. Dave wasn't typical anything. On his first day at training with us he nipped into the physio's room, picked up a pair of scissors and cut the sleeves off Ian's shirt. He then cut the tops off his socks before putting them back into the shoes. What Dave was saying to us was, 'Look, you tossers might cut up a shirt or some socks, but which of you would do it to the gaffer?' Ian took one look at the damage and worked out that no one except Dave would have had the bollocks to do that. The gaffer loved him for it.

Dave got us going in the tunnel before games and wound up the opposition by saying things no proper human being would say to another. With Dave, nothing was off-limits. Mums, dads, sisters, wives, girlfriends, they were all dragged into Dave's search for a man's weak spot. If they reacted, they were taking on a bloke who relished a fight. If they didn't, they were cowards.

Dave wouldn't admit when he was beaten. He struggled with his fitness and Ian would get the physio to run him till he dropped. Dave complained the gaffer was killing him and he wasn't taking any more. Then Ian walked into the changing room and Dave's mood changed. 'I'm still standing,' he belted out, not exactly improving Elton John's song but making his point. Ultimately that was why the gaffer signed him and why he survived in the game. For all his lunacy, you wanted him in your team.

Gareth

We didn't know whether we wanted Alen in our team or not. I felt we were a better side with Alen leading the attack but there was another view that in matches where we had our backs to the wall, he could be a passenger. This was especially true for away games. What was indisputable was that during Alen's time at the club it was impossible to have total harmony in the dressing room. It wasn't just that he was paid more than everyone else (and in many cases, vastly more) but that he contributed so little to the team's spirit. The best-paid guy happened to be the least committed. Robbie and several of the club's steady pros were never paid anything like Alen but they carried us through the difficult winter weeks when spirit in the dressing room counted for as much as talent on the pitch. When Steve McClaren took over at the club, he didn't see Robbie as a regular in our first eleven. He was, after all, a 33-year-old central midfielder and the manager probably thought he would need fresher legs alongside another seasoned player, Paul Ince. But Robbie didn't accept he was too old and fought for his place. He and Incey were critical to our survival in the Premiership in that season. What I particularly liked about Robbie was his ability to see beyond the game; to be more than Robbie Mustoe, professional footballer. He had overseen the building of his own house and was in the process of overseeing the building of another. Within the dressing room, he was hugely popular and I had tremendous respect for him.

Like me, Robbie is interested in how footballers are managed and was fascinated to see how Steve handled the players he had inherited. Robbie was also intrigued by my efforts to connect with our Croatian friend and would be there in the background, pulling faces as I tried again to find the way into Alen. Seeing I wouldn't be discouraged, Robbie would say. 'You're not giving up, boy, are you?' After the initial coolness melted, Alen answered my questions and there was something likeable about him. Something in his *hauteur* you had to admire. There was, of course, an ulterior motive to my humouring him. I wanted more from him on the pitch. He had the ability to do the most extraordinary things with the ball. He made intelligent runs that were often missed by his team-mates. His close control was out of this world and in one-on-one situations against the goalkeeper, he was as good a finisher as I've ever seen. Early in the season we were at Chelsea, trailing 2–1 when we got a last-minute penalty. Alen hadn't done a tap throughout the match. Yet when he placed that ball, I was never as confident about any player scoring from the spot as I was about him that day.

The disappointing thing about Alen for me was his lack of flexibility. 'This is how I am, take me or leave me.' He tried as hard as he wished to try, he gave as much to the team as he wished to give. Everything was on his terms. For all my perseverance with him, I was wasting my time. Robbie knew the score. One–nil to the Croat. Our relationship was destined to go only so far; marginally beneath the surface but no further. Alen never once asked a question about anything related to my life: England, my previous clubs, my family. Nothing. In the end, he was a challenge I was happy to leave in Steve's lap. Managers earn their money dealing with the difficult guys.

One day during that first season at Middlesbrough, Bill Beswick told Robbie and me an interesting story about an American basketball coach unhappy with the spirit in the locker room. He called a meeting but before the players arrived he positioned the chairs in various clusters around the room. When the players turned up, they were confused about where to sit. 'Okay,' said the coach, 'you and you in that corner, you four over there, you three in the middle, you five at the front, you two in the other corner and the four of you, over here.' When they had all sat down in their different groups, he said, 'Now you can see the way you are in this team. Divided into your little cliques. I'm leaving the room, you lot sort it out.' When he returned fifteen minutes later, the chairs and players were all together in the middle of the room. 'Let us keep it this way,' the coach said. Bill Beswick has a way of making you see things differently. He once asked Robbie to draw up a rooming list. Robbie thought it was a psychological test and spent twenty-five minutes working out the people who might be best suited to each other. Bill simply wanted to know the usual sharing arrangements.

Soon after the story about the basketball coach, Steve called a team meeting. We filed in and Robbie and I were keen to see where people sat. The chairs were lined up in three rows across the room. We sat in the middle of the second row and watched. The younger players went to the back row, hoping by sitting at the back that the manager would not catch their eye. Incey and Ugo Ehiogu sat close to us and people generally went where you expected them to go. Everyone was seated except Alen. By the time he strolled in there were just two empty seats. One was in the middle of the group, the other in the front row and slightly left of centre. As soon as Alen entered, Robbie nudged me. 'Here he comes.' We held our breath as he walked towards the front row. It appeared he was going to take a seat roughly where you expect the teacher's pet to sit. Wrong. He dragged the empty chair across the room to the back, close to the door through which he had just come in. That way he was near the exit, far away from Steve and detached from his own team-mates. Mustoe and Southgate almost convulsed with laughter on their chairs: 'Analyse *that*!'

Except you didn't need to be a psychologist to work it out. Alen was a loner. For him, football wasn't about the togetherness of the team. Was he different when he played for Croatia? Would he have pulled his chair away from his compatriots? I doubt it. Had he realized what Robbie and I were laughing at, he would have had a little laugh at himself. He was aware of his idiosyncrasies. He would laugh but he wouldn't change. He read the club's rules as an à la carte menu: 'I'll have this, this and this.' The rules said no mobile telephones at the training ground and everyone had to be in the changing room by ten for a 10.30 start. In would stroll Alen at 10.05, mobile phone glued to his ear. If you challenged him, he might shrug or feign ignorance. His grasp of English often depended upon what was being said or who was saying it. He would be on the training pitch before 10.30, what was the problem? If you tried to explain his behaviour undermined the manager's authority and set a bad example, his quizzical look would again remind you that English was not his first language.

Andy

On the morning of my first game at Wembley for Northampton, the 1997 Division Three play-off final against Swansea, about six of us went for a walk to the ground. We stayed at the nearby Hilton so it wasn't far. The hot-dog stalls and sandwich bars were being rolled into place and set up along Wembley Way. Inside the ground, we headed straight for the tunnel. Even at ten o'clock in the morning, with the stadium empty and silent, it had an unbelievable effect on us. Six years later and the memory still sends a tingle down my spine. We had grown up watching the FA Cup final and the picture of both teams lined up in the tunnel before the game was vivid in the minds of all of us. Now we would walk through that tunnel before playing the biggest match of our lives.

Five hours later we were lined up in the tunnel when all hell broke loose. Glancing behind me, I could see our centre-forward, John Gayle, standing toe-to-toe with Swansea's Carl Heggs. John was 6ft 3in and intimidating. He tried to wind up Carl but Carl was having none of it. The other lads tried to keep them apart. Roger Freestone, the Swansea goalkeeper, said, 'That's all I need, someone winding up John Gayle.' Roger, understandably, didn't want John's level of aggression any higher than it usually was. As we walked out, fireworks were being set off on the pitch and I thought, 'Hey, we've already had them in the tunnel.'

The following season we were in Division Two and Ian Atkins wanted to strengthen the squad. One of the players he went for was Carl Heggs. Heggsy turned up at Northampton during pre-season training, dressed in a nice suit and apparently keen to join us. He waited in reception to have talks with Ian. Word went round he was there and John Gayle went straight to reception. Heggsy was sitting down when John walked in. 'Hey, we've got some unfinished business,' said John.

'Leave it, I'm here to have talks with your gaffer. If I sign and you feel the same way, we can have a straightener.' As Heggsy spoke, he got to his feet just in case John was going to have a go.

His instinct was spot on. Bang! John caught Heggsy smack in the face and sent him flying across the receptionist's desk. Heggsy picked himself up, grabbed a computer off the desk, threw it at John and then landed a couple of decent punches of his own. These guys were heavyweights. Four or five lads jumped in and tried to separate them. The women at reception were petrified. Heggsy's eye was already swollen and John's lip was cut.

In walked Ian to meet his potential new signing. Heggsy's shirt was torn off his back, the swelling around his eye was getting bigger and the gaffer was smiling from ear to ear. If he had had any doubts about Heggsy, they were dispelled by the cut on John's lip. He was as good as signed. Next day he came into our changing room for the first time. His eye was more or less closed. No one was sure what to say. The ice was broken by John. Still bearing the marks of the previous day's set-to, he went straight over to Heggsy and in front of all the lads shook his hand and said, 'Respect, man, respect.' After that the two of them got on great.

No characters left in the game, they say.

Gareth

Alen was a nightmare for Steve. Here was a player inherited from the previous regime, an individual whose character and behaviour went against everything Steve believed in for a strong dressing room. He probably wanted to move Alen on but given his age, his injury record and his wages at Middlesbrough, there were no takers. Paying up his contract was not an option because the sums involved were too great. So Steve tried to focus on the positive: Alen could score. So we tried to forget his constant litany of injuries and illnesses. Six viruses during his two and a half years at Boro, according to the local newspaper. We learned to live with his indifference to what we were trying to create. But no matter how well we got on with it, the bottom line was the club could not move forward until he was moved out.

I dealt with Alen better than I had done with Stan Collymore. Patience where once there had been impatience, acceptance where once I had felt frustration. Most important of all, I did not allow Alen's attitude to affect my performance in the way Stan's had.

In the days after Alen vanished, there was plenty of talk among the lads. We believe some agreement must have been worked out with the club which paid him at least part of the remaining six months of his contract, otherwise Alen would never have gone – the wages were too good. There is also speculation that the club had to pay him a bonus for seeing out his contract, a reward for his 'loyalty' to Middlesbrough. Someone asks why he wasn't paid off earlier and the reason is simple: it would have cost too much. I think of other players who have left Boro recently: Steve Vickers to Birmingham, Curtis Fleming to Crystal Palace and my old sparring partner, Robbie Mustoe, who gave far more and got far less. Robbie would have loved to finish his Premiership career with Boro. But even the kitchen lady had to go, the club unwilling to match the offer of the local nursing home who came up with £50 a week more. I understand a business must be run as a business but it does grate that Super Al may have got a golden fucking handshake. People have given Alen everything for years and he's done them. 'Done them proper,' as Woody would say.

You may wonder at this but I bear Alen no malice. He treated football the way football treats most of the players: he screwed it. A scene from *One Flew over the Cuckoo's Nest* springs to mind, the point where the Chief suddenly reveals he could talk and understand all along. You fucker, Chief! Alen understood all along, of course he did, and we knew it. What was remarkable was the balls, the sheer brazenness with which he went about his business. At the end of the day, was he wrong? I ask that question again: was he wrong? I'm not sure he was. In most lines of work you earn as much as you can. They speak in America's professional sports of the

MEAT syndrome: Maximize Earnings at All Times. Alen adhered to the MEAT syndrome but that is no crime. That he could do this without making a major contribution to the team, though, highlights a weakness in the way football contracts are agreed.

But here is the greatest headfuck for me. He can even turn around and say he won the European Cup.

Andy

To us he was always Razor. Ray Warburton. Centre-back at Northampton Town from 1994 to 1998. What? You've never heard of him? Razor is one of the game's heroes. Goalkeepers get to know their centre-backs and it wasn't a coincidence that during the best years of my football life, Razor was centre-back. He was just six feet tall and thirteen and a half stones, smallish for a centre-half but Razor had what size and weight cannot give you. He had heart. If you were in the trenches with Razor, you had more than a chance. He's lived an anonymous life in the lower leagues but if you played with him or supported his team, you knew.

To the game, he gave more than ever he took. To each team, he gave 100 per cent and by God, that was a lot. Without being too sentimental I am proud to have played with him and it gives me a little buzz to recall big days when we were on the winning side.

He started professional football with his home-town club, Rotherham, and then moved to York City in his twenties. Early in his career, he broke his back. Two vertebrae had to be fused and the injury kept Razor out for a year. Medical opinion was that he would struggle to play again, but Razor came back and played ninety games in five seasons for York. Liverpool followed his progress, Ron Yeats was supposed to have watched him, Kenny

Dalglish was interested and stories in the *Sun* and the *Mirror* speculated that Razor was on his way to Anfield. Injury, though, plagued him and destroyed what chance he had. A disc above the fused area popped out. He had it pinned and was in a body cast for fourteen weeks. Again, they told him to pack it in. Razor came back and did his knee. Two operations later, he returned to the game but then broke his leg. For over two years, he was permanently injured and still he fought his way back. You found him in the gym first thing in the morning or straight after training in the afternoon. No one was going to take away his career.

He had been at Northampton for six months when I signed. In our time, he was the rock upon which the side was built; captain for almost five years; 169 league games; and third in a poll of Northampton fans to pick the greatest players in the history of the club. Being from Rotherham, he had a strong northern accent and though I gave him a hard time about that, it never bothered him. He was the gamest centre-half I ever played with and, without saying much, he was the best captain I have ever seen.

We played Fulham away at the time when Kevin Keegan was rebuilding the team. They had just signed Paul Peschisolido from West Bromwich Albion for £1.1m and every team in the league wanted to beat them. From the first minute they were all over us and Razor was typically brave, making blocks and crashing into people. Inside the box, the ball fell to one of their players. As he pulled the trigger, Razor dived across the line of fire. The ball went out for a corner, Razor stayed down. He lifted his hand to show me the damage. Blood was pouring from a gash in his wrist so deep you could see the bone. It almost made me sick and I immediately shouted at our physio, Dennis Casey, who raced on and got Razor off.

The sub didn't come on immediately and that amazed me. What were they playing at? The lad's wrist was hanging off. But five minutes later, stitched and strapped, Razor was back on the field. He didn't know if it was fractured but he hoped not. The pain was written in his face every time he tackled or challenged for a high ball but he never gave an inch. We drew 1–1 that day at Craven Cottage, which was a fantastic result for us. It was all down to Razor. He did go off before the end, but his commitment and attitude inspired those around him. A leader if ever there was one.

Another time we were in Cardiff for the first leg of the 1997 Division Three play-off semi-final. We knew going down there that if they got an early goal, their fans would get behind them and they would give us a going over. That morning we looked at Razor and noticed how he was walking like Tin Man. Legs, hips, back; zero flexibility. The operations had tightened things up. 'Not to worry, lads,' he said, 'I'll be looser by the time the game starts.' That day he was like 'a head on a stick', attacking balls in the air and powering them clear. At the end it was Cardiff 0, Tin Man 1. What was lovely about Razor was his willingness to die for the cause and the way he could inspire others to do the same.

We beat Cardiff 3–2 at home and were heading for the first of two appearances at Wembley in consecutive years. In Northampton it felt like we had made the FA Cup final. We were measured up for suits, shirts and ties. There was a factory in the town that produced Church's shoes – which are top of the range and can cost over £200 – and the captain was invited to bring the shoe sizes of everyone and choose a particular design at the factory. Of all the bloody people to pick the design, it had to be Razor. Northern lad without a touch of fashion sense, he chose black brogues. When the boxes arrived at the club, I despaired. 'Razor,' I said, 'my granddad wore shoes like this after the Second World War.' He looked at me and laughed. 'Cockney boy,' he was thinking, 'for once you will dress like a northern lad.'

We had some great times with Northampton. The following year we got to the Division Two play-off final after getting past

Bristol Rovers in the semi-final. They beat us 3–1 in the first leg – it should have been six or seven – and their centre-forward, Barry Hayles, destroyed us. At our level, Barry was world class. Our goal, scored by John Gayle, came late in the game but it didn't change anyone's opinion about who would go through. They were in a different class. Walking off the pitch, some of their players heckled our lads: 'Any spare tickets for Wembley, boys? We'll give you a decent price.'

Before the second leg at Northampton, there was an incident in the tunnel that decided everything. John Gayle began bouncing a ball off the head of a Bristol Rovers guy who turned round very quickly, as if to square up to John. 'What the fuck are you going to do?' John said before the bloke could get a word out. Poor Bristol lad was shit scared and every one of us noticed none of his mates were keen to have a go. We beat them 3–0 with Razor scoring one of the goals, Heggsy had the game of his life and we were back at Wembley. This time I chose the Church shoes and Razor stuck to football.

Razor was so good on those big days. Ever so quiet but always giving the impression that everything was under control. He played well against Grimsby in that second Wembley final and though we gave it all we had, we were beaten 1–0. I am not ashamed to admit I cried that day in Wembley. That night we had a reception at the team hotel but it was like a morgue. The next day the squad flew off for a week's break in the sun. Out there I roomed with Jason Dozzell, who had played at Ipswich and Spurs. Of course we weren't allowed to make calls from our rooms and Jason went down to reception to ring home. He was fuming on his return. His wife had opened a letter from the club that said he was no longer wanted by Northampton. Jason was a smashing fellow and didn't deserve to be treated like that. But that's the way football clubs behave. Even Razor, the club's greatest player and most loyal servant, got short shrift in the end.

Early in the 1998–99 season they pulled him in and said they had accepted an offer from local rivals Rushden & Diamonds. Razor was then thirty-one, Rushden were prepared to pay £60,000 for him and give him a wage increase. But it meant leaving the Football League and playing in the Conference, something Razor was loath to do. Anyway, he had spent almost five years at Northampton and loved the place. He knew they weren't going to match Rushden's offer so he asked chairman Barry Stonhill for a £60-a-week increase to help him to stay. The club wouldn't rise to that and Razor reluctantly moved to the Conference. We all followed his progress at Rushden & Diamonds, where he was the inspirational figure in their promotion to the Football League. His injuries then came back to haunt him. He played only one league game for Rushden and was sold on to Boston United. Injuries recurred there and Razor was shipped on to Aldershot where he's now returned to fitness and playing as well as ever.

When it's all over, he will be left with a lot of health problems. Back and knees particularly. I think of what a fantastic servant he has been to his various clubs and how, for very small money, he put his body through torture. I think too of how various clubs used and then discarded him. So when I hear stories of how Premiership players extract the last drop of blood from the bigger clubs, there is never a word of condemnation from me.

18

When the character of a man is not clear to you, look at his friends.
  Japanese proverb

Gareth

The pressure not to stand out from the crowd comes not just from inside the dressing room but from everywhere; especially from the media. During England's qualifying campaign for Euro 2004, I was asked by the FA to do an interview session with the Sunday newspaper journalists in the week of the away game in Liechtenstein. It struck me as odd that I should be doing the interview as I wasn't in the team at the time and on the evidence of the previous qualifier against Macedonia, I was fourth choice. Still, I have always found it easy to deal with the media and generally they have been very fair to me, so I spent almost an hour with the journalists before our departure for Liechtenstein.

In hindsight, it is easy to see there was an agenda. In the previous qualifying game against Macedonia, Sven-Goran Eriksson had chosen Jonathan Woodgate to partner Sol Campbell when Rio Ferdinand was injured. I was deeply disappointed because Jonathan had not previously been preferred to me. The journalists were obviously going to ask me about Sven, reckoning I might be feeling a little aggrieved. Rather than give the usual pat answers, I tried to be honest. I talked about going to Sven after I had been left out and asking him what I needed to do to improve. As I explained to the press men, it is easy to sulk and complain in private but I wanted Sven to know that this mattered to me and that though I was thirty-two, age hadn't lessened my desire to play for England. To be honest, Sven didn't really enlighten me but that didn't surprise me. Lots of managers struggle to give you reasons why they have picked someone else. The reason is often a simple one: they fancy the other guy more, but they can't bring themselves to tell you. Human nature.

What Sven said was I would always be part of his squad but that he picked the team. That was it. I half-expected this but still wanted him to understand my disappointment, otherwise it would be too easy for him to leave me out. And as I said to the journalists, I am an Englishman first, a footballer second; playing for my country means everything to me. When I return from international duty, I don't have Champions League matches to dilute the disappointment of not having played for England. If I expressed any disenchantment, I countered it with plenty of positive things about Sven and the set-up.

We talked also about the chemistry of the current England team and I expressed reservations about having a side that was young and lacking in senior pros. Of course, I had a vested interest because at this stage of my career I qualify as a senior pro. Still, the observation was genuine. I made the point that there was a danger in always wanting to find 'the next bright young thing'. From there we got talking about the collective character of the England team and I said many of the lads were young and quiet. Not many were comfortable speaking up and asking questions but in time they would grow in confidence and this would improve.

The character of our young players is now being shaped

in the clubs' high-tech academies. Today's generation of young stars don't clean boots, they don't mix with the senior players like we did as kids and they are not subjected to the banter that was central to the old way. As a result, a lot of them are not good at accepting criticism and getting involved in the endless football discussions that used to be common-place. Now, after dinner, the majority go to their room to watch their DVDs or call their agents.

I spoke openly and could sense the surprise in the room at my candidness. They were obviously going to focus on my disappointment at being left out for that Macedonia game but if they were being half-honest, they would have seen that what I said was balanced and fair. Most of them did. The *News of the World* and the *Sunday Mirror* went a different route and with the help of their headline writers produced pieces that didn't reflect what I had said. Basically, they printed the criticisms, excluded all the qualifying bits and conveyed an impression that I was having a go at Sven and my fellow players. I should have known better and accepted that you can't be open and straightforward with an audience needing headlines. It bothers me that we should have to be so guarded and so bland.

The timing couldn't have been more damaging. With Sol Campbell injured, Sven chose me ahead of Jonathan and put me in the team for the Liechtenstein game. Great, but the day after the match the Sunday newspapers would hit the streets and I had heard on the grapevine that the *News of the World* was going to sensationalize what I had said. I was annoyed, more at my own naivety than at the newspaper. I should have known better.

We won 2–0 in Liechtenstein and though it wasn't much of an England performance, the criticism of the side in the following day's papers was over the top. And, of course, my supposed slating of Sven and the team couldn't have surfaced at a worse time. It was three days before a hugely important qualifying match against Turkey and I was portrayed as being contemptuous of Eriksson and the England set-up. Sol was fit for the Turkey game and it was obvious he would be reunited with Rio in the centre of the defence. Sven put Jonathan on the bench and many people saw it as a rap on the knuckles for me. I don't believe it was. I spoke with Sven and briefly explained that what the two newspapers had reported was inaccurate. He said he didn't worry about such things.

I don't think there was anything sinister in his putting Jonathan on the bench. Danny Murphy had come on against Liechtenstein and done very well but Sven put Frank Lampard on the bench for Turkey and left out Danny. My feeling was that the same logic had applied in my case. He wanted to involve as many of the squad as possible. We played really well against the Turks, won 2–0, but when you don't play, it doesn't mean much. I drove away from the Stadium of Light that night with very mixed feelings.

Andy

Gareth called that Wednesday night and though the team had won well, he was pretty down. That stuff in the newspapers had got to him and the fact that he might have damaged his chances of playing for England again. I tried to joke with him that fifty-four caps wasn't bad for a lad who had spent so long trying to win John Pemberton's place in the Crystal Palace team. And I reminded him of how happy Freddie and I are that he had got to fifty international caps. A lot of people don't realize this but once a footballer gets his fiftieth cap for England, he receives two complimentary tickets for international games once he retires. Freddie and his dad are looking forward to his retirement.

Gareth

The first time I met Sven-Goran Eriksson was the day before his first match as England coach. He was pleasant, and a little shorter than I'd imagined. England were playing Spain at Villa Park. Damaged knee ligaments ruled me out of contention but as the team were staying just a couple of miles from where we lived at the time, it was an opportunity to drop in and let the physios look at my knee. I cleared it with Michelle Farrer, the team administrator. Sven was a manager with a formidable reputation and the season before he had been interested in taking me to Lazio. I would have jumped at the prospect of playing in Serie A, but while at Villa I never got to hear about Lazio's inquiry.

After Kevin Keegan's resignation as England manager, the FA's David Davies canvassed a number of the senior England players in Helsinki about who the new man should be. My feeling was that it should be Terry Venables but suggested to David that if they were intent upon going for a foreign coach, Arsène Wenger was the obvious choice. If he was unwilling to leave Highbury, then they should go for Sven-Goran Eriksson.

Before announcing his squad for the World Cup qualifying matches against Albania and Finland, Sven telephoned. 'Look, Gareth, I have a disappointment for you. I'm not going to pick you but the door is not closed.' I was only just back from injury and not having been in any previous squad of his, it wasn't like he was dropping me. The initial disappointment subsided and I buckled down to the job of

working my way up the England rankings again. Rio Ferdinand and Sol Campbell had become Sven's first-choice central defenders and it was going to be hard for anyone to
displace them. Steve McClaren and Bill Beswick spoke to
me about the importance of hanging in and not accepting
that Rio and Sol and Martin Keown were better players than
me. We have different attributes but I believed then and still
believe I am the best centre-back in England. Through the
season leading up to the World Cup, I worked harder than I
had ever worked and played the best football of my career.

Back in the squad, I got opportunities in friendly matches
but as a second-half substitute. Newspapers revealed that in
the official weekly reports on Premiership centre-backs, I
was consistently coming out on top. The ambition to regain
my England place never wavered, even when the team
achieved the brilliant 5–1 victory over Germany in Munich.
That was amazing. Beforehand, I worried that the German's
3–5–2 formation would overrun us in midfield but, at the
same time, if our two full-backs, Gary Neville and Ashley
Cole, could bomb forward, the Germans would be in trouble
out wide. On the Thursday at Bisham Abbey, the reserves
played as Germany in a training match against Sven's team.
Sure enough, Gary and Ashley hurt us with their running but
with three central midfielders, we were able to comfortably
retain possession. Great judge that I am, I suspected England
would be in trouble.

Psychology helped us because few thought we could win
in Germany and yet we knew we had to. Would the Germans
really want to win when a draw was enough? There is always
pressure when you play for England but that evening it was
less intense than normal for a game against Germany. Their
numerical advantage in midfield allowed them to control the
first fifteen minutes but having got the lead goal, they quickly

conceded one. That was important, and when they missed a clear chance to go 2–1 up, there was a sense that England could take advantage. Steven Gerrard's outstanding goal just before half-time and Michael Owen's early in the second half killed the Germans. After that, they were devastated and we just picked them off at our leisure.

We had played really well but the key to the game was how poorly Germany had defended. How could players such as Nowotny and Worns play that stupidly? Oliver Kahn walked off with his head bowed – how seldom we have seen that! Seeing them drained and dejected was an enjoyable experience. In our dressing room, the elation was mixed with disbelief. 'What a result, what a fucking result.' Even Sven couldn't keep the surprise from his voice: 'Honestly, boys, I expected us to get a good result but never, never did I believe we would score five goals against Germany in Munich.' When we got back to England that night some of the guys stayed up and had a few drinks, as they were entitled to. I just wanted to get to bed. It was late, a little past midnight, we had Albania on the following Wednesday and my own thought was, 'We're training tomorrow and I'm going to train bloody well.' Though results under Sven had been good, the defence was conceding goals and in my eyes it was not watertight. I still believed I could get into his eleven.

After Albania, there was just the game against Greece at Old Trafford and one of the most celebrated moments in England's recent history. David Beckham's free-kick was beautifully flighted and as it came in the last minute and guaranteed qualification for the 2002 World Cup, it was the stuff of fairytale. When the game ended, the capacity crowd at Old Trafford was delirious and England's players were understandably still on the pitch. 'Everyone out,' Sven-Goran Eriksson said. Not having played, I couldn't do it. I just didn't feel part of it. I hadn't played in any of the matches under Sven and would have felt an impostor out there. I pride myself on being a good member of the squad, helping the guys who are picked and training properly but there are certain things I will not do. Celebrating with the lads on the pitch that day was one of them.

The goal was to work my way up the pecking order and start England's opening game in the tournament against Sweden. My form for Middlesbrough was excellent and a number of 'experts' were predicting that I would be in the team. The one expert who mattered though didn't see it that way. Once the squad numbers were announced, it was easy to work out Sven's team. Rio and Sol would be his centre-backs, Martin and I were the back-up; numbers 15 and 16 in the twenty-three man squad.

Andy

I am looking at the inbox of my laptop and have come across e-mails I sent to Gareth during the World Cup. Actually, the first was sent by Freddie with a note from me tagged on at the end.

> Dear Gareth,
> Please could you send me your captain's armband from the friendly against Cameroon. I will be able to be captain with my friends when I play football. I have drawn this picture and got Dad to send it to you for good luck. Thank you,
>   Love,
>   Freddie
>   PS Could you get me the red England kit like yours.

Nord, it's nice to see Freddie is following in his dad's footsteps and taking liberties with people. He tortured me to send you this picture so my neighbour Alan scanned it and sent it to you.

   Speak to you soon,
   Woody

Then there was another short e-mail I banged off after the Sweden game.

Mate,
Just watched the Sweden game. Probably the only person in the country who was gutted to see Sol Campbell score. He wasn't totally impressive up to that point but the goal was his turning point. You will definitely get your chance. Hope all is well, mate. Speak to you soon,
   Woody

Gareth

Being listed No. 16 knocked the stuffing out of me. A few years before, I would not have dealt with it very well. Nowadays I do better. You don't want to be a pain in the arse to the other guys. So you say the right things, you encourage the lads who are picked and you play your part. But I am a professional footballer; sitting and watching means nothing to me. You remind yourself about the millions who would kill to be in your place but it does no good. Japan was my fourth major championship but only at Euro 96 did I feel truly part of things. Japan was a fascinating country and there will never be a World Cup like it but I came home feeling emotionally empty. When I said to people it was a fantastic experience, I was telling a lie. Mum and Dad came to the tournament and travelled round with Ted Sheringham's mum and dad. The thought struck me that they were having a better time than me. It is the curse of not being involved in the matches. But there was no way I wanted any of the lads in the team to pick up on my disappointment, so that meant making the best of a bad situation.

Over the years I have got close to Ted Sheringham and Martin Keown and have enjoyed spending time in their company. In the England set-up, it is generally the older players who are to be found sitting round the dinner table relating stories from times gone by and trading the latest gossip from each other's clubs. The younger guys tend to disappear to their rooms, and it is the same for the foreign players with whom I've played. The younger English lads don't realize what they are missing because there is so much to learn from listening to those who have been around for a while. If an Arsenal or Manchester United player mentioned something they did at training, I would make a mental note of it and wonder if it could be of benefit to my club. Loads of little things like that.

Ted and I have been in England squads since 1995. As a player and a man I have long admired him. He is a thinking footballer and asks questions of defenders that few other strikers ask. When he drops deep, what do you do? Who is picking him up as he ghosts late into the box? He is a leader too and will make tactical decisions on the pitch. His partnership with Alan Shearer was one of the best in my time as an England player. Whether or not he was in the starting eleven, Ted contributed to the squad. He and I were the two England players chosen for drug testing after England's excellent 0–0 draw at the Olympic Stadium, Rome, in 1997.

We sat with Demetrio Albertini; the two-hour wait for pee shortened by our smug celebration of a great result. Then we were drawn again for testing in Marseilles after England's 2–0 win over Tunisia in our first game at France 98. We lamented how rotten it was for the boys in the squad who hadn't played and what a shame they couldn't feel what we were feeling. Two days later I had done my ankle, two games later Michael Owen had replaced Ted. Mugs, that's what we were. No one cared a jot when the two of us ended up on the bench.

Ted has something about him that makes you think he will eventually go into management. Similarly, I can see Martin as a manager because he too is one of the game's thinkers. Martin and I share the belief that defence is a skill, an art seldom coached in England. We were both fortunate to have worked with Don Howe and Steve Harrison, two coaches who paid particular attention to that side of the game. Martin is very intense and trains exactly as he plays. You don't upset him in a five-a-side unless you want a battle. But he was good with the younger players, generous with his time and always prepared to pass on good advice. Sven was fortunate to have Ted, Martin and myself on the bench because we didn't bitch and we did help the other guys who weren't in the team. Maybe Sven deserves the credit for knowing the players and assembling a squad that was one of the most harmonious in my eight years at international level.

You could walk into the team room and see any combination of players and staff together. Dave Seaman complaining that he was giving away twenty years to Joe Cole at their computer game. Joe is as confident off the pitch as on it but his is an innocent cockiness that's easy to like. Joe and Owen Hargreaves both had great attitude: keen to learn, eager to try new things. Joe would speak with our Dutch physical therapist, Richard Smith, and next thing he would be doing a bit of boxing or some new fitness exercise. Once he walked into the physios' room and caught me having my umpteenth massage. 'Fuck me, Gate,' he said, 'I've seen you have that many rubs I'm expecting a genie to pop out of your arse.' Joe had a way of putting a smile on your face. Lying on the treatment table, the thought struck me that if management is to be my future, I could end up signing Joe Cole or Owen Hargreaves.

Danny Mills was another one of the younger brigade whom I got to know well. He has a son around the same age as our Mia and we were together a lot when the players' families were taken to Dubai before the World Cup. Danny reminds me of Stuart Pearce in that there is a lot more to him than the supposed hard man defender. I was pleased to see him come through the mistake he made against Sweden to have a good tournament. He has the pace and athleticism to be a very good defender if he gets the right coaching.

Our victories against Argentina and Denmark were good for the side and great occasions for the fans. After the win over Argentina I spoke to Woody on the telephone and could hear cars tooting their horns in the background. 'It's going mad here, mate,' Woody said. I looked around the team bus at the players who hadn't played. 'We're going fucking mad here too,' I said. The subs were genuinely pleased the team had won, pleased for the other lads, pleased for the country but as individuals you've got to say we were totally unfulfilled. And in the end it was not a good tournament for England and left me feeling decidedly flat.

Andy

I spoke to Gareth straight after the Argie game. I was on my way to see my financial adviser, Diane Leonard. It's guys at our end of the wage scale that need financial advice. Diane's office is in Purley and on the way I saw people dancing on the roundabouts and cheering wildly. You would have thought we had won the World Cup. As I was about to walk into her office, the phone rang. It was Gareth calling from the tunnel inside the stadium. I got the impression he had no idea about the feeling at home. Typical Nord, he said he thought Sol and Rio were brilliant. There was no malice or bitterness towards the lads, just a sense of disappointment he had not been involved.

As I put the phone down, the receptionist at Diane's said, 'That's a coincidence, I have just been talking to my mate who's watched the game in a pub and you've been talking to your mate too. Did he watch it in a pub too?' I said, 'No, my mate's out there playing for England.' She said. 'Yeah, right.' I found myself having to try to convince her I wasn't a bluffer. She wouldn't believe me. Diane then came to the reception area and put her receptionist straight. It annoyed me that I got sucked into that little conversation. Still does when I think of it now.

Gareth

For every game you thought you might just get on and when the third sub went on, the game ended for you. Against Brazil, Ted was the third sub and when he went on I took off my boots and sat back. Dejected. I sensed we weren't going to turn the game round and that meant I would never again play at the World Cup finals.

Walking from the field, Martin turned to me and said, 'Well, I think that's it for me now, this is probably the last time for me with England.' We were always competitors for the same position but it didn't stop us becoming friends and it was a poignant moment as we walked back to the dressing room. Like me, Martin hadn't had much of a World Cup but there was still sadness in his decision because playing for England had meant a lot and I could relate to that. I went to see David Seaman because his anguish at the end was certainly something I could understand. David wasn't the reason we were on the way home: as a team, we hadn't played well enough. Hadn't done so in the friendlies before the World Cup and didn't do it in the tournament itself.

We had a good first half against Sweden, played our best football against what turned out to be a poor Argentina side and that was about it. We defended very well as a unit and that gave us a platform, but from where I sat, we didn't have the game plan or the individual brilliance to go all the way. Seeing countries like France, Italy, Argentina and Spain go out, you began to believe anything was possible. But that was to forget the physical tiredness that affected many of our players. Some of our key men were not 100 per cent: David Beckham struggled, Michael Owen wasn't fully fit and Kieron Dyer was rushed back into the team after injury. The difficulties for Sven are the same that every England manager faces. For all the excitement and passion it generates, the Premiership is not where you want your players in the season leading into the World Cup. It is physically punishing and does not prepare players for the technical challenge of a World Cup. It wasn't coincidental that we were so poor in the second half of the Sweden and Brazil matches.

I looked at Brazil and marvelled at their physical condition. What do they do that we don't? The idea that they drag kids off the beach or out of the slums of Rio is romantic nonsense. These guys are magnificent physical specimens who are also technically outstanding. Time after time, they mount a serious challenge at the World Cup finals. Are their lifestyles better than ours? I imagine they are. Are they better coached? Again, my feeling is they probably are. For all the hype that is generated when England go to a major tournament, our record is pretty ordinary. Winners once, semi-finalists twice in the last fifty years and two of those three tournaments were held on home soil.

On the day before the Brazil match we trained at the stadium in Shizuoka and briefly saw the Brazilians who were having a run out on the pitch. I couldn't help noticing that when our lads looked at them, it was with a touch of awe. Ronaldo, Rivaldo, Roberto Carlos; it was like we saw them as superior to us. And when it came to the critical points in the match, we did not believe in ourselves. After their second goal, our self-belief just disintegrated. Like we knew all along that they were better than us.

Andy

I was on holiday in Portugal at the time of the Brazil match. Me, Anna, Freddie and Isobelle with Anna's parents and Anna's brother Iain, his wife, Theresa, and their two kids, Elle and Alex. It was an early morning match and in a lovely villa overlooking Quinta do Lago golf course, we watched England exit the World Cup. It was strange for me because, as a fan, I wanted the lads to win, but I secretly wanted them to lose so that Gareth would get home quickly and fly out to Portugal so we could have a few rounds of golf. Through the second half, I just wanted one of the centre-backs to pick up a little injury so that Gareth could come on. He hadn't played in the World Cup and I knew he would be down about that.

When the match ended, I was obviously disappointed England were out but quite relieved my mate's role as a shadow member of the squad was over. Maybe I am biased but I do believe he gets a raw deal at international level. The only England managers who fully believed in him were Terry Venables and Glenn Hoddle and Gareth was so unlucky at France 98. The only explanation I can come up with is that he is not 6ft 4ins tall and aggressive. Because he reads situations so well, he rarely makes last-ditch tackles and that also seems to tell against him. Biased or not, I feel he should have had seventy or seventy-five caps by now.

Gareth

As England players, we have to look at ourselves more critically. Especially, we have to take greater responsibility for our physical fitness. I am thinking particularly of young and talented English players who, if they do not settle for more disciplined and professional lifestyles, are going to lose good career opportunities to foreign players. This is a trend that is already evident in the Premiership.

What I took away from a disappointing World Cup was the camaraderie in our group. There were lads in the squad who didn't play but gave everything in training and tried to hide their frustration. I enjoyed all the chats and the banter with the staff. Much of my time with England nowadays is spent in the massage room. As well as having the rubs, that is where you catch up on the gossip. Steve Slattery and Terry Byrne did tremendous work and the new physical therapist, Richard Smith, brought a new dimension to our training and the treatment of injuries. Richard opened my eyes to a lot of things regarding proper preparation for an international footballer.

And what do I make of Sven? When the FA appointed him, I thought it was an enlightened decision. I imagined we would become cleverer in the way we played. While I don't think we're that much cleverer, we are now better organized. There are limitations to the job that make it difficult for any England manager and Sven faces the same problems his predecessors had to deal with. To a great degree, the quality of England's preparation depends upon the attitude of the bigger clubs. Sven has been reasonably successful and the 5–1 result in Munich was a monumental victory. We should not forget though that the same Germans played in the World Cup final long after England had gone home.

Sven has given us a definite and easily understood game plan without broadening our tactical approach. I feel we need to expand our game to succeed at the highest level. This could happen over the next couple of seasons, as some of England's best young players gain more experience. You've got to be able to change things depending upon the opposition and the circumstances of the match. Sven brings calmness to England's preparation which, given the media attention that surrounds every game, is an achievement.

My conversations with Sven have been few. He is a quiet man who likes to observe from a distance. When he speaks to the team, he keeps it simple, makes sense but doesn't inspire. His man-management has been good with some players, not great with others. He is easy to like but difficult to get to know. For me, he remains something of an enigma. On the training ground he watches more than he participates and delegates the coaching responsibilities to his assistants which, I guess, is good management. His way is to impart quiet confidence and keep the stress levels low in the dressing room. Players appreciate that. How we finally judge Sven will depend upon results. It is ever thus in football.

Andy

When we got back from Portugal, there was a parcel addressed to Freddie Woodman. True to his word, Gareth had sent my son the captain's armband with a load of other stuff. Within minutes Freddie was out on the street, wearing the armband, king of the road. He was the captain. The other kids were all making a fuss but Freddie played it down, just said it was a present from his godfather. When he gets older, I hope he realizes just how good Gareth has been to him. Right now he thinks it's how all godfathers treat their godchildren.

It could have got off to a better start though. The night Freddie was born, Gareth was one of the first people I rang. It was four in the morning. Bleary-eyed, he picked up the phone and when I said it was a boy and we had called him Freddie, he said, 'Brilliant, mate, I am chuffed for you, give our love to Anna and we'll speak in the morning.' First thing the next morning, he called. 'Listen, mate, I had the weirdest dream last night. In the dream you and Anna had a boy and you named him Freddie. I mean who would call their son Fred: Fred Flintstone, Fred West, Fred the tortoise?'

'It was no dream, mate, but if you hadn't spent your life going around half-asleep you might have known Alfred the Great was Fred to his friends.'

Once Gareth came down to London with Ali and Mia and the three of us, Nord, Freddie and I, went to the park to play football. Nord was wearing jeans and pumps, Freddie said he was David Beckham, I was David Seaman and Gareth was allowed to be Gareth. Within ten minutes, he was covered in mud as he and

Freddie tried to score goals against me. A few kids recognized Gareth and stood there watching, amazed that an England player should play for so long with a five-year-old.

19

The shifts of fortune test the reliability of friends.
  Cicero

Gareth

Not much in life turns out to be perfect.

  I have been a full-time footballer since the age of sixteen, the second half of my life spent earning extraordinary money playing the game I loved for much of the first half. Do I still love the game? Yes, but not in the pure, untainted way of my youth. When you do something for a living, it changes your attitude towards it. We speak of going to work rather than training, of having a boss rather than a manager. Bad results get to us and stay with us in a way that wasn't possible in the days before it became our profession. There have been particular disappointments for me, principally the frustration of not playing for one of the top clubs. I wanted to experience the pressure that comes with life at Manchester United, Arsenal or Liverpool, but the opportunity never came. Perhaps this was how it was meant to be: you are given so much but not all you want. Over the last few years I have felt too often that I may have to wait for a career in management to have a shot at fulfilment. A strange thought for a man still unsure about what he wants to do after his playing days are over. The attraction of managing at the highest level is countered by the knowledge of what such a life would mean for my family. Can you be a football manager and see your kids grow up?

That's the future, a distant land. I am now thirty-three but retirement still seems a long way off. My body has stood up well to the rigours of the Premiership and I intend to continue for as long as I can at the highest level. Even with the frustration of not having been at one of the big clubs, you can't say it's been a bad career. A friend who knows both Woody and I once suggested Woody seemed more content with his lot in football than I have been with mine.

Maybe there is some truth in that. I wanted more than I got. Woody, if I've read him correctly, got more than he expected. Yet in terms of achievement and financial reward, my career has been better than his. What young footballer setting out on the professional road would say no to the career I've had? Crystal Palace got to two League Cup semi-finals, an FA Cup semi-final and I captained them to win the Division One title in 1994. In six years at Aston Villa, we were always close. Four times in the Premiership's top six although never better than fourth. We won the League Cup, got to the Uefa Cup quarter-final and I captained the team in the FA Cup final. We also lost League Cup and FA Cup semi-finals. At Middlesbrough, there has been another FA Cup semi-final. That's six losing semi-finals and two final appearances, one of which we won. As bitter as the disappointments were, I am glad to have played in those games. Wouldn't Woody have wanted to play in those matches? You bet he would. Would he have changed his salary for a Premiership salary? Silly question.

Am I more satisfied with my career than Woody is with his? Probably not. He feels an understandable sense of achievement at having survived in the professional game for sixteen years and I reckon he has played over 350 league games, been twice part of promotion-winning teams and has twice been to Wembley for play-off finals. When I went to watch him play for Exeter City in his first season – 1994–95 – away from Crystal Palace, things weren't going well and his future seemed uncertain. We went to Torquay for a quiet beer and neither of us knew if he had a future in the game. It's turned out well for him.

We have never spoken about this but I believe Woody's dreams of playing at a high level disappeared a long time ago. After he was left out of the team at Northampton and forced to find another club, he decided survival was the name of the game. From then on, his ambition seemed to be to stay in the game for as long as he could. Woody, typical Woody, survived brilliantly. But professional football in the lower divisions is no schoolboy lark. It is tough work for unexceptional pay. It wears you down, blunts your edge, forces you to accept less. Down through the years, most of Woody's team-mates would have settled for the football lives they had. I don't imagine they have sacrificed too much and as time went on, they would have given up less and less. Woody doesn't spend much time lamenting what's he missed out on.

Though I've played out my football life in the Premiership, I am deeply conscious of what I've not had. Mixing with players at international level has only deepened my lack of fulfilment. These are the guys who because of their attitude and achievements are described as 'winners'. Being with them in England squads convinced me I could perform at the highest level. Because they played with Man United and won trophies didn't necessarily mean they were better than me. My career ambitions may now be unattainable, I may retire with regrets Woody may not have.

But the ultimate question for any professional athlete is

straightforward: could I have given any more? I don't believe I could. Everything I had as a player and a person went into my preparation and my performance. It still does. Was that good enough for the highest level? Yes, I believe it was. Throughout my career I played for clubs that simply weren't good enough to win the biggest trophies. Maybe I should have been more hard-headed off the field and made sure I got myself to a bigger club. I am not beating myself up over this. I think of our daughter, Mia, and young son, Flynn – when the time comes, how shall I judge them? All that I will ask is that they commit themselves 100 per cent to whatever they are doing. Then, there will be no recriminations. How could I ask more of myself?

I wonder about Woody's response to the last question.

Andy

Could I have worked harder? Without a doubt. Especially during the seven years at Crystal Palace. They were important years because they set me on the road to the lower leagues. So you've got a choice: you can rubbish me as a guy who didn't work hard enough or you can look at where I came from. Excuses, you may say. Realities, I say. My education in south London came not from the classroom but on the streets. Streetwise, I was called. A survivor. That's what I learned. If you needed money you played snooker or cards. You sold aftershave or tracksuits or fake perfume. What has this got to do with my football career at Crystal Palace? Everything.

The Woodmans were a Palace family, we lived a mile from the ground. Stanley Technical High School, where I got my formal education, was a stone's throw from Selhurst Park. When Palace took me as an apprentice at the age of fifteen, it was like a dream.

But you have to know who I was when that opportunity came. My background was a gambling background; my granddad, Ernie, was a bookmaker and on his busy days, I helped him. Every Sunday afternoon the men in our family would gather at my nan's in South Norwood where the women made sandwiches and the men played cards. My cousin Darren and I would be bankers for our dads, stacking the money to see who had the biggest pile. At the age of eight or nine, granddad Tom taught me how to play kaluki.

I joined South Norwood's snooker hall. It was located in a building called David House and it became my second home. With my friends Clement Salmons, Ashgar Naeem and Mark Smith, I was there from morning to night. We learned how to hustle. People thought they could take advantage of us and that was our ace card. By the time they realized we should be taken seriously, they'd lost their money. After being on the tables, we would play card games into the night. How many thirteen-year-olds can play kaluki, three-card brag, poker and shoot pontoon? And do it for large sums of money? For us it was a question of holding our nerve and we took pride in being able to do that. We learned to fiddle the fruit machines, to find and sell dodgy gear and never to pass up an opportunity to make money.

Once me and Ashgar were asked by a bloke if we could get hold of some weed. We were fourteen-year-olds, we didn't know what weed was but we said, 'Yeah, course we can.' That evening we went to Ashgar's house – he was Pakistani-cockney – and got some of his mum's herbs, mixed them in a coffee grinder and funnelled them into a small transparent plastic bag. The following day, we sold the bloke 'some weed'. Survivors we were, good at making money and not getting into big trouble. That was Andy Woodman when I signed for Crystal Palace.

Being signed by your local team is a dream for a kid but the actual experience was tough and demoralizing. We had a poor youth team, I played crap, let in loads of goals and had the nuts ripped out of me. Day in and day out. Not just by the coach, Alan Smith, but by senior pros at the club. My confidence was shot to pieces. Why didn't I train harder? Hindsight is a lovely thing. At the time I thought I was doing enough but knowing what I now know, I would have stayed there all afternoon every day. Back then I saw it differently. I was earning £27.50 a week as an apprentice, money I could earn in five minutes at the snooker hall. Yes, I was uneducated, couldn't see the bigger picture but that's where I came from. You survived, that's all you knew.

There were other difficulties. Through my first two years at Palace my life was different from the other lads' because my mum was dying of cancer. I was seventeen when she passed away. Other boys went home to a house where their mums were waiting for them, dinner was ready and their ironing was done. That is not to say my dad didn't do most of these things, he did, God bless him, and because of that he was my hero. But there is an emptiness about a house that doesn't have a mum. No one at Palace ever had a clue about that except Gareth. It affected my focus at a time when I didn't even know what the word 'focus' meant. That was me during the formative years of my career; not exactly primed for life at the top.

Had I the talent to go further? We'll never know that. But this isn't a regret because that's not how I see life. In the circumstances I didn't do badly at Palace. A lot of my time was spent with the first team, even though I was almost always on the bench, understudy to Nigel Martyn. But Nigel was a great bloke and I've got nothing but happy memories of those days. I got very close to making my league debut but it didn't happen. Ah well, no complaints. Since leaving Palace I have played over 350 league games, played at Wembley twice and survived in the game for seventeen years. Yeah, I was naive at the beginning; thought there was an easier life hustling in the snooker hall and selling dodgy gear. No matter. I am proud of the fact that regardless of the shit thrown at me, I came through it.

Yeah, I could have done more. But I've lasted longer than I thought I would after the terrible start at Palace. Are there regrets? Plenty of them but they don't cost me a thought because there is no regret comparable with my mum not being around. Perspective I find easy. What's more important: your mum or your football career? There are things you cannot change about your life, things you must accept. I have no problem accepting the limitations of my football career. It's been great fun. The only football fear I have is the fear of how I will survive without it. Even with all the shit, it has been a beautiful life.

I have always thought it's like being at school, except that in this world there is no teacher ticking you off. Monday to Friday, it's just one long laugh. You train hard but while you're training, you're having the fun that kids have. Totally immature: a Peter Pan world where you don't grow up. I'm thirty-two now and still up to the pranks I was as a fifteen-year-old. I know, unbelievable. But it makes us laugh, makes us feel good. The other Saturday our game was called off and I had teletext on in one room, Sky's *Soccer Saturday* in another and wanted to know what was happening in every game. My son, Freddie, now comes to see me play and I've seen how proud he is that his dad is out on the pitch, part of the game that he already loves. His pride in what I am doing – that's a big thing for me.

Gareth

Do I love the game as much now as in my youth? The answer is an emphatic no and that is one of the saddest things I have written.

You may think, 'He's one bitter and twisted old pro,' but

I am not. Physical fitness and the challenge of performing every Saturday afternoon remain huge priorities in my life. Behaving like a true professional is something I hold dear and at Middlesbrough I want to play in every match and do as well for them as I possibly can. Whatever I've got will be channelled into every game. Losing still hurts and even if I accept Boro cannot be Man United, there is still plenty of ambition. We can and should be a top-six team. That's where I want us to be. But no, I don't love the game as I once did.

Cynicism has coloured my view of the professional game. The attitude of some of the players, the behaviour of clubs, even the fans. Nothing appals me more than those endless and mindless phone-ins. Some guy, reacting to a defeat that afternoon, thinks the manager should be fired. Someone else agrees and in no time there's a bandwagon rolling. Spare me all of that. But the nonsense is everywhere. I've played with blokes happy just to pick up their money, with others who have given everything and been treated dismally by their clubs. Fairness doesn't come into it. Supporters call for loyalty from the players but it's a one-way street; expected from players but not reciprocated.

Steve Harrison, who coached me at Palace and Villa and now at Middlesbrough, tells me not to get cynical like so many others. But I am a bit. My experience when leaving Aston Villa had a deep impact. For two years I tried to get away from Villa, a year before my departure two big clubs wanted to take me but it didn't happen. Players with the right agent always seem to be able to get the move they want. Within football, no one believes everything is above board in the selling and buying of players but no one does anything about it. In general, agents have become far too influential.

When I was young, the professional game was a dream, but that dream is an illusion. Maybe I am a football man who has overdosed on the game and is now paying the price. Everything I have, physically and mentally, has been poured into my career for fifteen years. It has been an intense experience, perhaps too intense. I guess in any job you wise up to the pitfalls and see the shallowness of people. It is not just football but life. With age has come diminished respect for politicians, for the royals, for people that as a boy you thought were beyond reproach. Is that because we now have so much insight into their lives? Society is changing and standards are falling. Young people have less respect for their elders and an eighteen-year-old footballer that has done fuck-all can pick up fifteen grand a week.

I still care about the game, good-quality matches excite and inspire me. Perhaps there has been a bit too much mediocrity in my football life over the last few years. As a kid, I thought the top of the game would be packed with unbelievable quality. Now I work with international players who have poor technique and a lack of focus.

I love football but do not like the professional version. I am living with the reality, not the dream – the emperor without his clothes.

Epilogue

Friendship is not something you learn in school. But if you haven't learned the meaning of friendship, you really haven't learned anything.
  Muhammad Ali

Andy

27 April 2003
It is the last Sunday in April. Today Giovanni Gonzales is getting married and it is like a reunion of the Crystal Palace class of the early nineties. Gareth and Alison fly down from Leeds-Bradford and Clem Salmons, our old mate from the Bon Bonne nightclub days, picks them up at Heathrow. They come to our house and though we have not seen each other for almost six months, straight away we're on the same wavelength. They walk into the kitchen, I crack a joke and the girls laugh at our laughter. There is always excitement when we meet and today you can't miss it. Gareth's deep belly laugh hasn't changed, and in our kitchen he is once again the Gareth that the public doesn't know: the bloke with the great one-liners and the wicked sense of humour. It's a part of him I see as almost mine. Something that very few get to see. Gareth Southgate is what the public get, Nord is the bloke I know.

At the wedding the Palace boys see us together and later in the afternoon some of them come over and we talk about the old days. 'Nord and you were always together,' they say. This is the first time I have seen most of them since the day I packed the black bin-liner and walked out of Selhurst Park. We're talking almost ten years. They are pleased that the friendship between Nord and I survived our different career paths. Inside I am cheered by the fact that we are closer than the boys realize. The two teenagers that sat on Mitcham station's only platform have grown up together, had a lot of good times and shared our bad days. 'I don't know if I would do it that way,' Nord would say when I told him how I intended to worm my way out of some tight corner. What he meant was 'Don't be daft' and the message always got through because I read him like a book.

I look at Alison and Anna catching up on each other's life. We have all come a long way. It's funny too to be at Giovanni's wedding when it was at Giovanni's restaurant that Nord first fancied Ali. And Anna, watching him like a hawk, then swooped like one. 'That girl is in a relationship,' she said. It was a judgement and a warning, not a statement. Gareth never needed Barbara, his mum, watching over him as long as Anna was around.

Too early, the Southgates have to get back to Heathrow for their evening flight back up north. Saying their goodbyes Anna and Ali are again tearful and though we nod sarcastically, we're dead happy that the girls have such a good relationship. After Nord and Ali leave, I spend more time with some of the old Palace lads. We talk about each other's children, our managers, our contractual situations, our plans for life after football; the usual stuff for ageing footballers. These are good blokes and we talk about staying in contact and meeting up more often. But it won't happen. We'll return to our separate worlds, I'll be driving up and down to Oxford, organizing soccer schools for the kids, trying to sneak an odd game of golf with Anna's dad, John, and eventually we lose each other's phone numbers. 'Did you ever get round to calling Chris?' Anna will ask. 'Nah, but I meant to.'

Why was there one friendship that broke the rules, one that outlived the Palace years? There are countless reasons but no particular reason. What I do know is that it has been a huge part of my life, a bond that helped me through the bad times and made the good ones better. At Giovanni's wedding, I could sense the lads thinking, 'Woody's done well to stay friends with Gareth.' They are right but it's not for the reason they imagine. We've been mates for seventeen years; almost brothers from the time when we both earned £27.50 a week. No one could have made us as close as we are and that's something I'm proud of. Whatever my future holds, Nord will be part of it.

Gareth

About fifteen years ago Woody and I stood at a bar and watched two fortysomethings sharing a beer. They looked a little wistful; occasionally they brought up something from the past and reminisced. We eavesdropped for a bit and then took our drinks to a table. First question Woody asked: where will we be ten years from now? We didn't have a clue. We were Palace reserves at the time, not knowing if we would be in the game five years or five minutes. One thing we agreed and that was that no matter what happened, we would be having a beer and recounting past experiences like the two guys we had just been listening to.

I recall this incident because as I reread the pages of this book, I wonder if I've somehow given the impression that I haven't truly enjoyed my life. If that's the case, then it's the greatest cock-up since that penalty at Euro 96. If you brought me the fifteen years back to that bar and said: 'Gareth, you will play fifty-five times for England, be considered one of the best defenders in your league over eight or nine seasons and you will earn a salary that you cannot even imagine,' I would call you insane. It has been a privilege to play football for a living and a particular privilege to play at such a high level. I could never, and I don't think I did, abuse that privilege. I was blessed with a talent, not as great as that of many others, but I made the most of it.

For all the flaws of the professional game, I still love football and its people. Sometimes at training or after matches, I see kids queuing for autographs or waiting to catch a glimpse of their heroes. Seeing their enthusiasm is a joy: the delight when their side wins, the hurt after a defeat. They all want to play for their local team, then for one of the big professional clubs and, always, for their country. I was one of those kids and can vividly recall my first game for the school and the first time I saw a match under floodlights and the brightness of the colours. I would rush home from school to see England play on television and I think there are now kids doing that to watch the England team I play for. That has always been a surreal thought: it is almost incomprehensible that I could be to today's kids what my heroes were to me.

I am glad too that my start in the professional game happened at a time when attitudes were more lax and players were anything but professional. Back then the camaraderie in a team was far greater than it is now. The game was more fun when there was less money. It is not coincidental that the greatest friendships and characters I remember come mostly from the early part of my career. Back then there was a hunger and a spirit that you don't much see any more. That had a lot to do with a dressing room that was full of British players and where the only foreigner was the chap from Dublin. After an away victory, the team coach bubbled with enthusiasm – or with black humour when we lost. That kind of interaction comes only from playing a team game and we relished it.

I have loved meeting the characters, making the friendships

and learning about myself. Whatever you may think about my career, it has kept me engrossed. Not surprisingly, I learned more about life from that missed penalty than from any number of victories. Football has made me a more complete person. I think of it as a fantastic journey but one without a destination. The fun has been in the sharing of the experiences and that brings me to the heart of the matter.

When Woody and I sit down as fortysomethings to have that drink, what will we remember? I know for sure it will be as much about Mitcham station as Wembley stadium, more about Alan Smith than Glenn Hoddle. It will be more about friends than achievements. Laughter will outweigh regret, by a long, long way. We will look to our futures too and talk about our children. Will they enjoy life as much as we have, will they forge a friendship as strong as their fathers'? In a game as tough and as harsh as football and in the light of our different career paths, that has been the greatest achievement of all.